THE
LOW-CHOLESTEROL
OLIVE OIL
COOKBOOK

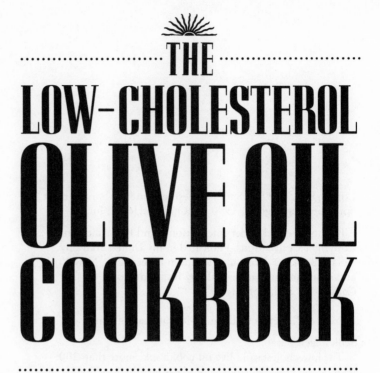

THE
LOW-CHOLESTEROL
OLIVE OIL
COOKBOOK

MORE THAN 200 RECIPES

**THE MOST
DELICIOUS WAY
TO EAT
HEALTHY FOOD**

*Sarah Schlesinger
& Barbara Earnest*

VILLARD BOOKS · NEW YORK · 1990

Copyright © 1990 by Sarah Schlesinger and Barbara Earnest
Foreword copyright © 1990 by Random House, Inc.

Library of Congress Cataloging-in-Publication Data

Schlesinger, Sarah.
    The low-cholesterol olive oil cookbook: more than 200
recipes, the most delicious way to eat healthy food/by Sarah
Schlesinger and Barbara Earnest.
        p.   cm.
    ISBN 0-394-58074-5   0-679-73288-8 (pbk.)
    1. Low-cholesterol diet—Recipes.   2. Cookery (Olive oil)
I. Earnest, Barbara.   II. Title.
RM237.75.S35   1990
641.5′638—dc20   89-70472

DESIGNED BY BARBARA MARKS
Manufactured in the United States of America
9 8 7 6 5 4 3 2
First Edition

To Sam's good heart, our continuing inspiration!

To Ruth Reed, and the many friends, associates, and health professionals whose willingness to share their time and knowledge made this book possible. Special thanks to Dr. Scott M. Grundy, Dr. Bruce Roseman, nutritionist Mary Beth Reardon, Diane Reverand, Robert Cornfield, the staff of the USDA Library in Beltsville, Maryland, Linda Russo of Food Communications, Dean and DeLuca, and Zabar's.

FOREWORD

For the past twenty years, my research has focused on understanding cholesterol metabolism and its role in coronary heart disease. During this time, two important links to coronary heart disease have been firmly established: one is that high serum cholesterol levels increase the risk for heart disease and the other is that high intakes of saturated fats and cholesterol cause elevations in serum cholesterol. As a result of these two relationships, current recommendations call for people to lower their serum cholesterol levels through diet. To help accomplish this, the amount of cholesterol and saturated fat in the diet should be limited. However, the removal of saturated fat can leave a caloric deficit. Other nutrients are needed to take its place. The key question is which nutrient best fills the void left by the decrease in saturated fat. The two possibilities are unsaturated fat and/or carbohydrate.

In the 1960s, a great deal of medical research was carried out to determine the answer to this question, the outcome of which was to recommend increased polyunsaturated fats in the diet. Gradually, this recommendation proved to be a disquieting alternative as more facts came to light about some of the potential side effects of polyunsaturates. For example, although polyunsaturates effectively reduce cholesterol levels when replacing saturated fats, they also lower high-density lipoprotein, or HDL. This effect is disturbing because the concentration of HDL cholesterol is inversely related to the risk for coronary heart disease. That is, HDL is seen as the "good" cholesterol and appears to be protective against risk for coronary heart disease. There were other reports showing that polyunsaturated fats will promote formation of tumors in laboratory animals and that they can suppress the immune system. To add to this uneasiness, there is no known population that consumes large amounts of polyunsaturated fats to attest to their long-term safety. Thus, concerns about recommending increasing amounts of polyunsaturated fats in the diet prompted my colleagues and me to reexamine the potential for the use of the other major form of unsaturated fat, namely monounsaturated fat.

In the studies carried out in the 1950s and 1960s by Drs. Ancel Keys, Mark Hegsted, and their associates, oleic acid, the major monounsaturated fat in the diet, was considered to have a neutral effect on serum cholesterol, neither raising nor lowering the level in the serum. This concept had been generally accepted along with the idea that polyunsaturated fats lower cholesterol levels and saturated fats raise cholesterol levels. Our approach to reexamine this concept was supported by one of Dr. Keys's other observations, namely, that the rate of coronary heart disease is low in the Mediterranean region, where large quantities of monounsaturated fat are consumed in the form of olive oil.

We designed a series of studies in which we compared dietary monounsaturated fat and polyunsaturated fat to saturated fat for their action on cholesterol levels. The results of these studies were very rewarding. We found that monounsaturates not only lower total cholesterol and LDL cholesterol, the so-called "bad cholesterol," but also do not lower HDL cholesterol, the "good cholesterol." Although polyunsaturated fat reduced the LDL level, it unfortunately lowered the HDL cholesterol as well. These findings have been received with wide interest, but, in truth, they are not a new discovery. Rather, the findings are the continuation of work of the earlier researchers who, after all, had made the original observation that the rate of coronary heart disease is low in the Mediterranean region.

What about carbohydrates? A prudent alternative to high polyunsaturates is a diet low in total fat and relatively high in carbohydrate. Carbohydrates effect is similar on cholesterol and its subfractions to that of polyunsaturates, that is, carbohydrates lower total cholesterol, LDL cholesterol and HDL cholesterol. Although undeniably effective for cholesterol lowering, high carbohydrate diets have a few drawbacks. For one thing, as mentioned above, carbohydrates lower HDL cholesterol. They also raise serum triglycerides, another blood lipid that carries some risk for coronary heart disease. High carbohydrate diets are low in fat, and fat is known to provide flavor and satiety to our food; as a result, many people find that it is not easy to adhere to very low fat diets for prolonged periods of time.

What then is the bottom line? What does all this mean to you and to me? For one thing, it means that there is increasing evidence that monounsaturates have a role in preventing coronary heart disease. Both the American Heart Association and the National Cholesterol Education Program have recommended a basic diet in which 20 to 30 percent of total calories come from fat. They suggest setting limits on both polyunsaturated fats and saturated fats in the diet to 7 to 10 percent of total calories. The remaining dietary fat calories should come from monounsaturates. The higher monounsaturated fat diet provides an alternate way to lower serum cholesterol through diet without resorting to very low fat diets that many people find unpalatable and unsatisfying. An important point for physicians to consider: A diet containing liberal amounts of monounsaturates can be recommended without concern about its safety. We have had centuries of experience with diets high in monounsaturates.

I am very pleased to be asked to write a foreword to this book because it provides a link with the research that we have been carrying out on monounsaturated fats at the Center for Human Nutrition. A difficult task for a research scientist is to establish a practical application for one's research discoveries. I have in fact been besieged with requests for information on the "alternative diet" and how best to implement it. I am happy to say that *The Low-Cholesterol Olive Oil Cookbook* answers this need.

Dr. Scott M. Grundy
Director
Center for Human Nutrition
University of Texas
Southwestern Medical Center

CONTENTS

THE
LOW-CHOLESTEROL
OLIVE OIL
COOKBOOK

THE HEALTH STORY

A century ago, an Italian physician named P. E. Remondino urged Americans to enrich their diets with olive oil, as an antidote for shriveled livers, mummified skin, constipation, and pessimism. As we learn more about the role of olive oil in helping to lower the risk of coronary artery disease, it becomes increasingly clear that we should have paid better attention to some of his advice.

Nutritionists are constantly seeking improved ways to put our cholesterol and fats in better balance by using natural adjustments in diet and life-style that don't require drugs and other forms of medical intervention. The renewed interest in olive oil is a byproduct of this investigative process.

In order to understand the importance of turning to monounsaturated olive oil as our primary source of fat calories, we first have to examine the role of cholesterol and fats in our diets.

THE ROLE OF CHOLESTEROL IN CARDIOVASCULAR DISEASE

Cardiovascular disease kills one American every minute. A million and a half people suffer heart attacks every year and six million are estimated to have coronary artery disease. Although some risk factors for this disease such as sex, age, and family history are beyond our control, others such as diet, smoking, blood pressure, weight, physical activity, and blood cholesterol levels are not. Forty million Americans are estimated to have dangerously high cholesterol levels. Coronary specialists have predicted that 30 to 50 percent of the potential victims of heart disease could be helped by lowering these levels.

Cholesterol is a white, waxy, tasteless, and odorless substance produced by our liver and intestinal tract and is also found in foods of animal origin. We will be using the term "cholesterol" to refer to the total amount of cholesterol in the blood. The cholesterol in our bloodstream is measured in milligrams per deciliter, or mg/dl.

Some cholesterol is necessary for making essential body substances such as cell membranes, bile acids, and sex hormones and performing other important bodily functions. Without cholesterol we could not stay alive. However, too much can be dangerous since cholesterol contributes to the buildup of fatty deposits on artery walls that can lead to heart attack and stroke.

Our cholesterol can be too high because of diet, lifestyle, or family history. Some people manufacture more cholesterol than their body needs. The amount of dietary cholesterol and saturated fats consumed in the food we eat each day can also contribute to elevated blood cholesterol.

Dietary cholesterol is found in foods of animal origin such as egg yolks, red meat, organ meats, and dairy products. Plant foods, including fruits, vegetables, and grains such as oats, do not contain cholesterol. Saturated fats are usually of animal origin and are solid at room temperature. Foods high in saturated fat include beef fat, lard, butter, cheese, and whole milk, as well as the three tropical oils: palm, palm kernel, and coconut oil.

Since cholesterol and fat are not soluble in water, they connect with proteins and travel through the body as lipoproteins. Two major kinds of lipoproteins deserve special attention: low-density liproprotein (LDL), often called "bad" cholesterol, and high-density lipoprotein (HDL), often called "good" cholesterol.

LDL is responsible for depositing cholesterol in tissues. The more LDL in the bloodstream, the greater the chances of its building up and attaching itself to the artery walls.

One role of HDL is to prevent the deposit of cholesterol on the artery walls. Consequently, the more HDL and the less buildup of cholesterol there is in the body, the lower the risk of developing heart disease.

However, when there is either very little HDL or too much LDL, the interior lining of the blood vessels can become clogged.

LDL is accompanied on its journey through the body by a special protein called "apolipoprotein B" or "Apo B." Apo B is a tough insoluble substance that tends to adhere to artery walls. Gradually LDL cholesterol and Apo B build up to form a material known as "plaque." Since arteries are only one twelfth of an inch in diameter in some spots, a very small amount of plaque can narrow an artery. The process of plaque formation is called atherosclerosis.

As the result of atherosclerosis, coronary arteries can become increasingly narrow and less able to expand and contract. When an artery becomes totally clogged, blood flow decreases and the heart muscles start to suffocate. Chest pain or a heart attack may result. Two thirds of deaths from cardiovascular disease in the United States are caused by the narrowing of these arteries that supply blood to the heart. High blood pressure may also result when the heart must work harder and harder to send blood through narrow arterial openings. High blood pressure can be both a cause and a warning of heart attack or stroke.

As we follow this chain of events, we can clearly see the importance of having a low LDL level and a high HDL level. Dr. William Castelli, the medical director for the Framingham Heart Study, calls HDL the number one blood fat factor in staving off heart attacks—an element even more important than total cholesterol or LDL levels. Therefore, as we plan a diet to help control our cholesterol level, we need to pay particular attention to preserving or boosting the beneficial HDLs.

The lower your ratio of HDL to total cholesterol, the better. For example, in men, the suggested ratio of HDL to total cholesterol is below 4.6. Some steps that can help you achieve and maintain a desirable HDL level are:

1. Substitute olive oil for the saturated fats in your diet. Dr. Scott M. Grundy, of the University of Texas Health Science Center in Dallas, has found that monounsaturated oils such as olive oil are more protective of HDL levels than polyunsaturated fats such as corn oil and soybean oil. Olive oil reduces total cholesterol without lowering HDL.

2. Eat more seafood. Omega-3 fatty acids in oily fishes such as salmon, mackerel, sardines, and white albacore tuna can boost HDL levels.

3. Add beans, oat bran, apples, and other foods high in soluble fiber to your diet. Studies done by Dr. James Anderson at the University of Kentucky College of Medicine showed that eating one cup of dried navy or pinto beans each day improved the HDL/total cholesterol ratio by 17 percent. A half a cup, or 40 grams, of dry oat bran daily can boost HDL by up to 15 percent in several months.

4. If you are heavy, lose weight. Getting rid of excess weight raises HDL.

However, losing weight if you are already at your recommended level will not boost HDL.

5. Participate in a regular exercise program. Aerobic exercise has been found to elevate HDL levels in addition to burning calories.
6. Don't smoke. As early as 1970, the Framingham Heart Study reported that cigarette smoking lowered the blood levels of HDL.
7. If you take vitamins, check with your physician or nutritionist for advice on which supplements might adversely or positively affect HDL levels.

FINDING OUT ABOUT YOUR OWN CHOLESTEROL LEVEL

Although cholesterol tests are now available from portable testing units at health fairs and shopping centers, it is also important to be tested under the supervision of a physician. Then you can count on receiving a correct analysis of your results and be sure that they will include LDL and HDL levels as well as total cholesterol levels.

Although the National Cholesterol Education Program (NCEP) has stated that a total cholesterol level of under 200mg/dl is a desirable level, 200–239 is borderline-high, and over 240 is high risk, many individual factors such as age, sex, heredity, and lifestyle need to be evaluated by your physician to determine the correct level for you.

If your physician determines that your cholesterol is in the desirable range, NCEP suggests that you maintain a diet strategy designed to promote low cholesterol levels. If you have an elevated cholesterol level, NCEP suggests a series of cholesterol and fat-restricted diets before drugs are considered. Even if drugs are taken, a cholesterol and fat-modified diet must still be followed.

The American Heart Association (AHA) recommends that we reduce our intake of dietary cholesterol to no more than 300 milligrams a day, or 100 milligrams per 1,000 calories consumed. Currently the average American eats 450 to 600 milligrams of dietary cholesterol a day.

The AHA further recommends that our total fat intake not exceed more than 30 percent of our daily diet. But merely reducing the quantity of total fat in our diet is not enough. We also have to become familiar with the three kinds of fat and learn to include the correct percentage of each type in our daily food plan.

FACTS ABOUT FATS

Fats are vital to good human nutrition. In addition to providing energy, fat contributes to a feeling of fullness, adds taste to foods, acts as a carrier for the fat-soluble vitamins A, D, E, and K, and furnishes essential fatty acids that are needed for life and growth.

Fats don't exist in an isolated form, but rather have to be extracted from the foods in which they are found. Butter is removed from cream by churning, lard is removed from animal tissues by heating, and vegetable oils are separated from seeds, nuts, or fruits by pressing or using chemical solvents. Soy, corn, peanut, cottonseed, sunflower, coconut, palm kernel, safflower, sesame, and rapeseed oils are extracted from plant seeds, while healthful olive oil and harmful palm oil are derived from the actual pulp of the fruit.

The terms saturated, monounsaturated, and polyunsaturated are used to classify fats according to their structures. These labels relate to the number of hydrogen atoms in the fat and the available openings that exist between the hydrogen and the carbon atoms. In a saturated fat, the openings are all filled up and, consequently, are solid at room temperature. In a monounsaturated fat, there is only one opening for hydrogen atoms. In polyunsaturated fats, there is more than one opening. Both monounsaturated and polyunsaturated fats are called unsaturated fats and are liquid at room temperature.

All fats are a blend of saturates, monounsaturates, and polyunsaturates. But the proportions vary greatly. Olive oil contains a higher amount of monounsaturated fat than any other oil.

Although past attempts to lower cholesterol in the diet have centered on foods that contain polyunsaturated fats, recently the focus has been shifting to the significance of eating more monounsaturated fat. This new attention to monounsaturates has been prompted in part by concerns about the other long-term health effects of consuming large quantities of polyunsaturated fats. While humans have been eating large amounts of monounsaturated fat in the form of olive oil for thousands of years, the consumption of large quantities of polyunsaturated vegetable oils is relatively recent. No population has existed for a long period of time on a diet in which polyunsaturates provided as much as 8–10 percent of its calories. In other words, there is no recorded experience from which to evaluate the consequences of long-term consumption at this rate. In addition, monounsaturated fats are naturally synthesized by the human body while polyunsaturated fats are not.

Some scientists are concerned that the highly reactive nature of polyunsaturated fats can cause them to oxidize and form carcinogenic compounds. Recent research has shown that high doses of polyunsaturates can promote cancer in laboratory animals, dramatically alter cell membranes, and may increase the risk of gallstones. The following possible links between polyunsaturates and cancer are being explored:

- Polyunsaturates may play a vital role in releasing free radicals. When oxygen or enzymes react with polyunsaturated fats to release their energy, a free radical is formed. A free radical is a chemical substance made by the body that contains an odd number of electrons. The odd number is the result of a free, high-energy electron attaching itself to a new atom, disturbing the atom's energy balance. The atom is anxious to get rid of this new electron as soon as possible, resulting in a sudden transfer of energy to adjacent body tissue. This process can lead to cancer if the free radicals are not neutralized by antioxidants.
- The more polyunsaturated fats contained in cell membranes, the more susceptible the cell may be to carcinogenic agents.
- Polyunsaturates may enhance cancer development by increasing a hormone called prolactin.
- Polyunsaturated fatty acids may inhibit the normal function of the immune system. Diets high in the N–6 polyunsaturated fatty acids found in safflower, corn, and soybean oils delay the maturation of suppressor cells, which act as brakes on the immune system. They also inhibit the formation of lymphocytes, resulting in a decline in immune responses.

Although current studies are not conclusive, these immunological effects of polyunsaturates as well as the possibility of a link between high polyunsaturate consumption and cancer make the increased consumption of monounsaturates a logical step.

RESEARCH ON THE DIETARY BENEFITS OF MONOUNSATURATES

An early hint at the value of monounsaturates came from the Seven Countries Study, begun in 1958, when researchers tracked various risk factors in healthy middle-age men including diet, blood pressure, weight, cigarette smoking, and exercise habits. When they correlated the data with the men's subsequent rates of heart disease, they discovered that the more saturated fat there was in a diet, the more mortality there was from heart disease. The Finns fared worst, followed by the Americans. The Greeks, Italians, and Japanese fared best. Since the Japanese ate very little fat in their diets, their results were not surprising. But unexpectedly the Greeks and Italians had less heart disease even though they consumed a high-fat diet. Most of their fat consumption was in the form of monounsaturated olive oil.

The Seven Countries Study continued over a fifteen-year period as people in traditional olive oil areas began to imitate the tastes of the more affluent populations of northern Europe and the United States. This resulted in their eating more meat and dairy products and cutting back on their olive oil intake. Some researchers noted an alarming increase in the concentration of cholesterol in the blood serum of the men in the Mediterranean area and saw many more coronary patients toward the end of the study.

International Congresses on the Biological Value of Olive Oil were held in 1969, 1975, 1980, and 1982 to review research findings related to the dietary benefits of monounsaturates.

During the 1980s, Dr. Scott M. Grundy, director for the Center for Human Nutrition at the University of Texas Southwestern Medical Center, and his associate, Dr. Fred H. Mattson, of the University of California at San Diego, became involved in studying the role of monounsaturates in human health.

Although saturated fats were long known as bad fats because they increased cholesterol and polyunsaturated fats were considered good fats because they did not increase cholesterol, the role of monounsaturated fats had been largely ignored in this country. Dr. Grundy became interested in reinvestigating the role of olive oil in the Mediterranean diet.

In one of their studies, Dr. Grundy and Dr. Mattson developed three liquid diets. They were identical in all nutrients except fats. One contained saturated fat, one polyunsaturated fat, and one monounsaturated fat. Each of the twenty patients in the study followed each diet for four weeks. After the four-week periods, they were tested for changes in cholesterol levels.

Their total cholesterol levels rose on the saturated fat diet, while they were lowered on the polyunsaturated fat diet. However the polyunsaturated diet lowered both their LDLs and their HDLs. The monounsaturated diet was equally effective in lowering total cholesterol levels but tended to target the LDLs for reduction and leave the HDLs alone.

In another experiment, Dr. Grundy studied eleven patients during three dietary periods, each lasting four weeks. He developed three liquid diets for them that differed only in the type of fat they contained. The first was high in saturated fatty acids (High-Sat) and the second was high in monounsaturated fatty acids (High-Mono). Each of these diets derived 40 percent of their total calories from fat and 43 percent from carbohydrate. The third diet (Low-Fat) derived 20 percent of its calories from fat and 63 percent from carbohydrate. The High-Mono diet lowered plasma cholesterol by 14 percent compared with the High-Sat diet which didn't alter it, while the Low-Fat diet brought down cholesterol by 8 percent. The average cholesterol level of the patients at the beginning of the investigation was 251 mg/dl. The High-Mono diet lowered LDLs by 21 percent while the Low-Fat diet lowered them by only 15 percent. The High-Mono diet did not cause an increase in triglycerides or a decrease in HDLs. Triglycerides are an important fat found in the blood and they often travel in close contact with cholesterol. There is a growing body of opinion that connects triglycerides with cardiovascular disease. In contrast, the Low-Fat diet raised the triglyceride level and lowered the HDLs.

These research results suggest that monounsaturated fats such as olive oil may be even more effective than polyunsaturated fat in reducing blood cholesterol levels and lowering the risk of heart disease. While polyunsaturates and monounsaturated fats lower total cholesterol about equally, monounsaturated fat appears to lower LDL cholesterol more effectively without lowering HDL cholesterol. In other words, monounsaturated fats reduce only the "bad" LDLs, leaving the good HDLs to do their work of carrying cholesterol away from the heart vessels. Polyunsaturated fats, however, reduce both LDL and HDL cholesterol.

Additional research links olive oil to two other heart disease–related areas, diabetes and blood pressure.

In a 1988 study, Dr. Grundy and his associates studied patients with Type II diabetes. The doctors controlled what the patients ate. Type II, or non-insulin-dependent diabetes, usually begins after age forty. Individuals suffering from Type II often have a family history of diabetes. While Type II diabetes patients have been encouraged to eat high-carbohydrate, low-fat diets, a growing body of research suggests that they may be better off replacing the saturated fat in their diet with unsaturated fat. In Dr. Grundy's experiment, half of the group ate a diet high in carbohydrates, such as fruits, vegetables, and grains, but very low in fat, for twenty-eight days. On this diet, 60 percent of total calories came from carbohydrates and 25 percent came from fat. The other half of the group ate a diet that had 35 percent of its calories from carbohydrates and 50 percent from fat, in the form of olive oil. The diets were identical in terms of fiber and protein. The groups were switched after the initial twenty-eight days.

When the Grundy team examined the results, they found that when patients consumed high-fat diets, their blood sugar was lower and they required less insulin, proof that their diabetes was under better control. The high-fat diet also produced lower levels of triglycerides and LDLs but higher levels of HDLs. Dr. Grundy's findings in this study reinforced those of earlier studies conducted by Dr. Gerald M. Reaven, a diabetes expert at Stanford University Medical Center.

A 1988 study by the Stanford Center for Research in Disease Prevention indicates that olive oil may also reduce high blood pressure, although the Center stresses that more research needs to be done to bear out this finding.

Combined with the Mediterranean experience, the findings of American researchers suggest that adding monounsaturated fat to our diets while reducing polyunsaturated fats is a prudent step to be taken in the fight against heart disease. On the basis of centuries of use, monounsaturates appear to have the benefits of polyunsaturated fats without their drawbacks.

It would not be wise to totally eliminate polyunsaturates from the diet because a small amount of these fats are needed by the body as "essential fatty acids." However, we should seek polyunsaturates from natural food sources rather than relying on highly processed oils. Remember that olive oil includes 9 percent polyunsaturated fat.

The following breakdown has been suggested by Dr. Grundy and endorsed by Dr. Kenneth Cooper, the father of aerobics and acknowledged international leader in the field of disease prevention, in his book *Controlling Cholesterol* (Bantam, 1988).
- Keep saturated fats below 10 percent of total calories.
- Keep polyunsaturates between 5 and 10 percent of total calories.
- Keep monounsaturates between 10 and 15 percent of total calories.

OTHER MEDICAL AND NUTRITIONAL BENEFITS OF OLIVE OIL
In addition to its heart-protective role, olive oil has numerous other medical applications. The most exhaustive review to date of all aspects of the olive oil–health relationship was carried out by the Italian medical researchers Publio Fiola and Mirella Audisio. Summarizing scores of studies in their publication "Olive Oil and Health" in 1986, Fiola and Audisio offer evidence that the olive's role in health and longevity goes far beyond the reduction of coronary risk.

Some of the areas discussed in "Olive Oil and Health" include:
- Digestion. Olive oil can also help the digestive system to function more efficiently. It is thought to reduce gastric acidity and to be effective in

protecting against ulcers and gastritis. It also stimulates bile secretion and regulates the emptying of the gallbladder, reducing the risk of gallstones.

- Intestinal functions. Olive oil is the edible fat most easily absorbed by the intestines and regulates the passage of food through the intestines. One or two tablespoons of olive oil has a positive effect as a laxative.
- Bone and brain development. Olive oil also promotes bone growth by fighting calcium loss and permits improved bone mineralization in both children and adults due to its chemical composition. It is considered a good food choice for expectant and nursing mothers since it encourages normal brain development in the infant before and after birth. At the other end of the spectrum, olive oil may be helpful in preventing the wear and tear of age on brain functions and the aging of organs and tissues in general.
- Energy. Olive oil is an excellent source of energy since it metabolizes readily thanks to its oleic oil content.

OTHER SOURCES OF MONOUNSATURATES

In addition to olive oil, there is one other oil currently on the market that has a high ratio of monounsaturates. This product is called canola oil.

Formerly known as rapeseed oil, canola oil is made from the rape plant. Canola oil is a staple of cooking in Canada, Japan, India, and China. It isn't as well known in America because it was banned for import here until 1985. In the past, rapeseed oil contained a high level of erucic acid, a fatty acid that has been linked to heart lesions and cardiac defects in test animals. For this reason, rapeseed oil was prohibited for sale in the United States. However, after the eurucic acid level was reduced to 0.5 percent, the Food and Drug Administration lifted import restrictions.

Canola oil is currently marketed as Puritan oil by Procter and Gamble and is used in a variety of processed foods as well.

Although canola oil and peanut oil both have large percentages of monounsaturates, olive oil has more. In addition, it has a much lower percentage of polyunsaturates than either canola oil or peanut oil.

Olives, avocados, and most nuts except walnuts and coconuts also contain a relatively high percentage of monounsaturates. While these foods can contribute to monounsaturate intake, they have a variety of limitations. Cured olives are high in sodium, nuts are high in saturated fats, and avocados are an unlikely choice for a daily diet staple. Although many animal products contain a relatively high percentage of monounsaturates, they also contain an excessive amount of saturated fat and cholesterol. One tablespoon of olive oil contains 1.9 grams of saturated fat, 1.2 grams of polyunsaturated fat, 10.3 grams of monounsaturated fat, and 125 calories.

HOW TO ADD OLIVE OIL TO YOUR DIET
Adding olive oil to your diet will take planning and a change in some of your current eating habits. Since it is a fat, eating too much of it could cause you to gain weight. Consequently, you have to use it to replace other fats currently in your diet rather than simply adding fat calories in the form of olive oil.

How to Calculate Your Fat Calorie Consumption:
1. Find out how many calories you should be eating each day to either maintain your weight if it is currently appropriate for your height and bone structure or to reduce it if you exceed your suggested weight range. Let's imagine, for example, that you will be eating 1,800 calories a day.
2. Multiply your total calories by 30 percent. This figure represents the maximum number of fat calories that you can eat every day. If you are eating 1,800 calories a day, you should eat no more than 540 calories (1800 × .30) in the form of fats.
3. To determine how many calories of saturated fats you can eat each day, multiply your total calorie intake by 10 percent. If you are eating 1,800 calories a day, fewer than 180 (1800 × .10) of these should be saturated fat.
4. To determine how many calories of polyunsaturated fat you can eat each day, multiply your total calorie intake by 5 percent. If you are eating 1,800 calories a day, approximately 90 (1800 × .05) of these can be polyunsaturated fat.

5. To determine how many calories of monounsaturated fat you can eat each day, multiply your total calorie intake by 15 percent. If you are eating 1,800 calories a day, 270 (1800 × .15) of these calories should be in the form of monounsaturated fat, ideally in the form of olive oil.

At the end of each of our recipes, you will find a list of the total fat, as well as the monounsaturated, polyunsaturated, and saturated fat counts of the combined ingredients. Each of these counts will be listed in both grams and calories for your convenience in computing your daily fat intake. Choose recipes that will provide the quantity of monounsaturated olive oil calories you need.

To determine the fat content of the other foods you eat, use a food guide that includes a breakdown of the three kinds of fat. We suggest *The Nutritive Value of Foods* (United States Department of Agriculture Human Nutrition Information Service Home and Garden Bulletin Number 72) that can be ordered from The Superintendent of Documents, U.S. Government Printing Office, Washington, D.C. 20402. Write to the GPO for a current catalogue for information on publication and postage charges.

Fat contents are often presented on packaged foods in the form of grams. Since there are 9 calories in each gram of fat, you can compute the number of fat calories by multiplying the number of grams by 9.

SAMPLE DAILY FAT CONSUMPTION GUIDE

Total Calories Consumed	30% Fat	10% Sat	5% Poly	15% Mono
3000	900	300	150	450
2000	600	200	100	300
1500	450	150	75	225

INCLUDING OLIVE OIL IN A HEART-HEALTHY DIET

While fats have a vital role to play in a cholesterol-lowering diet, they must be viewed as only one aspect of changing our overall approach to eating.

We need to focus on eating the correct number of calories, developing an exercise program and avoiding processed foods that contain sugar, sodium, additives, and preservatives. The ideal diet is one that is nutritionally sound and based on the Mediterranean tradition that includes less meat and high-fat dairy products and more fish, fresh fruit and vegetables, grains, and olive oil.

Complex carbohydrates (fresh fruits, vegetables, breads, and starches) should make up 50 to 60 percent of total calories; protein (fish, poultry, lean meat, dairy products, beans) should make up 10 to 20 percent. Fats (monounsaturates, polyunsaturates, and saturates) should make up no more than 30 percent.

SHOPPING LIST OF HEART-HEALTHY INGREDIENTS

- Buy "choice" or "good" graded beef including lean, well-trimmed chuck, loin, and round.
- Buy ground beef (round or chuck) with no more than 10 percent fat.
- Buy low-fat whole-grain or fat-free French and Italian bread.
- Buy cholesterol-lowering 100 percent oat bran to use as bread crumbs.
- Buy a chicken broth that has a reduced sodium content or low-sodium chicken bouillon.
- Buy one of the new cheeses made from skim milk products that are low in fat, cholesterol, and sodium.
- Buy 1 percent low-fat cottage cheese. Whirl it in an electric blender and use as a substitute for sour cream or ricotta cheese.
- Buy large fresh eggs but limit egg yolk consumption to two a week in all foods.
- Buy 1 percent or skim milk instead of whole milk.
- Buy skinned white meat poultry, which has a lower fat content than dark meat.
- Buy ground turkey with a fat content under 7 percent.
- Buy natural brown rice since its bran layer has recently been found to lower cholesterol.
- Buy white albacore tuna that is packed in either water or olive oil.
- Buy nonfat or low-fat plain yogurt.

OLIVE OIL BASICS

The long, rich tradition of the olive tree, which Sophocles described as "the tree that stands unequalled," is woven through the tapestry of human history.

Archaeologists have uncovered works of art that describe olive tree cultivation in the ancient world; many of the scenes they depict are still being acted out in the olive tree groves of the twentieth century.

Understanding how olives are grown and processed is a helpful tool in selecting olive oils and interpreting their labels. The steps in the process are harvesting, collection, grading, crushing, and pressing. Each of these stages influences the final flavor of the oil.

The trees thrive mainly in the Mediterranean climatic zone, which produces 95 percent of the world's olive crop.

The flowering of the olive tree takes place between April and June. The flowers produce tiny berries the size of pinheads, which subsequently fill out with flesh and develop a hardened stone.

The olives contain no oil until they are pastel green in color. At this point a chemical transformation begins to change sugars and organic acids into oil. This process continues until the olives have fully ripened and turned black.

Green olives are harvested from August to November; ripe olives are harvested from November to March. The degree of ripeness determines the taste of the olive and its oil. Olives that are harvested after they have turned black contain more oil than red-ripe olives, but their oil is more acidic. Growers try to pick their trees before January, allowing them to rest in January and February.

Since the olives are fragile and firmly attached to the tree, they are still frequently harvested by hand or with poles that have wooden or plastic comb heads. Workers balance on ladders and climb into the branches, snatching limbs with one hand and combing with the other. They may use small hand tools to strip the branches or use their hands, which they protect by wearing gloves or taping their palms.

While leaf ventilation and harvesting machines that can grasp and shake the trees have been introduced, the fragility of the crop and the weakness of new branches make mechanical harvesting difficult. However, with mechanical assistance, the daily harvest per picker triples. The machines knock down 80 percent of the olives and the rest are knocked down by hand or with poles. Using this method, a worker can pick from 1,000 to 1,700 pounds of olives a day.

Many experts feel that hand harvesting is essential to producing the finest quality oils since mechanical picking bruises the fruit and increases the acidity and tartness of the resulting oil. The importance of picking olives at the same stage of ripening and of similar size further complicates the use of mechanical devices. On the other hand, an increasingly scarce work force is adding pressure to the search for satisfactory new harvesting methods.

In the collection phase, canvasses, nets, or polyethylene covers are used beneath the trees to catch the falling olives and prevent them from touching the ground. Some resourceful growers even use open umbrellas placed upside down to catch the olives as they fall. Olives that touch the ground can become bruised and collect dirt, causing them to turn rancid.

The collected harvest is then poured into baskets and crates and picked over to clean out leaves, bits of twigs, and unsound olives. Some producers allow leaves to remain to heighten the green color of their oils. The olives are then graded according to their plumpness, stage of development, and quality either for oil or preserving. This process must be done by hand. Five kilograms of olives are needed to obtain 1 litre or 1½ cups of olive oil.

After cleaning, the olives are spread in thin layers on the floors of open-air sheds or packed in ice and stored for no longer than three days to prevent their fermenting. During this storage period, the water in their flesh evaporates, enabling them to more readily release a larger amount of oil. If olives are stored too long, they need to be chemically refined. Larger olive oil producers store their olives for extended periods to allow them to maintain year-round production schedules. As a result they often must rely on chemicals to process the damaged olives.

After the olives are removed from storage, they are bathed in cold water to get rid of any impurities before being sent to the mill to be crushed and pressed.

Oil, which makes up 20 to 30 percent of the olive, is contained in pockets within the fruit's cells. The crushing process breaks these cells, releasing all the oil from the olives. The olives are placed in a vat and crushed into a pulp by eight-ton granite or stainless steel millstones.

The next step, pressing, extracts oil from the smooth, thick milled olive paste. In the traditional pressing process, which has been used for more than three thousand years, twenty-pound loads of olive paste are spread on hemp or synthetic fabric pressing-bags, each with a hole in the middle. The bags are threaded on top of one another in batches of twenty-five to fifty between pressing plates on the vertical spindle of a cold screw or hydraulic press. When three hundred to four hundred tons of pressure is applied and the whole column is pressed downward, the pressing bags act like drainage tubes that allow the liquid to flow down the perforated central shaft onto the lower plate of the press while holding back the solids. This first pressing is accomplished without using much force and produces "first-pressed" oil. Second and third pressings use more power and produce successively inferior oil. According to custom, no heat or water is used in these first few pressings.

However, many larger producers have replaced the traditional cold hydraulic presses with centrifugal presses. Inevitably these time- and labor-saving devices are more damaging to the oil.

Regardless of the method used, the oil must be decanted, filtered, and settled after pressing. Since a percentage of the pressed fluid is water, the oil and water must be separated either by natural decantation or by passing the oil into a centrifuge with two spouts. A muddy-looking water referred to by workmen as "inferno" pours out of one spout, while oil spurts out of the other. Quality evaluation of the oil takes place at this time by mill technicians who taste the oils and measure their acidity.

If an oil is found to have less than 1 percent acidity and is considered perfect in flavor and aroma, it is called "extra-virgin." This oil must have a richness and depth of flavor that captures the essence of the olive itself. If it has an acid level of 1 to 3 percent, it is called "virgin" olive oil and has a sharper taste.

The new "extra-virgin" and "virgin" oil is usually cloudy and is allowed to settle in huge crockery jars in cool cellars. It will have an extremely strong, peppery flavor for several months. The oil can be stored as long as necessary until the producer is ready to bottle it.

If filtration is desired, the oil is filtered through cotton before bottling. Although the sediment is filtered out of most oils, some producers believe that the sediment contains a rich olive flavor that should be left in. If you notice that your oil is cloudy with bits of sediment floating around on the bottom of the bottle, accept it as a natural part of the oil-producing process. After filtration, a final quality check is made before bottling to be sure that oxidation has not altered the taste.

Olive oil that does not meet the exacting standards of extra-virgin or virgin oil along with the pulp or "inferno" that remains after the initial pressing are processed further to improve acidity and remove off-flavors. Refining methods include the use of chemicals, bleaching, and steam heating. The resulting oil is pale, very fluid, and almost devoid of flavor. If marketed in this form, it is called "refined" olive oil. It may also be blended with 5 to 10 percent virgin olive oil to improve its flavor and color. The resulting product is usually sold as "pure" olive oil.

If the level of acidity of one of these refined oils has been reduced to less than 1 percent by chemical treatments, this tasteless, artificially deacidified product can be labeled and sold as "extra-virgin oil." In other words, the name "extra-virgin oil" doesn't automatically refer to a superior oil product, when purchasing imported oils. If you buy olive oil produced in the United States, it is subject to FDA regulations prohibiting the use of the term "extra-virgin" on chemically processed oils.

Refined oil is the type of olive oil most readily available to American customers. The words "pure" or "100 percent" on a label merely indicate that the oil has been refined of impurities and was not processed from any source other than olives. They are not indicators of quality. Pure oils have a nutritive value equal to finer oils but may actually be a blend of virgin and refined oils. In the United States refined oils may also be simply labeled as "olive oil."

OLIVE OIL LABELING

Olive oil that does not meet the exacting standards of extra-virgin or virgin oil is processed further to improve acidity and to remove off-flavors. Refining methods include neutralization, deodorization, and bleaching. The resulting oil is pale, has a very mild flavor and a very low acidity. Refined olive oil has the same fatty acid composition as virgin and extra-virgin olive oil. "100% Pure" olive oil is a blend of 5 to 20 percent virgin or extra-virgin olive oil with refined oil. The art of blending is what determines the taste, color, and aroma characteristics unique to each brand.

Oil that is chemically extracted from the pulp or residue of pressing is crude olive pomace oil. Even after refining, this oil is not allowed to be called olive oil under EEC regulations. Unfortunately, some olive pomace oil sold in the United States is not clearly labeled. On some brands the word "pomace" is either missing, disguised, or can only be found in small type on the side or back of the container. An unrealistically low price may indicate the use of olive pomace oil by the packer.

Olive oil produced in the United States is subject to FDA regulations; however, these safeguards are of minimal help since they apply only to oils produced in this country at a time when 97 percent of the olive oil consumed here is imported.

In the area of imported oils, consumer protection is largely in the hands of the International Olive Oil Council (IOOC), which has established standards for the international olive oil community to employ on a self-regulatory basis.

As the number of olive oil products on the American market increases, the consumer has to be sensitive to the exact meaning of the manufacturer's claims. For instance, one of the most popular oils sold in this country is Filippo Berio Mild and Light. Filippo Berio began to market this oil to satisfy Americans who wanted to consume olive oil for health reasons but disliked strong-tasting and -smelling oils. "Extra light" refers to the flavor and color of the oil and not its fat or calorie content.

One clue to identifying a genuine 100 percent extra-virgin olive oil is its cost. Since they are produced in smaller quantities, these oils are both more expensive and less widely available in the United States than chemically refined olive oils. The names of the growers and their orchards are often included on the labels of expensive oils.

You can do a simple test at home to verify the product descriptions on olive oils that you purchase. Place ¼ cup of olive oil in a cup and refrigerate it for two days. Chemically refined oils will turn into a solid mass, while genuine extra-virgin oils will create small granules of fat suspended in liquid oil.

COOKING WITH OLIVE OIL

Olive oils differ in quality, smoke point, color, flavor, and aroma. Each type of olive oil has its own purpose. Genuine extra-virgin oil has the richest, deepest flavor and captures the essence of the olive itself, but isn't appropriate for every dish. Since cooking reduces the flavor of extra-virgin oil, it's a waste of money to use it in baking, sauces, or recipes in which other ingredients might overpower its taste.

Genuine extra-virgin oil is best served at room temperature because high heat can destroy its delicate flavor. Save it for salads and other cold dishes or trickle it over hot dishes just before serving so the rich flavor can be fully enjoyed. Use it in dishes where it is the featured ingredient. For example, genuine extra-virgin oil would be a good choice for a pasta that will only be sauced with oil and garlic.

Use lesser quality oils in dishes where the flavor will be dominated by the other ingredients. Their lighter nature allows the flavors of the food to come through, and they are usually preferred for sautéeing and frying.

Cooking oils should not be allowed to smoke since the chemical structure of fats and oils is changed when heated beyond the smoking point. Olive oil, unlike seed oils, remains stable at relatively high temperatures because of its antioxidant and high oleic acid content. Pure olive oils have smoking points ranging from 406 to 468° F.

Since some genuine extra-virgin olive oils have a smoking point of as low as 300° F., and begin to lose flavor at 140° F., using genuine extra-virgin olive oil in high temperature cooking is not necessary. One possible exception is a new extra-virgin olive oil called La Tavola di Lorenza de Medici which has been developed especially for cooking at higher temperatures. This new oil from Apulia in southern Italy is not as intensely fruity or rich in flavor as typical extra-virgin olive oils and can be used for sautée-ing. (Available from De Medici Import, P.O. Box 20504, Columbus Circle Station, New York, 10023.)

Olive oil, like wine, also offers a wide range of flavors, colors, and aromas that vary with the nature of the soil and climate where the olives were cultivated and the type of olive used. In fact, olive oil is the only cooking and salad oil that offers a variety of natural flavors.

Flavors can vary from bland to peppery and can be described as mild (delicate, light, and almost buttery tasting), semi-fruity (stronger with more olive taste), fruity (oil with a strong olive flavor), pizzico (oil with a peppery accent), rustic (hearty oil), and sweet.

Colors can range from delicate straw hues to emerald green. While dark, intense color may signal a fruity flavor and lighter colors may indicate a nuttier flavor, this is not always the case since oils are often blends of several varieties of olives. Like wines, olive oils have vintages caused by changes in growing conditions that affect color and flavor. In fact, you might buy two very green oils and discover that one is intensely peppery and the other light and fruity.

Since no two olive oils are alike they should be chosen as you would choose wine, by personal taste preference and budget considerations. Beware of oils that have a thick, greasy appearance or those that are thin, pallid, and watery. Also avoid those that have been stored in the sun or have a copper tint.

Finally, olives oils, which are actually fruit juices, can differ according to the regions where they are grown. There are sixty different types of olive trees in the fifteen major oil-producing areas of Italy alone.

The four major olive oil–producing countries are Italy, France, Greece, and Spain.

- Italian olive oil *(olia di oliva)* is considered by many people to be the finest in the world, particularly those oils produced in the Tuscany and Chianti regions. These oils are very rich with an intense olive taste, a peppery flavor, and a deep, almost emerald-green in color.
- The Italian Riviera and Liguria produce an oil that is green-gold in color and more subtly flavored.
- The French Riviera and Provence produce an oil *(huile d'olive)* that is even more delicate. It's known for its sweet, fruity flavor and its light, golden-yellow color.
- Spanish olive oil *(aceite de oliva)* has a strong assertive flavor with a thick consistency.
- Greek olive oil is also thick but has a lighter olive flavor. Spanish and Greek oils are generally less expensive than the Italian and French oils.
- California oils range from rich, olivey, Italian-style oils to delicate French-style oils. Since most are produced on a small scale, they are quite expensive and have difficulty competing with the imports of equal quality that can be more cheaply manufactured abroad. While there were once sixty small olive oil producers in California, the dramatic increase in imports has reduced this number to five or six.

OLIVE OIL PRICES

The price of olive oil is generally two to five times higher than other edible oils due to the nature of olive cultivation and processing. Unlike an annually sown crop such as soybeans, olive trees grow very slowly, bearing fruit after five years and reaching full maturity after twenty years. The costs of plowing, fertilizing, pruning, pest control, harvesting, and production take large jumps each year.

Olive oils currently on the market may range in price between $2.98 and $40 for a sixteen-ounce bottle. Prices vary according to oil quality.

CHOOSING OLIVE OILS

To begin with, you'll want to buy one costlier genuine extra-virgin oil and one lesser quality oil. Buy the smallest quantity you can or split bottles with friends and neighbors as you try different brands. Gradually expand your selections to include a cross-section of olive oils of different grades and prices from several countries so you can experiment with a broad range of flavors and aromas.

Remember to select cold-pressed oils whenever possible. Although this phrase suggests that the oil has been removed without heat and is therefore more nutritionally sound, some heat may have actually been used in the extraction process. The important word is "pressed" since it indicates that oil has been produced by an expellor method.

The best way to taste olive oil is by dipping crusty bread or lightly steamed vegetables into it or sipping it from a spoon or a tiny cup. If you are tasting several oils at the same time, use mineral water, club soda, or white wine to cleanse the palate between tastings. A fatty sensation in the throat or a highly acidic taste are both negative signs. Olive oil experts also put drops of oil on the backs of their wrists like perfume or sprinkle the oil on their hands, which they rub together and smell to test for aroma.

Although we will be suggesting in some recipes that you use either an extra-virgin, flavorful oil or a milder, lighter flavored oil as a general guideline, we have not limited you to using specific types of olive oil in our ingredient lists. Rather, we suggest that you experiment with a variety of oils. By varying the oils you use to prepare a dish, you can create an endless array of taste experiences. You may wish to consider using milder, less fruity olive oils in fish and soup recipes and fruity, more flavorful oils with more robust meat and tomato-sauced dishes, but this is largely a matter of personal taste.

Another logical way to experiment is to use Italian oils when making Italian recipes, Spanish oils when making selections with a Spanish flavor, and Greek oils when working with Greek preparations. For instance, the earthy peasant character of Greek oil will add an authentic taste to dishes like Moussaka and Greek Salad.

Due to the increased interest in olive oil, your supermarket may offer a variety of moderately priced oils for you to choose from in the condiment and gourmet sections. If you are looking for a broader selection, investigate the nearest ethnic grocery, specialty deli, gourmet shop, or natural food store. Again, your best guide to olive oil selection is a reliable food merchant who knows something about the producers whose oils he is stocking.

STORING OLIVE OIL

Light is harmful to olive oil, so it should be stored in a cool, dark place. Keep it away from dampness and do not expose it to heat, light, or air for any length of time. You can pour olive oil into a green glass wine bottle with a cork to prevent spoilage from ultraviolet rays. It can also be stored in stainless steel or glazed ceramic.

Avoid buying olive oil in plastic containers because some of the compounds used in the manufacture of the plastic may be absorbed by the oil. If you have to buy oil packaged in plastic, transfer it to a glass or stainless steel container after you open it since contact with oxygen can trigger the chemical reaction.

Olive oil has less of a tendency to turn rancid than most other oils due to its low iodine value. Olive oil does not improve with age. If stored correctly, fine olive oils can be kept for at least a year. Oils are most flavorful for the first two months and begin to lose their tangy olive taste after twelve months.

If you are worried about having the oil spoil, you can store it in the refrigerator. The flavor will remain intact, but the oil will get cloudy. You can use the cloudy oil or wait until it returns to room temperature. You can speed up the process by placing the bottle under warm tap water for a few minutes. Another alternative is to keep a small amount of oil on your kitchen shelf while storing the larger bottle in the refrigerator.

OLIVE OIL SPRAY PRODUCTS

Olive oil sprays are useful for coating cooking pans, pasta and toast, or for making salads. However some commercial sprays are a combination of olive oil, alcohol, lecithin, and chemical propellants. Look for aerosol cans of olive oil cooking spray which contain no alcohol or fluorocarbons. Better yet, create your own by purchasing a plastic pump-spray bottle and filling it with olive oil. If the bottle doesn't spray evenly, spread the oil with a basting brush.

OLIVES

Since table olives are frequently high in sodium as a result of the processing methods used to preserve and package them, we have used them only as a garnish or recipe ingredient in small quantities. Green olives usually have considerably more sodium than black olives. For instance, the USDA analyzes four green olives as containing 312 milligrams of sodium, while four ripe black olives have only 68.

To avoid excess sodium, buy olives packed in oil instead of brine whenever possible. Rinsing brine-soaked olives is helpful but cannot remove all the sodium absorbed by the fruit through long months of curing. If you purchase dry, oil-packed olives that are too bitter for your taste, you can simmer them for 5 to 10 minutes and drain them before using.

Olives range from 4 to 18 calories each, depending on their size.

TWENTY EASY WAYS TO ADD OLIVE OIL TO YOUR DIET
1. Keep a cruet of extra-virgin olive oil on your dining table and sprinkle it on salads, soups, stews, and pasta.
2. Toss hot or cold vegetables with 2 tablespoons of olive oil, freshly grated black pepper, and a squeeze of fresh lemon juice.
3. Toss salad greens with olive oil, then with lemon juice or vinegar. Tossing with oil first will keep the greens from wilting.
4. Dip raw vegetables in a dipping sauce made with extra-virgin olive oil and freshly ground black pepper.
5. Stir-fry vegetables with two tablespoons of olive oil, 2 minced garlic cloves, and a sprinkling of fresh herbs.
6. Make vegetable sauces by sautéeing finely diced vegetables in olive oil. Add wine and stock and simmer.
7. Use olive oil to replace the rich taste of meat or meat broth in your favorite soup and stew recipes.
8. Reduce the saturated fat in butter sauces by substituting a stock thick-

ened with olive oil. Boil a fish or chicken stock and thicken it by adding a steady stream of olive oil. Add additional stock as needed and simmer. Season by adding a few tablespoons of wine.

9. Bake cubes of winter vegetables such as fresh pumpkin in olive oil, parsley, and garlic.

10. Rub potatoes with olive oil before baking for added crispness. Serve with more olive oil, herbs, and pepper.

11. Add a tablespoon of olive oil to water when boiling pasta to prevent the pasta from sticking to the pot. Toss cooked pasta with a tablespoon of olive oil immediately after draining.

12. To add flavor, first brown meat in olive oil when braising it before cooking in liquid.

13. When broiling or roasting meats or poultry, brush with olive oil to seal in the natural juices.

14. Pan-broil meat, poultry, or fish in an uncovered skillet lightly coated with olive oil.

15. Prepare pancake and waffle batter using light flavored olive oil. Also use olive oil to grease the griddle.

16. Substitute light flavored olive oil for other liquid oils in baking recipes. It is particularly compatible with fruit cakes and fruit muffins.

17. Pop corn in olive oil and drizzle some extra oil over the top of the popped corn.

18. Use olive oil as a spread for bread and rolls instead of butter or margarine. When dining out, ask your waitress for a cruet of olive oil for this purpose.

19. Make croutons by sprinkling ½-inch cubes of French bread with olive oil and black pepper. Bake at 400° F. until toasted.

20. Sauté bread crumbs with olive oil and paprika until golden brown. Add to steamed vegetables and salads.

USING THE RECIPES

....

NUTRIENT ANALYSIS

Following each recipe, you will find a nutritional analysis that includes:

    a. Calories (cal) per serving

    b. Grams (gm) of protein

    c. Grams of carbohydrate

    d. Grams of dietary fiber

    e. Milligrams (mg) of cholesterol

    f. Total fat (in grams and cholesterol)

    g. Saturated (sat) fat (in grams and calories)

    h. Polyunsaturated (poly) fat (in grams and calories)

    i. Monounsaturated (mono) fat (in grams and calories)

We have used Nutritionist III software to produce these nutrient analyses. The primary sources for the Nutritonist III Data Base are the USDA Handbooks #8–1 through #8–16.

The analyses of meat, poultry, and seafood ingredients are based on a single portion serving of meat, poultry, or seafood of 4 ounces. When a choice of ingredients is suggested (i.e., 1 percent or skim milk), we have based our analysis on the first ingredient listed.

Total fat calories are not always equal to the total of saturated, polyunsaturated, and monounsaturated fat calories in the nutrition counts due to gaps in currently available data on food values.

Due to inevitable variations in the ingredients you may select, nutritional analyses should be considered approximate.

SUPER-QUICK RECIPES

Our ⊙ symbol in the upper left corner of a recipe indicates a combined preparation and cooking time of 35 minutes or less.

APPETIZERS AND SNACKS

EGGPLANT CAVIAR 🅖
RAW VEGETABLES WITH TANGY CHEESE DIP 🅖
MUSHROOMS WITH OIL AND LEMON 🅖
GARLIC CHICKEN BITES
WALNUT-ORANGE CHICKEN BITES
LADY MEATBALLS
ECUADORIAN SHRIMP SEVICHE
CRAB SALAD COCKTAIL 🅖
TUNA CAPONATA
BRUSCHETTA 🅖

Eggplant Caviar

.... ● ....

This dish is often called "poor man's caviar" in southern France. Since real caviar is not only expensive but high in cholesterol, this delicious substitute is a bargain in more ways than one. Serve it at room temperature or chilled as a spread with crackers or toast.

2 eggplants, about 1 pound each
¼ cup minced scallions
1 clove garlic (or 1 shallot or 2 scallions), minced
2 teaspoons lemon juice
½ teaspoon dried basil leaves
¼ cup extra-virgin flavorful olive oil
¼ teaspoon black pepper

1. Preheat oven to 400° F. Cut eggplants in half lengthwise and place on a baking sheet with their cut-sides facing down. Bake for 20 minutes or until they are fork-tender.
2. Take eggplants out of oven and remove the pulp from the skin. Puree pulp in a blender. Spoon into a medium bowl.
3. Combine eggplant pulp with remaining ingredients. Serve at room temperature or chill for 1 hour.

VARIATION
Omit the basil. Add ¼ teaspoon of crushed dried red pepper for a spicier spread.

YIELD
Serves 4

PREPARATION TIME
15 minutes

COOKING TIME
20 minutes

NUTRIENT ANALYSIS
Calories per serving: 185
Protein: 2 gm
Carbohydrates: 16 gm
Dietary fiber: 6.4 gm
Cholesterol: 0 mg
Total fat: 14 gm (126 cal)
Sat fat: 2 gm (18 cal)
Poly fat: 1.4 gm (12.6 gm)
Mono fat: 10 gm (90 cal)

Raw Vegetables with Tangy Cheese Dip

YIELD
4 servings

PREPARATION TIME
10 minutes

NUTRIENT ANALYSIS
Calories per serving: 147
Protein: 4.5 gm
Carbohydrates: 1.6 gm
Dietary fiber: 0.05 gm
Cholesterol: 1.6 mg
Total fat: 13.9 gm (125 cal)
Sat fat: 2.1 gm (19 cal)
Poly fat: 1.2 gm (10 cal)
Mono fat: 10 gm (90 cal)

Prepare a tray of raw vegetables such as asparagus spears, broccoli and cauliflower florets, scallions, carrot and celery sticks, turnip wedges, green bell pepper strips, mushrooms, snow peas, radishes, cucumber and zucchini chunks, cherry tomatoes, and green beans. Serve with an assortment of whole grain crackers or pita bread wedges and a bowl of Tangy Cheese Dip.

10 tablespoons 1 percent low-fat cottage cheese
2 teaspoons red wine vinegar
¼ cup extra-virgin flavorful olive oil
1 teaspoon grated orange rind
1 clove garlic (or shallot), minced
1 tablespoon chopped scallions
¼ teaspoon black pepper

Process all ingredients at medium speed in blender container or food processor, until thoroughly blended. Use a rubber spatula to push down mixture to blend well.

VARIATIONS

- Omit orange rind and red wine vinegar. Add 1 tablespoon caraway seed, 1½ teaspoons sweet paprika, 1 tablespoon chopped celery, 2 tablespoons chopped radish.
- Omit red wine vinegar and orange rind. Add 1 teaspoon Dijon-style mustard, ½ teaspoon dried tarragon, 1 tablespoon chopped fresh parsley, ½ teaspoon anchovy paste.
- Add ½ teaspoon curry powder.
- Omit orange rind. Add ¼ cup chopped mushrooms and 1½ tablespoons fresh dill.

- Omit orange rind and scallions. Add 1 tablespoon minced fresh mint, 1 tablespoon minced fresh dill, and 1 tablespoon fresh chives.
- Omit orange rind. Add 2 tablespoons chopped cucumber, 2 tablespoons chopped radish, 1 tablespoon chopped green bell pepper, 1 tablespoon chopped fresh parsley, 1 tablespoon chopped fresh dill.
- Add ¼ cup chopped black olives.
- Add ¼ cup chopped blanched almonds.
- Omit red wine vinegar and orange rind. Add ½ cup chopped canned clams, drained; 1 tablespoon chopped fresh parsley, 2 tablespoons lemon juice.
- Add crushed dried red pepper to taste.
- Omit orange rind. Add 6 cooked, chopped medium shrimp.
- Add 2 tablespoons chopped cucumber.
- Omit orange rind. Add ½ ripe avocado, peeled, pitted, and chopped; 1 tablespoon fresh dill and 1 tablespoon fresh chives.

Mushrooms with Oil and Lemon

······· ⓒ ·······

YIELD
6 servings

PREPARATION TIME
10 minutes

COOKING TIME
8 minutes

NUTRIENT ANALYSIS
Calories per serving: 180
Protein: 1.6 gm
Carbohydrates: 4 gm
Dietary fiber: 1.4 gm
Cholesterol: 0 mg
Total fat: 18 gm (164 cal)
Sat fat: 2.6 gm (23 cal)
Poly fat: 1.7 gm (15 cal)
Mono fat: 13 gm (119 cal)

Select young mushrooms with a cream-colored or white cap surface. This dish should be served warm or at room temperature with the oil it was cooked in.

1 pound fresh mushrooms, rinsed and dried (avoid
    soaking)
½ cup extra-virgin flavorful olive oil
1 clove garlic, cut in half
¼ teaspoon salt
1 tablespoon lemon juice
1 tablespoon chopped fresh parsley

1. Cut off bottoms of stems of mushrooms.
2. Heat oil in a skillet over medium heat, and sauté garlic clove until it turns light brown. Remove garlic and discard.
3. Add mushrooms to oil and sauté for 1 minute. Add salt. Sauté mushrooms, stirring constantly, for 4 additional minutes.
4. Add lemon juice and parsley to skillet and stir to combine with mushrooms.
5. Remove from heat and serve.

VARIATION
Mexican Mushroom Appetizer: Add ⅛ teaspoon crushed, dried red pepper and ½ teaspoon dried oregano.

Garlic Chicken Bites

....

These crispy chicken nuggets are seasoned with garlic, cayenne, and black pepper. Serve warm and dip in a honey-mustard sauce or the Chili Pepper Barbecue Sauce (p. 245).

2 boneless chicken breasts (1 pound), skinned and cut
    into bite-sized strips
½ cup extra-virgin olive oil
4 cloves garlic, minced
¼ teaspoon black pepper
½ cup finely ground bread crumbs (or oat bran)
¼ teaspoon cayenne

1. Marinate chicken strips in olive oil, garlic, and pepper for 30 minutes. Drain off excess marinade. Preheat oven to 475° F.
2. Mix bread crumbs with cayenne. Dip both sides of chicken strips in mixture.
3. Arrange strips in one layer on a baking sheet. Bake for 15 minutes. Turn and bake 5 minutes more until browned.

YIELD
4 servings

PREPARATION TIME
15 minutes + 30 minutes of marinating

COOKING TIME
20 minutes

NUTRIENT ANALYSIS
Calories per serving: 475
Protein: 37 gm
Carbohydrates: 10 gm
Dietary fiber: 0 gm
Cholesterol: 94 mg
Total fat: 32 gm (284 cal)
Sat fat: 5 gm (46 cal)
Poly fat: 3.2 gm (29 cal)
Mono fat: 21 gm (191 cal)

Walnut-Orange Chicken Bites

YIELD
4 servings

PREPARATION TIME
*10 minutes + overnight
marinating time*

COOKING TIME
10 minutes

NUTRIENT ANALYSIS
Calories per serving: 315
Protein: 35 gm
Carbohydrates: 1.9 gm
Dietary fiber: 0.1 gm
Cholesterol: 94 mg
Total fat: 17.5 gm (157 cal)
Sat fat: 3.1 gm (28 cal)
Poly fat: 2 gm (18 cal)
Mono fat: 11.4 gm (102 cal)

Marinate the chicken in orange juice and sherry overnight and sauté it immediately before serving. Serve with toothpicks on a bed of lettuce or watercress.

2 tablespoons sherry
¼ cup orange juice
Outer rind of ½ orange, cut into thin strips
¼ cup extra-virgin olive oil
¼ teaspoon black pepper
*2 boneless chicken breasts (1 pound), skinned and cut
    into 1-inch pieces*

1. Combine the sherry, orange juice, orange rind, 2 tablespoons of oil, and pepper in a glass bowl.
2. Add the chicken pieces and marinate overnight.
3. Drain chicken on paper towels. Save the orange rind and discard the marinade.
4. Heat remaining olive oil in a skillet and sauté chicken pieces, while stirring, for 10 minutes until tender. Stir in orange rind and remaining oil immediately before removing from skillet.

Lady Meatballs

These Syrian meatballs, also called *Kadin Budu,* are made with rice, Parmesan cheese, and dill. Serve very hot on toothpicks. They can be made ahead and reheated when ready to serve.

½ cup cooked rice
1 pound lean ground turkey (or lamb or ground beef)
½ cup grated onion
¼ cup chopped fresh parsley
½ cup grated Parmesan cheese
5 tablespoons extra-virgin flavorful olive oil
2 egg whites, beaten
¼ cup chopped fresh dill (or 2 teaspoons dried dill)
¼ teaspoon black pepper
½ cup all-purpose flour (or ¼ cup flour and ¼ cup oat bran)

1. Combine rice, meat, onion, parsley, cheese, 2 tablespoons of the olive oil, egg whites, dill, and pepper in a bowl.
2. Knead well and form into twenty egg-shaped ovals.
3. Roll ovals in flour.
4. Heat remaining oil over medium heat in a large frying pan. Sauté ovals for about 5 minutes until brown on one side. Turn carefully and sauté other side for 3 minutes or until brown. Remove and drain on paper towels.
5. Keep in a covered casserole in a warm oven until ready to serve. If refrigerating to serve later, reheat in a covered casserole at 325° F. for 20 minutes until warmed through.

YIELD
20 small meatballs (4 servings)

PREPARATION TIME
20 minutes (not including cooking rice)

COOKING TIME
10 minutes

NUTRIENT ANALYSIS
Calories per serving: 455
Protein: 43 gm
Carbohydrates: 19 gm
Dietary fiber: 1.2 gm
Cholesterol: 104 mg
Total fat: 22 gm (198 cal)
Sat fat: 5.1 gm (45 cal)
Poly fat: 1.7 gm (15 cal)
Mono fat: 14 gm (126 cal)

Ecuadorian Shrimp Seviche

YIELD

8 servings

PREPARATION TIME

*30 minutes + overnight
marinating time*

COOKING TIME

5 minutes

NUTRIENT ANALYSIS

Calories per serving: 228
Protein: 13 gm
Carbohydrates: 13 gm
Dietary fiber: 1 gm
Cholesterol: 100 gm
Total fat: 14 gm (128 cal)
Sat fat: 2 gm (18 cal)
Poly fat: 1.4 gm (12 cal)
Mono fat: 10 gm (90 cal)

S eviche, a multi-flavored Mexican specialty, is an appetizer of fresh fish or shellfish that is "cooked" in freshly squeezed fruit juices. This Ecuadorian version of seviche uses a medley of fruit juices and can be served like a shrimp cocktail in individual lettuce-lined goblets.

*1 pound fresh medium or large shrimp, peeled and
    deveined*
1/4 cup water
1/2 teaspoon salt
1 tablespoon black pepper
*1 cup fresh fruit juice (juice of 3 lemons, 4 limes, and
    1/2 orange)*
1 large red onion, very thinly sliced
2 large ripe tomatoes, very thinly sliced
1 clove garlic, minced
1/2 cup extra-virgin olive oil
1/2 tablespoon white horseradish
1 cup chili sauce
1/4 cup chopped fresh parsley
1/4 cup chopped fresh cilantro (Italian parsley)

1. Rinse shrimp in running water, put in a medium saucepan, and add 1/4 cup of water. Cover pan and simmer over low heat until water boils, then remove from heat immediately.

2. Let stand for 3 or 4 minutes, then remove shrimp from water. Strain shrimp water from pan and refrigerate for use the following day when you assemble the seviche.

3. Place the shrimp in a glass bowl with 1/4 teaspoon of the salt, 1/2 teaspoon of the pepper, and half the fruit juice. Stir, cover, and let marinate in the refrigerator overnight.

4. In a second glass bowl, combine sliced onions and to-

matoes. Add garlic, olive oil, and remaining salt, pepper, and fruit juice. Cover bowl and marinate overnight.

5. Before serving, combine shrimp and vegetable mixtures. Stir in horseradish, chili sauce, parsley, cilantro, and water set aside from steaming shrimp. Mix well and serve. Serve with additional chili sauce on the side.

Crab Salad Cocktail

Olive oil gives a new dimension to this favorite Maryland delicacy. Serve the crab mixture mounded into empty crab shells or use it as a stuffing for hollowed-out cherry tomatoes.

1 pound cooked crabmeat
3 tablespoons minced fresh parsley
¼ cup extra-virgin flavorful olive oil
Juice from 1 large lemon
¼ teaspoon white pepper

1. Shred the crabmeat in a bowl with a fork and combine with parsley.

2. Add oil and lemon juice. Sprinkle with white pepper. Stuff shells or tomatoes and chill thoroughly before serving.

YIELD
4 servings

PREPARATION TIME
10 minutes

NUTRIENT ANALYSIS
Calories per serving: 237
Protein: 20 gm
Carbohydrates: 2.4 gm
Dietary fiber: 0.2 gm
Cholesterol: 113 mg
Total fat: 16.2 gm (146 cal)
Sat fat: 2.4 gm (21 cal)
Poly fat: 2.8 gm (25 cal)
Mono fat: 10.4 gm (94 cal)

Tuna Caponata

YIELD
6 servings

PREPARATION TIME
30 minutes

COOKING TIME
20 minutes

Traditionally, caponata is served at room temperature; however, it can also be served hot or chilled. You can present it as an hors d'oeuvre with French bread or as a side dish with broiled meat or fish.

6 tablespoons extra-virgin flavorful olive oil
1 medium eggplant (about 1 pound), peeled and cut into
  ¾-inch slices
¼ teaspoon black pepper
1 cup chopped celery
2 medium onions, chopped
1 medium red bell pepper, cut into ¾-inch chunks
1 small yellow squash, cut in half lengthwise, then into
  ½-inch slices
1½ cups chopped ripe tomatoes (or 1½ cups drained
  chopped canned tomatoes)
¼ cup red wine vinegar
½ teaspoon fresh thyme leaves (or ¼ teaspoon dried)
¼ teaspoon ground cloves
1 teaspoon sugar
8 green olives, rinsed in cold water, pitted and chopped
1 7½-ounce can white albacore tuna, packed in olive oil
  or water-pack tuna mixed with 1 tablespoon of olive
  oil

1. Heat 4 tablespoons of the olive oil in a large skillet. Add eggplant and season with pepper. Cook over high heat until eggplant is lightly browned, about 8 minutes. Remove with slotted spoon and set aside in a large bowl.
2. Add 2 more tablespoons of olive oil to skillet and sauté celery for 5 minutes over medium heat. Add onions and cook 2 minutes more or until onions are soft. Add red peppers and squash to skillet and sauté for 4 minutes more.
3. Add tomatoes, cover, and cook over moderate heat for

6 minutes. Return eggplant to skillet, stir, and simmer over low heat for 5 minutes.

4. In a small saucepan, heat vinegar, thyme, cloves, sugar, and olives for 30 seconds.

5. Add vinegar mixture to skillet. Cover and simmer for 5 more minutes.

6. Flake the tuna and sprinkle on top of the caponata immediately before serving.

Bruschetta

YIELD
4 servings

PREPARATION TIME
10 minutes

COOKING TIME
5 minutes

NUTRIENT ANALYSIS
Calories per serving: 303
Protein: 6.6 gm
Carbohydrates: 37 gm
Dietary fiber: 1.7 gm
Cholesterol: 0 mg
Total fat: 13.6 gm (122 cal)
Sat fat: 1.9 gm (17 cal)
Poly fat: 1.2 gm (10 cal)
Mono fat: 10 gm (90 cal)

Bruschetta is the Italian ancestor of our American version of garlic bread. It can be prepared with or without the tomato slices. Serve on a platter with slices of low-fat mozzarella cheese and green Italian olives.

8¹⁄₂-inch thick slices French or Italian bread
2 cloves garlic, cut in half
¹⁄₄ cup extra-virgin flavorful olive oil
2 medium, ripe tomatoes, thinly sliced
¹⁄₂ teaspoon black pepper

1. Toast bread until lightly browned on both sides under a broiler.
2. Rub top of bread with garlic. Return slices to broiling tray.
3. Sprinkle olive oil over bread slices. Top with tomato slices and pepper.
4. Broil close to flame for 1 minute and serve at once.

VARIATION
Mince garlic and spread on bread.

SOUPS

BEAN-LEEK SOUP
SPINACH CHICK-PEA SOUP
CUBAN BLACK BEAN SOUP
SPLIT PEA SOUP
LIMA BEAN SOUP
MINESTRONE WITH PESTO ⊜
SOUP WITH PISTOU GARNISH
GREEK LENTIL SOUP
GAZPACHO
GARDEN CARROT SOUP
TOMATO-HERB SOUP
GREEK BOUILLABAISSE
ZUPPA DA PESCE
FISHERMAN'S STEW
CODFISH SOUP

BEAN SOUPS

....

Beans are low in fat and cholesterol-free. In addition, research has proven them effective in lowering harmful low-density lipoproteins (LDLs) in blood cholesterol.

Sort through beans before cooking them, removing any that are discolored and any pebbles or other particles that may be present.

There are two ways to soak dried beans to prepare them for cooking.

1. Rinse and soak the beans overnight in enough water to cover the beans plus two extra inches to compensate for absorption. When drained the next morning, they're ready to use.
2. The quicker method is to cover the beans with water in a large pot and bring to a boil for 2 minutes. Remove from the heat and soak for an hour. After draining and rinsing, they're ready to use.

Lentils don't need to be soaked. Other varieties of small beans such as green peas may also indicate on their packages that soaking isn't necessary.

Bean-Leek Soup

YIELD
4 servings

PREPARATION TIME
20 minutes

COOKING TIME
40 minutes

NUTRIENT ANALYSIS
Calories per serving: 393
Protein: 15 gm
Carbohydrates: 38 gm
Dietary fiber: 9.6 gm
Cholesterol: 1.0 mg
Total fat: 21 gm (187 cal)
Sat fat: 3.1 gm (28 cal)
Poly fat: 2.1 gm (19 cal)
Mono fat: 13.9 gm (125 cal)

This easy-to-prepare soup combines mild, sweet leeks with deep-red kidney beans and round, golden chick-peas, and then adds fresh string beans for good measure. Serve topped with fresh parsley and croutons.

⅓ cup extra-virgin flavorful olive oil
2 leeks, chopped
2 stalks celery, chopped
2 cloves garlic, minced
4 cups low-salt chicken broth
1 teaspoon dried thyme leaves
1 teaspoon dried marjoram leaves
1 bay leaf
¼ teaspoon black pepper
1½ cups cooked kidney beans
1½ cups cooked chick-peas
*1 pound fresh string beans, ends trimmed and cut into
    1-inch pieces.*

1. Heat olive oil in a large, heavy soup pot over medium heat and sauté leeks, celery, and garlic until tender.
2. Add broth, thyme, marjoram, bay leaf, pepper, kidney beans, and chick-peas. Bring ingredients to a boil, then lower heat to simmer for 25 minutes.
3. Add string beans and simmer for 10 minutes more.

Spinach Chick-Pea Soup

Chick-peas, with their nutlike flavor, are found in cuisines ranging from Lebanon to Provence..This soup includes spinach, mint, garlic, and parsley. Serve with cracked wheat bread and Tomatoes with Parsley (p. 74).

1½ cups canned chick-peas
6 cups low-salt chicken broth
1 cup fresh spinach, rinsed, cooked, drained, and chopped
    (or 10 ounces of frozen chopped spinach, squeezed to
    remove excess liquid)
⅓ cup extra-virgin flavorful olive oil
4 slices French or Italian bread, cut into ½-inch squares
4 cloves garlic, minced
¼ cup finely chopped fresh mint (or 1 teaspoon dried)
2 teaspoons finely chopped fresh parsley
4 sprigs mint

1. Drain chick-peas well. Place in a large, heavy soup pot, add broth, and simmer over low heat for 10 minutes.
2. Add spinach to soup and simmer for 10 more minutes.
3. While soup is cooking, heat ¼ cup of the olive oil over high heat in a skillet. Add bread, reduce heat to low, and cook, turning the squares until they are lightly browned.
4. Mash garlic with back of large spoon in bottom of a large serving bowl. Stir in mint, parsley, and remaining olive oil, 1 tablespoon at a time. Stir until the olive oil is completely absorbed.
5. Raise heat to high and bring soup to a quick boil. Pour soup into the large serving bowl on top of herb mixture. Stir with a large spoon and scatter croutons on top. Garnish with mint sprigs.

YIELD
4 servings

PREPARATION TIME
20 minutes

COOKING TIME
30 minutes

NUTRIENT ANALYSIS
Calories per serving: 398
Protein: 14 gm
Carbohydrates: 35 gm
Dietary fiber: 1.9 gm
Cholesterol: 1.5 gm
Total fat: 22.5 gm (202 cal)
Sat fat: 3.6 gm (32 cal)
Poly fat: 2 gm (18 cal)
Mono fat: 14 gm (128 cal)

Cuban Black Bean Soup

YIELD
4 servings

PREPARATION TIME
30 minutes plus bean soaking time (overnight)

COOKING TIME
1 hour and 10 minutes

NUTRIENT ANALYSIS
Calories per serving: 238
Protein: 11 gm
Carbohydrates: 13 gm
Dietary fiber: 1.9 gm
Cholesterol: 1.5 mg
Total fat: 16 gm (143 cal)
Sat fat: 2.5 gm (23 cal)
Poly fat: 1.7 gm (15 cal)
Mono fat: 11 gm (98 cal)

This satisfying soup features small oval-shaped black turtle beans accented with a subtle mix of garlic, oregano, cumin, and red pepper. For a spicier soup, add ½ teaspoon of Easy Blender Rouille (p. 266).

¼ cup extra-virgin flavorful olive oil
½ cup chopped onion
½ medium green bell pepper, chopped
1 tablespoon minced fresh cilantro (or 1 teaspoon dried parsley)
4 cloves garlic, minced
1 tablespoon red wine vinegar
1½ quarts low-salt chicken broth
5 ounces dried black turtle beans, sorted, rinsed, and soaked
½ teaspoon dried oregano leaves
½ teaspoon ground cumin
1 teaspoon cayenne pepper

1. In a large, heavy soup pot, heat oil over medium-high heat. Add onion, green pepper, cilantro, and garlic and sauté for 6 minutes.

2. Add vinegar and sauté for 1 minute longer. Add chicken broth, black beans, oregano, cumin, and pepper.

3. Bring to a boil. Reduce heat to low and let soup simmer for 55 minutes or until beans are tender. Remove from heat and let soup cool.

4. Puree about half of the soup, 2 cups of soup at a time, in a blender at low speed or in food processor.

5. Return puree to pot containing remaining soup and cook, stirring, until well heated.

Split Pea Soup

Split peas are available in green and yellow, the yellow peas having a less pronounced flavor, but both are good. Top soup with croutons or add ¼ cup of warm, cooked rice in the bottom of each soup bowl. Serve with rye rolls and Shredded Carrot-Turnip Slaw (p. 72).

¼ cup extra-virgin flavorful olive oil
2 medium onions, chopped
2 cloves garlic (or 1 shallot or 2 scallions), chopped
1 cup dried split peas, sorted and rinsed
6 cups water
½ cup sliced carrots
1 stalk celery, chopped
1 bay leaf
¼ teaspoon black pepper

1. Heat olive oil in large, heavy soup pot over medium heat and sauté onion and garlic 5 minutes or until softened.
2. Stir in split peas, water, carrots, celery, bay leaf, and black pepper.
3. Reduce heat and simmer for 2 hours, stirring frequently.

YIELD
6 servings

PREPARATION TIME
20 minutes

COOKING TIME
2 hours

NUTRIENT ANALYSIS
Calories per serving: 173
Protein: 5.9 gm
Carbohydrates: 18 gm
Dietary fiber: 0.9 gm
Cholesterol: 0 mg
Total fat: 9.5 gm (86 cal)
Sat fat: 1.3 gm (12 cal)
Poly fat: 0.8 gm (7 cal)
Mono fat: 7 gm (60 cal)

Lima
Bean
Soup

YIELD

4 servings

PREPARATION TIME

*30 minutes + bean soaking
time (overnight)*

COOKING TIME

1 hour and 15 minutes

NUTRIENT ANALYSIS

Calories per serving: 365
Protein: 13 gm
Carbohydrates: 30 gm
Dietary fiber: 4.8 gm
Cholesterol: 1.0 mg
Total fat: 22 gm (198 cal)
Sat fat: 3.4 gm (30 cal)
Poly fat: 2.2 gm (20 cal)
Mono fat: 15.6 gm (140 cal)

The special richness of olive oil replaces the salty meats often used to provide flavor in bean soups in this hearty wintertime Tuscan favorite. Additional olive oil can be added at the table.

1 pound dried lima beans, sorted and rinsed
1 quart low-salt chicken broth
2 bay leaves
2 teaspoons dried oregano leaves
6 tablespoons extra-virgin flavorful olive oil
⅓ cup chopped fresh parsley
4 cloves garlic, minced
5 tablespoons lemon juice

1. Place beans in a large bowl, cover with two extra inches of water, and soak overnight.

2. Drain beans and pour into a large, heavy soup pot. Add broth, bay leaves, oregano, and olive oil. Bring to a boil over high heat, then reduce heat to low, cover, and simmer for 1 hour.

3. Puree half the beans and half the liquid in a blender or food processor. Pour the puree back into the soup pot containing the remaining beans and liquid.

4. Add the parsley, garlic, and lemon juice. Simmer for 15 minutes.

Minestrone
with
Pesto

Serve this quick version of minestrone with Oregano Parsley Pesto (p. 264) and grated Parmesan cheese.

¼ cup mild, light flavored olive oil
½ cup chopped onion
½ cup chopped fresh or canned tomatoes
½ cup chopped carrots
1 cup chopped green cabbage
1 cup chopped zucchini
4 cups water
3 scallions, chopped
½ cup diced, peeled potatoes
½ cup chopped fresh mushrooms
2 tablespoons Oregano Parsley Pesto (or other pesto sauce)
Salt (optional)
Black pepper to taste

1. Heat olive oil over medium heat in a large soup pot and sauté onion until tender, about 4 minutes.
2. Add tomatoes, carrots, cabbage, zucchini, water, scallions, potatoes, and mushrooms. Cover and cook at a gentle boil for 18 minutes or until vegetables are tender. Add pesto, salt (if desired), and pepper and turn off heat.

YIELD
4 servings

PREPARATION TIME
15 minutes

COOKING TIME
22 minutes

NUTRIENT ANALYSIS
Calories per serving: 228
Protein: 1.8 gm
Carbohydrates: 11 gm
Dietary fiber: 2.6 gm
Cholesterol: 0 mg
Total fat: 20.6 gm (186 cal)
Sat fat: 2.9 gm (26 cal)
Poly fat: 1.9 gm (17 cal)
Mono fat: 15 gm (134 cal)

Soup with Pistou Garnish

YIELD
4 servings

PREPARATION TIME
30 minutes

COOKING TIME
40 minutes

A fragrant puree of basil, garlic, and olive oil is added to this hearty, nourishing vegetable, bean, and pasta soup just before serving. Serve with Herb Bread (p. 276) and spread with Pine Nut Parmesan Pesto (p. 264).

SOUP
½ cup chopped celery
½ cup chopped onion
1½ cups fresh green beans, ends removed and cut into 1-inch pieces or 1 10-ounce package frozen cut green beans
¾ cup sliced carrots
3 medium potatoes, peeled and cut into 1-inch cubes
2 medium zucchini, sliced
2 medium tomatoes, coarsely chopped
2 bay leaves
¼ teaspoon black pepper
¾ cup elbow macaroni
1 cup cooked drained red kidney beans

PISTOU
3 cloves garlic, minced
½ cup fresh basil leaves, well packed
¼ cup extra-virgin olive oil

TOPPING
½ cup grated Parmesan cheese

1. Place celery, onions, beans, carrots, potatoes, zucchini, tomatoes, bay leaf, and black pepper in a large, heavy soup pot. Add enough water to cover plus 2 inches. Bring to boil over high heat, then reduce heat to low, and simmer for 20 minutes or until vegetables are crisp-tender.

2. Add macaroni and kidney beans. Raise heat to high and bring to a quick boil. Reduce heat to medium and cook for 15 minutes more.

3. Prepare pistou by blending garlic, basil, and olive oil in blender or food processor until smooth, scraping down the sides of the container as needed.

4. Spoon equal portions of the pistou into four soup bowls. Add soup to bowls and garnish with Parmesan cheese.

NUTRIENT ANALYSIS
Calories per serving: 450
Protein: 16 gm
Carbohydrates: 59 gm
Dietary fiber: 9.8 gm
Cholesterol: 10 gm
Total fat: 19 gm (171 cal)
Sat fat: 4.5 gm (40 cal)
Poly fat: 1.6 gm (14 cal)
Mono fat: 11 gm (100 cal)

Greek Lentil Soup

YIELD
6 servings

PREPARATION TIME
20 minutes

COOKING TIME
1 hour and 20 minutes

Lentils are one of the oldest cultivated foods. They're extremely versatile, tasty, and packed with nutrition —high in vegetable protein, iron, minerals, and vitamins A and B. The Chilean lentil is brown, yellow, or gray and the Persian lentil is red-orange. All are good. Serve this hearty soup with Garlic Bread (p. 275) and Marinated Mixed Vegetable Salad (p. 71). Greek Lentil Soup can be refrigerated up to 3 days. When reheating, you may want to add extra liquid to compensate for thickening.

½ pound dried lentils, sorted (about 1¼ cups)
1 bay leaf
12 black peppercorns
½ teaspoon dried thyme leaves
½ teaspoon dried marjoram leaves
6 tablespoons extra-virgin flavorful olive oil
1 onion, chopped
2 cloves garlic, minced
2 carrots, chopped
2 stalks celery, chopped
1 cup canned whole plum tomatoes, with juice, roughly
  chopped
6 cups low-salt chicken broth

1. Pour lentils into a colander and rinse with cool water.
2. Tie bay leaf, peppercorns, thyme, and marjoram in a small square of cheesecloth.
3. Heat olive oil in a large, heavy soup pot over medium heat and sauté onions and garlic for 2 minutes. Add carrots and celery and cook for 1 minute more.
4. Add lentils and cheesecloth square to soup pot. Stir in tomatoes and broth. Bring soup to boil over moderate

heat. Reduce heat to low and simmer, covered, for 1 hour and 15 minutes or until lentils are tender. Discard herbs and cheesecloth.

VARIATION

Add 1 cup diced cooked chicken 15 minutes before the cooking time is completed.

NUTRIENT ANALYSIS
Calories per serving: 220
Protein: 9 gm
Carbohydrates: 14 gm
Dietary fiber: 4.1 gm
Cholesterol: 1 mg
Total fat: 15 gm (137 cal)
Sat fat: 2.4 gm (21 cal)
Poly fat: 1.6 gm (14 cal)
Mono fat: 10.6 gm (95 cal)

VEGETABLE SOUPS

Fresh vegetables are especially good in soups. Choose vegetables that are in season for the most flavorful soups. When served with reduced-fat cheeses and whole grain breads there is no meal that is more satisfying and simple to prepare.

Gazpacho

YIELD
6 servings

PREPARATION TIME
30 minutes

COOKING TIME
(croutons) 10 minutes

Gazpacho, which was created in the southern Spanish province of Andalusia, is sometimes called "the salad soup." Since the climate in Andalusia is particularly hot, the popularity of Gazpacho was greatly heightened by the fact that it is traditionally served icy cold. Gazpacho can be served as the first course of a formal meal, as an appetizer, or as a main dish.

In this recipe, basic Gazpacho is served with a bowl of crunchy croutons. Small bowls of garnishes such as chopped red onions, cucumbers, seeded bell and jalapeño peppers, hard-cooked eggs, and cilantro leaves can also accompany the Gazpacho.

2 medium cucumbers, peeled and chopped
5 medium tomatoes, peeled and chopped
1 large red or Bermuda onion, chopped
1 medium green bell pepper, seeded and chopped
2 cloves garlic, minced
2 cups crumbled stale French bread, crusts removed
4 cups cold water
3 tablespoons red wine vinegar
2 tablespoons lemon juice
¼ cup extra-virgin flavorful olive oil
1 tablespoon tomato paste

CROUTONS
1 cup ¼-inch bread cubes, crusts removed
¼ cup extra-virgin olive oil

1. In a large glass bowl, combine cucumbers, tomatoes, onion, green pepper, garlic, and crumbled bread.
2. Stir in water, vinegar, and lemon juice.
3. Ladle the mixture in 2-cup portions into a blender and

process until reduced to a puree. Return puree to the bowl, and beat in olive oil and tomato paste with a wire whisk.

4. Tightly cover bowl and refrigerate for a minimum of 2 hours. Whisk again immediately before serving.

5. Make croutons while soup is chilling. Heat ¼ cup olive oil in a skillet over moderate heat. Drop in bread cubes and cook, turning frequently with a wide spatula. Cook until crisp and lightly browned on all sides. Serve on the side to sprinkle on the soup when served.

VARIATIONS

- Add herbs such as parsley, mint, oregano, or chives after blending the gazpacho and before chilling it.
- Add ½ cup of shredded ham, lean roast beef, or crab meat just before serving.

NUTRIENT ANALYSIS

Calories per serving: 404
Protein: 8.5 gm
Carbohydrates: 48 gm
Dietary fiber: 3.8 gm
Cholesterol: 0 mg
Total fat: 21 gm (189 cal)
Sat fat: 3.1 gm (28 cal)
Poly fat: 1.7 gm (14.6 cal)
Mono fat: 13 gm (117 cal)

Garden Carrot Soup

YIELD
4 servings

PREPARATION TIME
20 minutes

COOKING TIME
50 minutes

NUTRIENT ANALYSIS
Calories per serving: 306
Protein: 13 gm
Carbohydrates: 28 gm
Dietary fiber: 2.9 gm
Cholesterol: 1.5 mg
Total fat: 16 gm (144 cal)
Sat fat: 2.6 gm (23 cal)
Poly fat: 1.7 gm (15 cal)
Mono fat: 11 gm (98 cal)

When shopping for carrots, look for firm, bright orange-yellow carrots with fresh, crisp green tops. They are an excellent source of vitamin A and potassium and also supply some B vitamins, vitamin C, and calcium. Serve with Turkey Salad (p. 88) and Italian bread.

¼ *cup extra-virgin flavorful olive oil*
½ *cup chopped onion*
½ *cup chopped scallions*
1 *clove garlic, minced*
5 *carrots, scrubbed and shredded*
1 *medium potato, peeled and diced*
6 *cups low-salt chicken broth*
1 *cup fresh shelled peas (or 10-ounce package of frozen peas, thawed and drained)*
½ *teaspoon dried tarragon leaves*
¼ *teaspoon dried thyme leaves*
¼ *teaspoon dried marjoram leaves*
¼ *teaspoon black pepper*

1. Heat olive oil over medium heat in a large, heavy soup pot and sauté onion, scallions, and garlic until softened, about 5 minutes. Add carrots and potatoes and sauté for 5 minutes more.
2. Raise heat to high and add broth to pot. Bring to a boil, then reduce heat to medium, cover loosely, and cook for 30 minutes or until potatoes are tender.
3. Transfer soup to a blender in 2-cup batches and puree until smooth.
4. Return soup to pot over medium heat. Add peas, tarragon, thyme, marjoram, and pepper. Cook for 10 minutes if using fresh peas or 5 minutes if using frozen.

Tomato-Herb Soup

This fragrant soup is based on a recipe that is traditionally prepared in a frying pan in Provence. It features thyme, which is thought to be a tonic and stimulant as well as marjoram, which is thought to cleanse the body of impurities. Serve with Chef's Salad Valencia (p. 63).

3 medium onions, chopped
4 medium tomatoes, chopped
¼ cup extra-virgin flavorful olive oil
3 cloves minced garlic (or 1 shallot or 2 scallions), minced
1 bay leaf
1 teaspoon dried thyme leaves
¾ teaspoon dried marjoram leaves
¼ teaspoon black pepper
8 cups water
8 slices French bread, toasted in oven
½ cup grated Parmesan cheese

1. Heat olive oil in large, heavy soup pot over medium heat and sauté onions until lightly browned. Add tomatoes and cook for 5 minutes more.
2. Raise heat to high and add garlic, bay leaf, thyme, marjoram, pepper, and water. Bring to a boil, reduce heat to medium, and cook for 15 minutes.
3. Puree soup, 2 cups at a time, in blender or food processor, or force through a food mill.
4. Return soup to pot and reheat soup to boil over high heat. Place two slices of toasted bread in each serving bowl. Ladle soup over bread and top with cheese.

YIELD
4 servings

PREPARATION TIME
15 minutes

COOKING TIME
25 minutes

NUTRIENT ANALYSIS
Calories per serving: 400
Protein: 13 gm
Carbohydrates: 46 gm
Dietary fiber: 4 gm
Cholesterol: 9.9 mg
Total fat: 17.7 gm (159 cal)
Sat fat: 4.4 gm (40 cal)
Poly fat: 1.4 gm (12 cal)
Mono fat: 11 gm (100 cal)

FISH SOUPS AND STEWS

Seafood soups and stews are low in fat and rich in protein, potassium, and phosphorus. Large, round or oval pots or roasting pans that are no more than 6 inches deep with a non-stick surface are the best choices to use while preparing these soups and stews. Crusty bread, green salad, and fruit desserts are ideal accompaniments to these dishes. See On the Side, the chapter for recipes for making rouille, a fiery sauce to serve "on the side" with fish soups.

Greek Bouillabaisse

YIELD
6 servings

PREPARATION TIME
20 minutes

COOKING TIME
1 hour

Mediterranean bouillabaisse was named for the earthenware pot in which it was cooked by Greek fishermen who prepared their fresh catch and made it go further by adding water, olive oil, and lemon juice. Traditionally, bouillabaisse is a combination of several varieties of fish, which can be ocean or fresh-water fish. Serve with Basic Rouille (p. 265), a fiery sauce that is added at the table. Garnish with croutons and accompany with lemon wedges.

½ cup extra-virgin flavorful olive oil
2 medium onions, thinly sliced
2 small potatoes, peeled and diced
2 small carrots, diced

1 stalk celery, chopped
3 celery tops, chopped
½ cup finely chopped fresh parsley
1 clove garlic, minced
4 ripe or canned tomatoes, peeled and chopped
2 quarts water
¼ teaspoon black pepper
1 large bay leaf
¼ cup dry white wine
2 pounds fish (choose red snapper, sea bass, porgies,
    whitefish, halibut, cod, swordfish or flounder, which
    has been washed, scaled, and cut into serving-size
    pieces)
½ cup unbleached all-purpose flour
½ cup raw long-grain rice
¼ teaspoon powdered saffron
2½ tablespoons lemon juice

1. Heat olive oil in a large, heavy soup pot over medium heat and sauté onions, potatoes, carrots, celery, celery tops, parsley, garlic, and tomatoes until almost soft, about 15 minutes.

2. Raise heat to high, add water, pepper, and bay leaf, and bring to a boil.

3. Add wine, reduce heat to low, and simmer for 20 minutes.

4. Sprinkle fish with flour. Wrap fish in a 36-inch square of cheesecloth and add to pot. Simmer for 10 minutes.

5. Remove cheesecloth and fish with two large spoons and place on a platter to cool.

6. Add rice and saffron and simmer for 25 additional minutes until rice is cooked.

7. Untie cheesecloth, remove and discard any skin and bones, then return fish to pot. Add lemon juice and serve.

Zuppa da Pesce

YIELD
6 servings

PREPARATION TIME
20 minutes

COOKING TIME
25 minutes

NUTRIENT ANALYSIS
Calories per serving: 495
Protein: 63 gm
Carbohydrates: 3.6 gm
Dietary fiber: 0.2 gm
Cholesterol: 175 mg
Total fat: 24 gm (216 cal)
Sat fat: 3.4 gm (30 cal)
Poly fat: 3.4 gm (30 cal)
Mono fat: 15 gm (134 cal)

This version of Zuppa da Pesce, made with a combination of fish and shellfish, is oven-baked and simmered in its own aromatic juices.

½ *cup extra-virgin flavorful olive oil*
2 *cloves garlic, chopped*
1 *sea bass or other solid fish such as trout, about 2–2½*
    pounds, cleaned
18 *littleneck clams, well scrubbed and rinsed*
12 *mussels, well scrubbed and rinsed*
½ *pound, raw shrimp, shelled and cleaned*
¼ *teaspoon black pepper*
½ *cup chopped fresh parsley*

1. Preheat oven to 350° F.
2. Heat olive oil and garlic over medium heat in a deep ovenproof casserole.
3. Place fish on bottom of casserole. Top with clams, mussels, and shrimp.
4. Sprinkle with pepper and parsley.
5. Cover tightly and bake for 25 minutes. Baste with juices several times. Fish should be opaque and flake with a fork when the Zuppa da Pesce is done. The clams and mussels will open when done.

Fisherman's Stew

Clams are the special ingredient in this wine-laced sea-food stew that is served over crispy, brown bread triangles. Serve with a tossed green salad dressed with Anchovy Vinaigrette (p. 240).

1 cup finely chopped onions
½ medium green bell pepper, seeded and chopped
3 medium-sized tomatoes, finely chopped
3 cloves garlic (or 1 shallot or 2 scallions), minced
¼ teaspoon black pepper
18 littleneck clams, well scrubbed and rinsed
½ cup extra-virgin flavorful olive oil
2 pounds mixed fish steaks or fillets (bass, cod, swordfish, halibut, haddock, red snapper, or pollock), boned and cut into 2-inch pieces
1½ cups white wine
6 slices bread, cut diagonally into two triangles
¼ cup finely chopped fresh parsley

1. Combine onions, green pepper, tomatoes, garlic, and pepper in a bowl.
2. Place clams in bottom of a large, heavy soup pot. Pour in ⅓ cup olive oil. Sprinkle one third of the vegetable mixture over clams. Add half the fish. Add another third of the vegetables on top of fish. Then add remaining half of fish and final layer of vegetables.
3. Pour in wine and bring to a boil over high heat. Reduce heat to low. Cover tightly and simmer for 30 minutes until clams are open and fish flakes easily.
4. While soup is cooking, heat remaining oil in a 10- to 12-inch skillet. Add bread and brown well on both sides.
5. Place two triangles of bread in each soup plate. Ladle soup over bread, then arrange clams and fish on top. Sprinkle with parsley.

YIELD
6 servings

PREPARATION TIME
30 minutes

COOKING TIME
35 minutes

NUTRIENT ANALYSIS
Calories per serving: 542
Protein: 45 gm
Carbohydrates: 24 gm
Dietary fiber: 1.7 gm
Cholesterol: 64 mg
Total fat: 24 gm (216 cal)
Sat fat: 3.5 gm (32 cal)
Poly fat: 3 gm (27 cal)
Mono fat: 14.8 gm (133 cal)

Codfish Soup

YIELD
4 servings

PREPARATION TIME
20 minutes

COOKING TIME
35 minutes

NUTRIENT ANALYSIS
Calories per serving: 537
Protein: 49 gm
Carbohydrates: 38 gm
Dietary fiber: 3.3 gm
Cholesterol: 70 mg
Total fat: 19 gm (171 cal)
Sat fat: 2.7 gm (24 cal)
Poly fat: 3 gm (27 cal)
Mono fat: 11.6 gm (104 cal)

You can use either fresh or frozen codfish in this easy-to-prepare, inexpensive soup. Serve it with French bread and a bowl of Parmesan cheese to sprinkle on top. Serve with a salad of apple chunks, diced celery, and seedless grapes dressed with One Egg Blender Mayonnaise (p. 243).

¼ *cup extra-virgin flavorful olive oil*
1 *cup chopped onion*
2 *cloves garlic, minced*
2 *cups canned tomatoes, liquid reserved*
½ *cup minced fresh parsley*
1 *bay leaf*
1 *teaspoon dried thyme leaves*
¼ *teaspoon black pepper*
4½ *cups water*
½ *cup dry white wine*
1 *teaspoon grated orange peel*
4 *medium potatoes, well scrubbed and cut into 1-inch cubes*
1½ *pounds fresh or frozen codfish fillets, cut into ½-inch cubes (thaw frozen fish in refrigerator)*

1. Heat olive oil in large, heavy soup pot over medium heat and sauté onion 5 minutes or until lightly browned. Add garlic and cook for 1 minute more.
2. Stir in tomatoes. Add parsley, bay leaf, thyme, and pepper. Cook for 10 minutes until most liquid has evaporated from tomatoes.
3. Raise heat to high, add water, liquid from tomatoes, wine, orange peel, potatoes, and fish, and bring to a boil.
4. Reduce heat to medium, cover, and cook about 15 minutes until potatoes are just tender.

SALADS

SUGAR SNAP AND CARROT SALAD
ASPARAGUS VINAIGRETTE
MARINATED MIXED VEGETABLE SALAD
SHREDDED CARROT-TURNIP SLAW
TRI-COLOR PEPPER SALAD
TOMATOES WITH PARSLEY
BROCCOLI SALAD
PUERTO RICAN AVOCADO SALAD
CAULIFLOWER SALAD
ISRAELI SALAD
GREEK SALAD
SYRIAN POTATO SALAD
QUICK WHITE BEAN SALAD
DILLED LENTIL SALAD
GREEN BEAN SALAD
SALAD NIÇOISE
RICE SALAD
CHEF'S SALAD VALENCIA
TURKEY SALAD
ORANGE, ONION, AND BLACK OLIVE SALAD

MARINATED ZUCCHINI AND CHEESE SALAD

SALAD

3	large tomatoes, cut in wedges	
	or	
2 cups	cherry tomatoes	500 mL
2	medium zucchini, thinly sliced	
2	green onions, chopped	
2 cups	diced BLACK DIAMOND Cheddar Cheese	500 mL
1 14-ounce can	hearts of palm, drained and sliced (optional)	1 398 mL can

DRESSING

¾ cup	olive or vegetable oil	175 mL
½ cup	red wine vinegar	125 mL
2 cloves	garlic, minced	2 cloves
1¼ teaspoons	dried basil	6 mL
1 teaspoon	granulated sugar	5 mL
¼ teaspoon	dry mustard	1 mL
1 teaspoon	salt	5 mL
	Pepper to taste	

In large bowl, toss together salad ingredients. In covered container, combine dressing ingredients; shake well. Toss salad with dressing. Cover and refrigerate overnight to blend flavours. Drain and serve on lettuce or spinach leaves.

Makes about 6 servings.

Note: Store leftover dressing in covered container in refrigerator.

...a's prize-win-
...nted with dill
...h Oven-Fried
...33).

...s removed
...d pieces

...a vegetable
...4 minutes or
...r, drain, and put in salad bowl.

2. Steam carrots in steamer for 2 to 3 minutes. Remove from steamer and add to salad bowl. Chill.

3. Blend scallions, dill, parsley, vinegar, and olive oil in a blender until smooth. Season with pepper and pour over peas and carrots. Cover and chill for several hours.

4. Add radishes before serving.

Sugar Snap and Carrot Salad

YIELD
6 servings

PREPARATION TIME
20 minutes + 2 hours chilling time

COOKING TIME
5 to 7 minutes

NUTRIENT ANALYSIS
Calories per serving: 227
Protein: 4 gm
Carbohydrates: 14 gm
Dietary fiber: 8 gm
Cholesterol: 0 mg
Total fat: 18 gm (165 cal)
Sat fat: 2.6 gm (24 cal)
Poly fat: 1.6 gm (15 cal)
Mono fat: 13 gm (119 cal)

Asparagus Vinaigrette

YIELD
4 servings

PREPARATION TIME
10 minutes

COOKING TIME
5 minutes

NUTRIENT ANALYSIS
Calories per serving: 238
Protein: 6 gm
Carbohydrates: 11 gm
Dietary fiber: 2.8 gm
Cholesterol: 0 mg
Total fat: 21 gm (189 cal)
Sat fat: 3 gm (27 cal)
Poly fat: 2.0 gm (18 cal)
Mono fat: 15 gm (135 cal)

When buying asparagus, look for firm, well-rounded spears of similar size. Avoid spears with open or wilted tips. Cut or snap off the tough white ends before using. Served with Baked Fish Steaks (p. 114) and Sautéed Potatoes with Red Pepper Oil (p. 160).

2 pounds fresh asparagus
6 tablespoons extra-virgin flavorful olive oil
2 tablespoons lemon juice
¼ teaspoon black pepper
1 clove garlic, minced
1 tablespoon minced onion or scallions
1 tablespoon minced fresh parsley

1. Microwave or steam asparagus 5 minutes, just until barely tender.
2. In a small bowl, combine oil, lemon juice, black pepper, garlic, onion, and parsley . Mix well and chill.
3. Arrange asparagus on serving dish and pour dressing over spears to cover well.

VARIATION
Omit the onion, parsley, and lemon. Add 2 tablespoons wine vinegar and ½ teaspoon dry mustard.

Marinated Mixed Vegetable Salad

An assortment of seasonal vegetables are steamed with oil and vinegar dressing and then marinated for 2 hours and garnished with parsley and lemon wedges. Serve with Fish in Foil (p. 112) and Potato Pancakes (p. 172).

1 cup fresh green beans, ends trimmed and cut into
    ½-inch pieces
1 cup fresh yellow wax beans, ends trimmed and cut into
    ½-inch pieces
2 medium carrots, cut into ¼-inch slices
1 large red bell pepper, cut into 1-inch squares
1 ear large kernel corn, cut from the cob
½ cup extra-virgin flavorful olive oil
3 tablespoons wine vinegar
1 clove garlic, minced
½ teaspoon dried thyme leaves

1. Steam green beans, wax beans, carrots, pepper squares, and corn in a vegetable steamer with about 1 inch of water for 5 minutes or until crisp tender.
2. Drain vegetables and return to pan. Combine olive oil, vinegar, garlic, and thyme. Pour over vegetables and stir well.
3. Cover pan and steam vegetables and dressing for 5 minutes more.
4. Transfer vegetables and dressing to a glass dish. Spoon dressing over vegetables and marinate at room temperature for 2 hours.

VARIATION
Substitute vegetables of your choice such as peas, baby lima beans, cauliflower florets, or mushrooms.

YIELD
6 servings

PREPARATION TIME
*10 minutes + 2 hours
marinating time*

COOKING TIME
10 minutes

NUTRIENT ANALYSIS
Calories per serving: 205
Protein: 2 gm
Carbohydrates: 11 gm
Dietary fiber: 2.8 gm
Cholesterol: 0 mg
Total fat: 18.4 gm (166 cal)
Sat fat: 2.6 gm (24 cal)
Poly fat: 1.7 gm (16 cal)
Mono fat: 13 gm (120 cal)

Shredded Carrot-Turnip Slaw

YIELD
5 servings

PREPARATION TIME
20 minutes

NUTRIENT ANALYSIS
Calories per serving: 178
Protein: 1.4 gm
Carbohydrates: 12.8 gm
Dietary fiber: 3.2 gm
Cholesterol: 0 mg
Total fat: 15 gm (131 cal)
Sat fat: 2 gm (19 cal)
Poly fat: 1.3 gm (12 cal)
Mono fat: 11 gm (95 cal)

Carrots, turnips, cabbage, apples, and radishes are marinated in a honey-vinaigrette dressing. Buy turnips that are firm, smooth, and fairly round. Avoid those that have obvious fibrous roots and yellow, wilted tops.

2 large carrots, shredded
1 medium turnip, peeled and shredded
4 cups shredded green cabbage
1 red apple, cored and thinly sliced
¾ cup sliced radishes
2 scallions, thinly sliced
⅓ cup mild, light flavored olive oil
¼ cup cider vinegar
1 teaspoon honey
½ teaspoon black pepper

1. Combine carrots, turnip, cabbage, apple, radishes, and scallions in a salad bowl.
2. Combine oil, vinegar, honey, and pepper in a small bowl with a wire whisk. Pour over vegetables and chill for several hours before serving.

Tri-color Pepper Salad

A simple salad of sautéed bell peppers is a delightful garnish for any meal. It can be eaten warm or prepared in advance and served cold.

¼ cup mild, light flavored olive oil
1 red bell pepper, cut into 2-inch julienne strips
1 yellow bell pepper, cut into 2-inch julienne strips
1 green bell pepper, cut into 2-inch julienne strips
2 cloves garlic (or 2 shallots or scallions), minced
1 teaspoon dried basil leaves
1 tablespoon chopped fresh parsley
¼ teaspoon salt (optional)
¼ teaspoon black pepper

1. Heat olive oil in a large skillet over medium heat. Add peppers and garlic and sauté for 15 minutes until soft.
2. When peppers are soft, add basil, salt, and black pepper. Mix well and serve at room temperature or chilled.

YIELD
4 servings

PREPARATION TIME
10 minutes

COOKING TIME
15 minutes

NUTRIENT ANALYSIS
Calories per serving: 136
Protein: 0.7 gm
Carbohydrates: 3.8 gm
Dietary fiber: 0.8 gm
Cholesterol: 0 mg
Total fat: 14 gm (124 cal)
Sat fat: 1.9 gm (18 cal)
Poly fat: 1.3 gm (11 cal)
Mono fat: 10 gm (90 cal)

Tomatoes with Parsley

YIELD
6 servings

PREPARATION TIME
10 minutes

NUTRIENT ANALYSIS
Calories per serving: 227
Protein: 5.1 gm
Carbohydrates: 7.5 gm
Dietary fiber: 3.0 gm
Cholesterol: 6.6 mg
Total fat: 21 gm (187 cal)
Sat fat: 4.1 gm (38 cal)
Poly fat: 1.6 gm (15 cal)
Mono fat: 14 gm (126 cal)

Parsley is the most popular of all cooking herbs and appears in all Mediterranean cuisines. When you bring fresh parsley home from the market, rinse it, shake it, and wrap it in a damp paper towel, then store in a jar or plastic bag in the refrigerator. Parsley stored in this manner will stay fresh for two weeks or more. Serve Tomatoes with Parsley as a side dish with Linguine with Oil and Garlic (p. 188).

1 clove garlic (or 2 shallots or 1 scallion), minced
½ cup extra-virgin flavorful olive oil
3 tablespoons wine vinegar
¼ teaspoon salt (optional)
¼ teaspoon black pepper
4 cups well-packed fresh parsley leaves
½ cup grated Parmesan cheese
4 medium tomatoes, thinly sliced

1. Process garlic, olive oil, vinegar, salt (if desired), and pepper in a blender container or shake well in a small, covered jar.
2. Pour dressing over parsley. Add Parmesan cheese and mix well.
3. Put tomato slices in a glass bowl. Add parsley-cheese mixture and toss well.

VARIATION
Omit cheese. Add ½ pound steamed green beans and 3 scallions, minced.

Broccoli
Salad

Blanched broccoli is mixed with avocado in a mustard-flavored dressing. Serve with Pan Sautéed Fish (p. 120).

3 cups broccoli florets
1 onion, sliced and separated into rings
1/2 cup sliced fresh mushrooms
1/4 pound feta cheese, crumbled into small pieces
3 tablespoons lemon juice
4 tablespoons olive oil
1 clove garlic, minced
1/2 teaspoon dried oregano leaves
1/4 teaspoon black pepper

1. Drop the broccoli in boiling water over high heat and quickly bring water to a second boil. Remove broccoli. Drain and chill.
2. Toss broccoli with onion, mushrooms, and cheese.
3. Combine lemon juice, olive oil, garlic, oregano, and pepper in an electric blender or in a small bowl using a wire whisk. Pour over broccoli mixture, toss, and serve.

YIELD
4 servings

PREPARATION TIME
2 minutes

COOKING TIME
5 minutes

NUTRIENT ANALYSIS
Calories per serving: 246
Protein: 8 gm
Carbohydrates: 12 gm
Dietary fiber: 5.6 gm
Cholesterol: 25 mg
Total fat: 20 gm (180 cal)
Sat fat: 6.2 gm (57 cal)
Poly fat: 1.5 gm (14 cal)
Mono fat: 11.3 gm (102 cal)

Puerto Rican Avocado Salad

YIELD

6 servings

PREPARATION TIME

15 minutes

NUTRIENT ANALYSIS

Calories per serving: 366
Protein: 3 gm
Carbohydrates: 19 gm
Dietary fiber: 5 gm
Cholesterol: 0 mg
Total fat: 33 gm (299 cal)
Sat fat: 4.8 gm (43 cal)
Poly fat: 3.4 gm (30 cal)
Mono fat: 23 gm (206 cal)

Since avocados are also high in monounsaturates, you'll be getting a double portion of monounsaturate calories by eating this citrus-accented tropical salad. Serve with Broiled Fish Steaks (p. 114).

3 ripe avocados
1 cup drained, unsweetened juice-pack pineapple chunks
½ cup mild, light flavored olive oil
¼ cup wine vinegar
¼ teaspoon lime juice
⅛ teaspoon ground black pepper
1 teaspoon sugar (optional)
1 small head red leaf lettuce, rinsed and drained
2 oranges, peeled and separated into sections

1. Cut avocados in half, lengthwise. Remove pits and carefully scoop out pulp. Avoid cutting into outer shells.
2. Cut avocado pulp into ½-inch pieces and mix with pineapple chunks in a medium bowl.
3. In a small bowl mix olive oil, vinegar, lime juice, pepper, and sugar with a wire whisk until well mixed. Pour over avocado and pineapple chunks.
4. Spoon salad back into empty shells. Place each filled shell on a lettuce leaf on individual salad plates. Garnish with orange slices. Refrigerate until ready to serve.

Cauliflower Salad

Cauliflower is marinated in a zesty paprika dressing and sprinkled with chopped egg-white and parsley. Serve with broiled boneless chicken breasts and Zucchini Fritters (p. 166).

1 small head cauliflower, cut into florets with stems removed
2 teaspoons lemon juice
¼ cup extra-virgin flavorful olive oil
2 tablespoons wine vinegar
1 clove garlic, mashed
1 teaspoon paprika
⅛ teaspoon cayenne pepper
3 tablespoons minced hard-cooked egg white
1 tablespoon chopped fresh parsley

1. Place cauliflower in a saucepan with 1 inch of boiling water. Add lemon juice. Cover and cook over low heat for 12 minutes. Drain and cool.

2. Combine olive oil, vinegar, garlic, paprika, and cayenne in a blender or in a small bowl with a wire whisk until well blended.

3. Pour over cooled cauliflower and marinate for 2 hours. Garnish with egg white and parsley and serve.

YIELD
4 servings

PREPARATION TIME
20 minutes

COOKING TIME
12 minutes + 2 hours marinating time

NUTRIENT ANALYSIS
Calories per serving: 155
Protein: 3.8 gm
Carbohydrates: 6.5 gm
Dietary fiber: 2.7 gm
Cholesterol: 0 mg
Total fat: 14 gm (124 cal)
Sat fat: 2 gm (17 cal)
Poly fat: 1.2 gm (11 cal)
Mono fat: 10 gm (90 cal)

Israeli Salad

YIELD
Serves 4

PREPARATION TIME
15 minutes

NUTRIENT ANALYSIS
Calories per serving: 144
Protein: 1 gm
Carbohydrates: 5.8 gm
Dietary fiber: 1.9 gm
Cholesterol: 0 mg
Total fat: 13.8 gm (124 cal)
Sat fat: 2 gm (18 cal)
Poly fat: 1.3 gm (11 cal)
Mono fat: 10 gm (90 cal)

Salad is served with almost every Israeli meal including breakfast. The ingredients for this dish are frequently kept on the tables in kibbutz dining halls so that members of the collective community can make their own fresh salads. Serve with Baked Fish Steaks (p. 114) for a quick and easy supper.

2 ripe tomatoes, chopped
1 cucumber, peeled and chopped
1 green bell pepper, seeded and chopped
¼ cup chopped fresh parsley
¼ cup extra-virgin flavorful olive oil
3 tablespoons lemon juice
¼ teaspoon black pepper
¼ teaspoon salt (optional)

1. Mix chopped tomatoes, cucumber, green pepper, and parsley in a large bowl.
2. Add olive oil and toss salad.
3. Add lemon juice, pepper, and salt (if desired) and toss again to mix well.

Greek
Salad

A traditional Greek Salad is easy to assemble. Try serving it on pita rounds for a special treat for lunch or a light supper.

1 clove garlic, cut in half
4 cups romaine lettuce or mixed salad greens, rinsed, dried, and cut into 2-inch pieces
8 red radishes, cut in half
10 ripe olives, rinsed
1 red onion, thinly sliced and divided into rings
1 green bell pepper, seeded and thinly sliced
1 medium cucumber, thinly sliced
1 ripe medium tomato, cut in wedges
¼ teaspoon black pepper
¼ teaspoon dried dill
½ teaspoon dried oregano leaves
2 tablespoons red wine vinegar
½ cup extra-virgin flavorful olive oil

1. Rub a large salad bowl with the cut garlic clove.
2. Place romaine, radishes, olives, onion, green pepper, cucumber, and tomato in bowl. Add black pepper, dill, oregano, and vinegar. Toss.
3. Add olive oil and toss again.

VARIATION
Garnish with anchovies and feta cheese.

YIELD
4 servings

PREPARATION TIME
20 minutes

NUTRIENT ANALYSIS
Calories per serving: 283
Protein: 2.2 gm
Carbohydrates: 88 gm
Dietary fiber: 2.8 gm
Cholesterol: 0 mg
Total fat: 28 gm (258 cal)
Sat fat: 4 gm (36 cal)
Poly fat: 2.5 gm (23 cal)
Mono fat: 21 gm (188 cal)

Syrian Potato Salad

YIELD
4 servings

PREPARATION TIME
10 minutes + potato boiling time

NUTRIENT ANALYSIS
Calories per serving: 250
Protein: 3 gm
Carbohydrates: 29 gm
Dietary fiber: 3.1 gm
Cholesterol: 0 mg
Total fat: 15 gm (136 cal)
Sat fat: 2 gm (19 cal)
Poly fat: 1.3 gm (12 cal)
Mono fat: 10.6 gm (96 cal)

In this salad, potatoes are tossed with olive oil, lemon juice, and onions, then topped with olives, tomatoes, and mint. Serve with broiled chicken.

1 pound potatoes, boiled, peeled, and cubed
¼ cup extra-virgin flavorful olive oil
Juice of 1 lemon
1 medium onion, finely chopped
¼ teaspoon black pepper
1 tablespoon dried mint
1 tablespoon chopped fresh parsley
8 cured olives, rinsed and drained
2 ripe medium tomatoes, sliced

1. Toss potatoes with olive oil.
2. Add lemon juice, onion, pepper, and mint.
3. Garnish with parsley, olives, and sliced tomatoes.

Quick White Bean Salad

This easy-to-make salad is made with canned beans and can be garnished with black olives and lemon slices. Serve with Citrus-Herb Baked Chicken (p. 100).

1 28-ounce can Great Northern white beans (or cannellini beans), well drained
¼ cup extra-virgin flavorful olive oil
¼ cup lemon juice
1 tablespoon wine vinegar
¼ teaspoon salt (optional)
¼ teaspoon black pepper
1 tablespoon Dijon mustard
¼ cup chopped fresh parsley
¼ teaspoon dried oregano leaves
1 red onion, thinly sliced
1 ripe tomato, sliced
1 green bell pepper, seeded and sliced

1. Drain beans and put in a large bowl.
2. Combine olive oil, lemon juice, vinegar, salt (if desired), pepper, and mustard with a whisk. Pour over beans and mix well.
3. Add parsley, oregano, red onion, tomato, and green pepper. Toss well.

YIELD
4 main course servings

PREPARATION TIME
20 minutes

NUTRIENT ANALYSIS
Calories per serving: 380
Protein: 16.5 gm
Carbohydrates: 49 gm
Dietary fiber: 0.8 gm
Cholesterol: 0 mg
Total fat: 15 gm (134 cal)
Sat fat: 2 gm (18 cal)
Poly fat: 1.3 gm (11 cal)
Mono fat: 10 gm (90 cal)

Dilled
Lentil
Salad

YIELD

4 servings

PREPARATION TIME

15 minutes

COOKING TIME

30 minutes

NUTRIENT ANALYSIS

Calories per serving: 201
Protein: 5 gm
Carbohydrates: 16.8 gm
Dietary fiber: 4 gm
Cholesterol: 0 mg
Total fat: 14 gm (125 cal)
Sat fat: 2 gm (18 cal)
Poly fat: 1.2 gm (11 cal)
Mono fat: 10 gm (90 cal)

Make lentil salad by dressing freshly cooked lentils with a lemon-oil dressing, then tossing them with tomatoes and scallions. It is one of the most delicious ways to eat this excellent source of protein. Serve with Chicken Pronto (p. 94).

1 cup dried brown lentils, sorted and rinsed
2 cups water
1 large carrot, thinly sliced
1 medium onion, chopped
1 clove garlic, minced
¼ cup extra-virgin flavorful olive oil
Juice of 1 lemon
¼ teaspoon black pepper
2 teaspoons chopped fresh dill or ½ teaspoon dried dill
1 medium ripe tomato, chopped
3 scallions, chopped

1. Simmer lentils in water in a large pot over low heat for 20 minutes until cooked. Add carrots and cook for 5 minutes more until lentils and carrots are soft.

2. In a medium skillet sauté onions and garlic in 2 tablespoons of the olive oil 5 minutes or until soft. Combine with lentils and carrots.

3. Add lemon juice, remaining olive oil, pepper, and dill to lentils.

4. Toss with tomatoes and scallions and serve warm or refrigerate and serve cold.

Green
Bean
Salad

Shop for green beans that are fresh and bright green. Avoid limp, spindly beans or those bulging with seeds. Serve with Sirloin Steak with Onion Sauce (p. 135) and Mexican Cauliflower (p. 171).

1 pound fresh green beans, washed and ends trimmed (or
    frozen beans if fresh are not available)
⅛ teaspoon black pepper
¼ cup minced red or Bermuda onion
¼ cup minced fresh parsley
¼ cup extra-virgin flavorful olive oil
2 tablespoons wine vinegar (or lemon juice)

1. Steam green beans for 5 to 10 minutes until tender but still crisp. (Or beans can be microwaved.) Drain well.
2. Place cooked beans in a flat soup plate or deep serving platter. Sprinkle with pepper, onions, and parsley.
3. Drizzle olive oil and vinegar over beans.
4. Refrigerate until chilled, about half an hour.

VARIATION
Slice 2 ripe tomatoes and place on larger platter next to the beans. Double the amount of onions, parsley, and dressing and drizzle over the beans and tomatoes. Chill.

YIELD
4 servings

PREPARATION TIME
15 minutes + 5 to 10 minutes
bean steaming time

NUTRIENT ANALYSIS
Calories per serving: 164
Protein: 2.4 gm
Carbohydrates: 10.5 gm
Dietary fiber: 2.4 gm
Cholesterol: 0 mg
Total fat: 14 gm (125 cal)
Sat fat: 1.9 gm (18 cal)
Poly fat: 1.3 gm (12 cal)
Mono fat: 10 gm (90 cal)

Salad Niçoise

YIELD
4 servings

PREPARATION TIME
30 minutes + potato cooking and bean steaming time

Salad Niçoise, a classic French salad, is an inspired blend of tuna, green beans, potatoes, and olives. Serve with crusty French bread for a complete meal.

1 pound green beans, trimmed and cut into 1-inch pieces
3 medium red potatoes, cooked and sliced
6 tablespoons extra-virgin flavorful olive oil
1 tablespoon wine vinegar
1 clove garlic, minced
1 teaspoon Dijon mustard
¼ teaspoon salt (optional)
¼ teaspoon black pepper
¼ teaspoon dried thyme leaves
½ teaspoon dried basil leaves
½ teaspoon dried tarragon leaves
4 large leaves romaine lettuce, rinsed and drained
1 green bell pepper, seeded and thinly sliced
2 stalks celery, thinly sliced
1 cup cherry tomatoes, cut in half
1 7-ounce can albacore tuna, packed in olive oil or water, drained
6 stuffed green olives, rinsed
6 black olives, rinsed and drained
1 small red onion, thinly sliced and separated into rings
¼ cup chopped fresh parsley
3 scallions, chopped
3 hard-cooked egg whites, quartered

1. Steam green beans for 5 to 10 minutes until crisp tender. Drain and refrigerate.
2. Boil potatoes until tender; drain, slice, and refrigerate.
3. Whisk olive oil, vinegar, garlic, mustard, salt (if de-

sired), pepper, thyme, basil, and tarragon in a small bowl until well blended; or put dressing ingredients in a small jar and shake well. Refrigerate while assembling salad.

4. Arrange lettuce, beans, potatoes, green peppers, celery, and tomatoes in a salad bowl. Flake tuna with a fork over salad. Top with olives.

5. Sprinkle onions, parsley, scallions, and egg whites on top.

6. Mix the olive oil dressing well and drizzle over salad. Serve as assembled and toss at the table.

VARIATION

Add 1 or 2 ounces of anchovies to the salad. We have left them out because of their high sodium content.

NUTRIENT ANALYSIS
Calories per serving: 431
Protein: 24 gm
Carbohydrates: 36.5 gm
Dietary fiber: 5.4 gm
Cholesterol: 20 mg
Total fat: 24 gm (215 cal)
Sat fat: 3.2 gm (29 cal)
Poly fat: 2.5 gm (23 cal)
Mono fat: 15 gm (145 cal)

Rice
Salad

....

YIELD

4 servings

PREPARATION TIME

*15 minutes
(not including cooking rice)
+ 1 hour sitting time*

COOKING TIME

5 minutes

NUTRIENT ANALYSIS

Calories per serving: 340
Protein: 9 gm
Carbohydrates: 39 gm
Dietary fiber: 0.8 gm
Cholesterol: 7.4 mg
Total fat: 17.5 gm (158 cal)
Sat fat: 2.4 gm (22 cal)
Poly fat: 1.6 gm (14 cal)
Mono fat: 12.4 gm (112 cal)

This combination of cooked rice, herb dressing, tuna, and raw vegetables can be served with One Egg Blender Mayonnaise (p. 243).

3 tablespoons chopped scallions
5 tablespoons extra-virgin flavorful olive oil
2 cups cooked rice
1 tablespoon wine vinegar
2 teaspoons lemon juice
1/4 teaspoon Dijon mustard
1 clove garlic
1/4 teaspoon dried thyme leaves
1/8 teaspoon dried tarragon leaves
1/4 teaspoon black pepper
1 tablespoon chopped fresh parsley
*1/4 cup white albacore tuna, packed in water or olive oil,
    drained and flaked*
2 tablespoons finely chopped green bell pepper
2 tablespoons chopped cucumber
2 tablespoons finely chopped carrots
2 tablespoons minced dill pickle

1. Stir fry scallions in 2 tablespoons of olive oil for 1 minute in a large skillet. Add cooked rice and stir to coat with oil.

2. While rice cools, combine vinegar, lemon juice, mustard, garlic, thyme, tarragon, and pepper in a small bowl with a wire whisk.

3. Pour dressing over rice and mix well.

4. Stir in parsley, tuna, green pepper, cucumber, carrots, and dill pickle.

5. Allow to sit at room temperature for 1 hour before serving.

Chef's Salad Valencia

In this delicious Spanish variation of chef's salad, rice is added, and chicken or turkey replace the high cholesterol and high sodium ham and cheese ingredients. Serve with Scones with Herbs and Parmesan (p. 290).

3 tablespoons finely chopped red or Bermuda onion
1 tablespoon minced fresh parsley
½ teaspoon dried tarragon leaves
1 clove garlic, cut in half and crushed
1 cup extra-virgin flavorful olive oil
⅓ cup wine vinegar
2 cups cooked rice
½ green bell pepper, chopped
1 cup cooked chicken or turkey, cut into bite-sized pieces
10 ripe black olives, rinsed and drained
2 small tomatoes, cut in quarters
1 small head red leaf lettuce or 4 large leaves romaine
    lettuce
3 hard-cooked egg whites, quartered

1. In a small bowl, combine onion, parsley, tarragon, garlic, and olive oil with a wire whisk. Let stand for 25 minutes.
2. In a medium bowl, mix rice with green pepper and chicken or turkey.
3. Remove garlic from dressing. Pour half of the dressing over rice mixture and toss well. Chill in refrigerator for 1 hour.
4. While rice mixture is chilling, soak olives and tomatoes in ½ cup of dressing.
5. Rinse and dry the lettuce leaves and circle a platter with them. Mound chilled rice and poultry in center of platter. Scoop olives and tomatoes out of marinade and sprinkle them over rice mixture. Place egg whites around the edges.
6. Drizzle the remaining dressing over the salad.

YIELD
4 servings

PREPARATION TIME
30 minutes + 30 minutes standing time for dressing and 1 hour chilling time for salad (not including cooking rice or chicken)

NUTRIENT ANALYSIS
Calories per serving: 425
Protein: 13 gm
Carbohydrates: 29 gm
Dietary fiber: 1.4 gm
Cholesterol: 20 mg
Total fat: 29 gm (265 cal)
Sat fat: 4.3 gm (39 cal)
Poly fat: 2.6 gm (24 cal)
Mono fat: 20.7 gm (187 cal)

Turkey Salad

YIELD
4 servings

PREPARATION TIME
20 minutes

COOKING TIME
*10 minutes + 15 minutes
marinating time*

NUTRIENT ANALYSIS
Calories per serving: 411
Protein: 26 gm
Carbohydrates: 5 gm
Dietary fiber: 1.5 gm
Cholesterol: 60 mg
Total fat: 32 gm (296 cal)
Sat fat: 5.1 gm (46 cal)
Poly fat: 3.1 gm (28 cal)
Mono fat: 21.4 gm (193 cal)

For this salad, marinated turkey is tossed with a tangy dressing and combined with tomatoes, scallions, and olives. Serve with steamed green beans and yellow squash tossed with Basic Pesto (p. 264).

4 turkey cutlets (1 pound)
½ cup olive oil
3 scallions, sliced
¼ teaspoon black pepper
3 tablespoons wine vinegar
1 teaspoon Dijon mustard
2 tablespoons mayonnaise
1 cup cherry tomatoes, cut in half
½ cup black olives, rinsed
2 tablespoons chopped fresh parsley
4 large leaves romaine lettuce, rinsed and drained

1. Sauté turkey cutlets in 2 tablespoons olive oil until lighty browned and tender, approximately 5 minutes on each side. Cool and cut into cubes.
2. Combine turkey cubes and scallions in a glass bowl and sprinkle with pepper.
3. In a small bowl, mix 2 tablespoons of olive oil and 1 tablespoon of wine vinegar. Stir into turkey mixture. Marinate 15 minutes.
4. While turkey is marinating, combine mustard, mayonnaise, and remaining vinegar and oil in a small bowl with a wire whisk.
5. Pour dressing over marinated turkey and stir. Add cherry tomatoes, olives, and parsley. Toss and serve on lettuce leaves.

Orange, Onion, and Black Olive Salad

Navel oranges, red onions, and black olives are tossed with a spicy lemon and oil dressing for this salad. Serve with Pasta with Chicken and Peppers (p. 193).

2 seedless oranges, peeled and cut into thin slices
1/4 cup thinly sliced red onion, separated into rings
8 pitted black olives, rinsed and sliced into rings
1 teaspoon paprika
1 clove garlic, minced
1 teaspoon ground cumin
1/8 teaspoon cayenne pepper
1 tablespoon orange or lemon juice
4 tablespoons mild, light flavored olive oil
1/4 teaspoon white pepper
2 tablespoons minced fresh parsley

1. Place oranges, onion, and olives in a salad bowl.
2. Combine paprika, garlic, cumin, cayenne pepper, orange juice, olive oil, and white pepper in blender or in a small bowl with a wire whisk.
3. Pour over oranges, onions, and olives and toss to coat. Serve at room temperature or refrigerate until chilled. Garnish with parsley.

VARIATION
Omit olives and red onions. Add 4 grated red radishes and 3 diced scallions.

YIELD
4 servings

PREPARATION TIME
15 minutes

NUTRIENT ANALYSIS
Calories per serving: 171
Protein: 1.2 gm
Carbohydrates: 10 gm
Dietary fiber: 1.7 gm
Cholesterol: 0 mg
Total fat: 15 gm (136 cal)
Sat fat: 2.1 gm (19 cal)
Poly fat: 1.3 gm (12 cal)
Mono fat: 10.8 gm (97 cal)

POULTRY

CHICKEN PRONTO
CHICKEN VERDE
GARLIC CHICKEN
SPICY MEXICAN CHICKEN
EASY BAKED CHICKEN BREASTS
COLD CHICKEN WITH LIME DRESSING
CITRUS-HERB BAKED CHICKEN
OVEN-FRIED CHICKEN
CHICKEN CURRY
CHICKEN COUSCOUS
RAPID CHICKEN IN WINE SAUCE
STIR-FRIED CHICKEN WITH VEGETABLES
PAELLA

POULTRY

Chicken and turkey are loaded with B vitamins and minerals and contain less fat than veal, lamb, beef, or pork. Smaller, younger birds contain less fat than larger, older birds. Chicken broilers have less than 10 percent fat, while roasters have 12 to 18 percent. Poultry white meat has less fat and less cholesterol than dark meat. The breast is the least fatty area and has the highest percentage (63 percent) of edible meat of any chicken part.

The skin contains at least half of the poultry's total saturated fat count; there is a layer of fat under the skin and several large fat deposits near the tail. Consequently, if you remove and discard the skin when you cook poultry, you can cut the fat calories in half.

The skin can be removed either before or after cooking. Whole chickens used for roasting need their skins left on as a protective layer to prevent the meat from drying out during the roasting period. Remove the skin when eating after the chicken is cooked.

Cooking tips:

Rinse chicken quickly under cold running water and pat dry with paper towels. It will brown better when dry.

Chicken is done when clear yellow fluid, with no pink traces, appears when meat is pierced.

Wash all cooking utensils used on chicken, particularly knives and cutting boards, before using on other foods to avoid carrying bacteria.

Chicken
Pronto

YIELD
4 servings

PREPARATION TIME
8 minutes

COOKING TIME
22 minutes

NUTRIENT ANALYSIS
Calories per serving: 358
Protein: 37 gm
Carbohydrates: 3.7 gm
Dietary fiber: 0.6 gm
Cholesterol: 95 mg
Total fat: 19 gm (170 cal)
Sat fat: 3.4 gm (31 cal)
Poly fat: 2.2 gm (20 cal)
Mono fat: 12.1 gm (109 cal)

Sauté boneless chicken breasts in olive oil and serve with tomato, garlic, and olives in a wine-yogurt sauce. Serve with Tomato Dolma (p. 169).

1 pound chicken breasts, skinned and boned
¼ cup mild, light flavored olive oil
¼ teaspoon black pepper
¼ teaspoon salt (optional)
1 medium tomato, chopped
6 pitted black olives, rinsed
1 clove garlic (or 2 scallions), minced
½ cup dry sherry or dry white wine
¼ cup low-salt chicken broth
¼ cup low-fat yogurt

1. Brown chicken breasts in oil in a large skillet for about 15 minutes or until lightly browned. Sprinkle with pepper and salt (if desired) and transfer to covered serving dish. Keep warm.
2. Add tomato, olives, garlic, sherry, and chicken broth to skillet. Bring sauce to a boil and reduce heat. Simmer for 7 minutes. Add yogurt gradually while stirring. Continue heating until sauce is warmed through. Do not allow to boil.
3. Pour sauce over chicken and serve.

Chicken Verde

Smother baked chicken breasts with a pesto-style green sauce. Serve with steamed zucchini and Sautéed Potatoes with Red Pepper Oil (p. 160).

1 pound boneless chicken breasts, skinned and cut in half
    (or turkey breast)
½ cup plus 2 tablespoons extra-virgin olive oil
¼ teaspoon black pepper
Juice of 1 lemon
2 cloves garlic
3 cups chopped fresh basil, parsley, or a combination
3 tablespoons grated Parmesan cheese
2 tablespoons pine nuts

1. Preheat oven to 350° F.
2. Rub chicken with 2 tablespoons olive oil and sprinkle with black pepper. Place chicken in baking dish.
3. Cover and bake for 45 minutes or until lightly browned.
4. While chicken is cooking combine lemon juice, remaining olive oil, garlic, basil or parsley, and cheese in an electric blender and blend until smooth.
5. Serve chicken covered with green sauce and sprinkled with pine nuts.

YIELD
4 servings

PREPARATION TIME
15 minutes

COOKING TIME
45 minutes

NUTRIENT ANALYSIS
Calories per serving: 544
Protein: 39 gm
Carbohydrates: 7.1 gm
Dietary fiber: 1.9 gm
Cholesterol: 98 mg
Total fat: 40.8 gm (367 cal)
Sat fat: 7 gm (62 cal)
Poly fat: 4.2 gm (38 cal)
Mono fat: 27.7 gm (249 cal)

Garlic Chicken

YIELD
4 servings

PREPARATION TIME
20 minutes

COOKING TIME
1 hour and 45 minutes

NUTRIENT ANALYSIS
Calories per serving: 355
Protein: 37 gm
Carbohydrates: 12 gm
Dietary fiber: 1.5 gm
Cholesterol: 93.9 mg
Total fat: 18 gm (159 cal)
Sat fat: 3.1 gm (28 cal)
Poly fat: 2.2 gm (19 cal)
Mono fat: 11.4 gm (102 cal)

Despite the large number of garlic cloves used in this popular dish, the finished flavor is surprisingly subtle. After the chicken is roasted, you can remove the cooked garlic cloves, peel and squeeze them from their hulls, and spread them on slices of toasted bread. When available substitute fresh herbs for the dried herbs in this recipe. Serve with Spinach and Rice (p. 182).

¼ cup extra-virgin olive oil
2 pound chicken cut into serving pieces (yields 1 pound of meat)
1 medium onion, chopped
4 stalks celery, chopped
2 medium carrots, chopped
2 tablespoons chopped fresh parsley
2 whole heads garlic, separated into unpeeled cloves (about 25 cloves)
¼ cup dry white wine
¼ cup water
½ teaspoon dried thyme leaves
½ teaspoon dried basil leaves
½ teaspoon dried rosemary leaves
½ teaspoon dried oregano leaves

1. Preheat oven to 350° F. Heat olive oil in a heavy skillet and sauté chicken for about 15 minutes over medium heat until lightly browned.
2. Put onion, celery, carrots, and parsley in bottom of a large ovenproof casserole. Layer chicken over vegetables. Tuck garlic cloves between chicken pieces. Pour wine and water over chicken. Sprinkle with thyme, basil, rosemary, and oregano.
3. Cover casserole and bake for 1½ hours. Don't lift the cover until cooking time is completed. Skin chicken before eating.

Spicy Mexican Chicken

This stove-top simmered chicken dish contains a diverse selection of spices and nuts. Add more chili powder if you prefer a hotter flavor. Serve with Black Beans (p. 184) and corn muffins.

½ cup unbleached all-purpose flour (or ¼ cup oat bran and ¼ cup flour)
1½ pounds boneless breasts, skinned and cut in half (or 1 pound turkey breast)
6 tablespoons extra-virgin olive oil
2 medium green bell peppers, diced
1 large onion, diced
¼ teaspoon ground cinnamon
½ teaspoon ground cloves
1 teaspoon chili powder
1 clove garlic, crushed
¼ cup dry roasted, unsalted peanuts
2 cups low-salt chicken broth
1 teaspoon dried oregano leaves
¼ cup cornstarch
¼ teaspoon ground black pepper

YIELD
6 servings

PREPARATION TIME
20 minutes

COOKING TIME
1 hour and 10 minutes

NUTRIENT ANALYSIS
Calories per serving: 421
Protein: 40 gm
Carbohydrates: 17 gm
Dietary fiber: 1.5 gm
Cholesterol: 94.2 mg
Total fat: 21 gm (190 cal)
Sat fat: 3.7 gm (33 cal)
Poly fat: 3.2 gm (29 cal)
Mono fat: 13.1 gm (118 cal)

1. Put flour in a bag. Shake one piece of chicken at a time in the bag to coat. Heat 4 tablespoons oil in a heavy skillet over medium heat, and sauté the chicken 15 minutes until lightly browned on both sides. Set chicken pieces aside.
2. Add remaining oil to skillet and sauté peppers and onion until tender. Add cinnamon, cloves, chili powder, garlic, peanuts, broth, and oregano. Heat until simmering.
3. Spoon out ½ cup of sauce and blend with cornstarch. Return this mixture to casserole, and simmer until sauce thickens.
4. Add chicken pieces to sauce, cover, and simmer over low heat for 45 minutes or until chicken is tender. Sprinkle with pepper and serve.

Easy Baked Chicken Breasts

YIELD
4 servings

PREPARATION TIME
15 minutes

COOKING TIME
1 hour

NUTRIENT ANALYSIS
Calories per serving: 430
Protein: 38 gm
Carbohydrates: 30 gm
Dietary fiber: 2.5 gm
Cholesterol: 94 mg
Total fat: 18 gm (159 cal)
Sat fat: 3 gm (28 cal)
Poly fat: 2.2 gm (20 cal)
Mono fat: 11.4 gm (102 cal)

This is a simple baked stew for an occasion when you long for something hearty and delicious that requires minimal effort. Serve with broccoli or a green salad with Basic Vinaigrette (p. 240).

1 pound boneless chicken breasts, skinned and cut in half
   (or turkey breast)
4 large potatoes, peeled and cut into eighths
1 cup coarsely chopped tomatoes
½ teaspoon black pepper
1 teaspoon dried oregano leaves
¼ cup extra-virgin olive oil
6 large mushrooms, sliced
1 tablespoon chopped fresh parsley

1. Preheat oven to 350° F. Place chicken in an ovenproof casserole. Add potatoes, tomatoes, pepper, oregano, olive oil, and mushrooms.
2. Bake, uncovered, for 1 hour. Baste ingredients with sauce from the casserole every 20 minutes. Remove from the oven and sprinkle with parsley.

Cold Chicken
with Lime
Dressing

Toss poached chicken with celery, red pepper, and scallions, then dress it with a tangy lime marinade. Serve with Syrian Potato Salad (p. 80).

1 pound chicken breasts, skinned and cut in half (or
    turkey breast)
1 teaspoon grated lime peel
¼ cup fresh lime juice
¼ teaspoon crushed dried red peppers
½ teaspoon ground cumin
½ cup extra-virgin olive oil
1 cup thinly sliced celery
1 cup diced red bell peppers
½ cup chopped scallions
⅓ cup chopped dry roasted, unsalted peanuts
8 large romaine lettuce leaves, rinsed and drained

1. Poach the chicken breasts in just enough water to cover. Bring to a boil over medium heat. Immediately reduce heat to low and simmer, covered, for 15 minutes until meat has lost its pinkness. Remove breasts and drain. Cool and debone. Cut meat into ¼-inch strips.
2. To make dressing, combine lime peel, lime juice, dried red peppers, cumin, and olive oil with a wire whisk.
3. Put chicken strips, celery, red bell peppers, and scallions in a large bowl.
4. Add dressing to chicken and vegetables. Toss well and refrigerate for 1 hour. (To avoid a pickling effect, do not marinate the chicken in lime juice for longer than three hours.)
5. Sprinkle with peanuts just before serving on romaine leaves.

YIELD
4 servings

PREPARATION TIME
30 minutes

COOKING TIME
*15 minutes + 1 hour
marinating time*

NUTRIENT ANALYSIS
Calories per serving: 545
Protein: 39 gm
Carbohydrates: 19 gm
Dietary fiber: 3.1 gm
Cholesterol: 94 mg
Total fat: 35.8 gm (322 cal)
Sat fat: 5.8 gm (52 cal)
Poly fat: 4.7 gm (42 cal)
Mono fat: 23.6 gm (212 cal)

Citrus-Herb
Baked
Chicken

YIELD
4 servings

PREPARATION TIME
10 minutes

COOKING TIME
1 hour 15 minutes

NUTRIENT ANALYSIS
Calories per serving: 309
Protein: 36 gm
Carbohydrates: 1.3 gm
Dietary fiber: 0 gm
Cholesterol: 94 mg
Total fat: 17.6 gm (158 cal)
Sat fat: 3.1 gm (28 cal)
Poly fat: 2.1 gm (20 cal)
Mono fat: 11.4 gm (103 cal)

Baked whole chickens are easy to prepare. They make an inexpensive family meal or enough chicken for salads, crêpes, sandwiches, and more. This recipe and its variations are made from the same basic cooking method using olive oil with a series of flavor twists. Serve baked chicken with Puffed French "Fried" Potatoes (p. 173) and Asparagus Vinaigrette (p. 70).

1 3-pound roasting chicken
½ teaspoon black pepper
2 cloves garlic, mashed (or 1 shallot or 2 scallions, minced)
¼ cup lemon juice
¼ cup extra-virgin flavorful olive oil
1½ teaspoons dried thyme leaves

1. Preheat oven to 450° F. Wash chicken inside and out. Pat dry with a paper towel. Sprinkle with pepper.
2. Rub chicken with garlic inside and out and place on a roasting rack with the breast-side up.
3. Mix lemon juice and oil together and pour over chicken, rubbing in lightly.
4. Sprinkle thyme over chicken.
5. Reduce oven temperature to 350° F. and put chicken in oven. Baste with drippings every 15 minutes for about 1 hour and 15 minutes or until the joints pull away easily. Remove skin before eating.

ORANGE-CUMIN BAKED CHICKEN
Omit lemon juice and thyme. Mix the juice of a small orange and 1 teaspoon of powdered cumin with the olive oil. Pour over chicken and rub in lightly; bake.

· ·

CALYPSO BAKED CHICKEN

Omit garlic, lemon juice, and thyme. Mix 2 tablespoons lime juice with the olive oil and rub in the chicken, inside and out. Cover the chicken with thin slices of 1 lime and 1 small onion; bake.

GARLIC-PAPRIKASH BAKED CHICKEN

Omit lemon juice and thyme. Use 3 minced cloves of garlic instead of 2 and mix with olive oil. Pour over chicken and rub in lightly. Sprinkle with 2 teaspoons paprika; bake.

Oven-Fried Chicken

....

YIELD
Serves 4

PREPARATION TIME
10 minutes

COOKING TIME
1 hour

NUTRIENT ANALYSIS
Calories per serving: 440
Protein: 37 gm
Carbohydrates: 16 gm
Dietary fiber: 0.4 gm
Cholesterol: 94 mg
Total fat: 24.5 gm (220 cal)
Sat fat: 4.1 gm (37 cal)
Poly fat: 2.7 gm (24 cal)
Mono fat: 16.4 gm (147 cal)

Chicken is coated with cornmeal, flour, and paprika before frying in the oven using this easy-to-fix method. Serve with Mexican Cauliflower (p. 171) and a salad of oranges, bananas and romaine leaves with Citrus Dressing (p. 237).

½ cup unbleached all-purpose flour (or oat bran or wheat germ)
¼ cup cornmeal
¼ teaspoon black pepper
½ teaspoon paprika
1 pound boneless chicken breasts, skinned and cut in half (or turkey breast)
6 tablespoons extra-virgin olive oil

1. Preheat oven to 350° F. Pour flour, cornmeal, pepper, and paprika into a paper bag. Place chicken in bag, one piece at a time, and shake until well coated.
2. Put chicken in a medium baking dish and pour olive oil over it. Bake for 1 hour, until browned. Turn chicken several times while baking.

Chicken Curry

This dish combines chicken with onion, garlic, tomatoes, pine nuts, and curry powder. Serve over steamed rice and garnish with toasted almonds. Accompany with spiced apples dusted with nutmeg.

1 pound boneless chicken breasts, skinned and cut in half (or turkey breast)
½ cup unbleached all-purpose flour (or oat bran or wheat germ)
¼ teaspoon black pepper
6 tablespoons extra-virgin olive oil
1 cup chopped onion
1 clove garlic, chopped
½ cup chopped green bell pepper
1½ teaspoons curry powder
½ teaspoon dried thyme leaves
2 cups diced fresh or canned tomatoes

1. Preheat oven to 350° F. Pat chicken with paper towels. Combine flour and pepper and sprinkle over both sides of chicken breasts.
2. Heat the olive oil in a large skillet over medium heat. Sauté chicken 15 minutes until lightly browned.
3. Remove from skillet with a wide cake turner and place in a large heatproof casserole.
4. Sauté onions, garlic, green pepper, curry powder, and thyme. Sauté in skillet 5 minutes until lightly browned. Add tomatoes. Stir until heated through.
5. Pour tomato mixture over chicken in casserole. Bake, uncovered, for 30 minutes until chicken is tender.

YIELD
4 servings

PREPARATION TIME
15 minutes

COOKING TIME
1 hour and 15 minutes

NUTRIENT ANALYSIS
Calories per serving: 294
Protein: 38 gm
Carbohydrates: 20 gm
Dietary fiber: 2.0 gm
Cholesterol: 94 mg
Total fat: 6.5 gm (59 cal)
Sat fat: 1.6 gm (14 cal)
Poly fat: 1.3 gm (12 cal)
Mono fat: 3 gm (27 cal)

Chicken Couscous

YIELD
4 servings

PREPARATION TIME
20 minutes

COOKING TIME
1 hour and 5 minutes

Couscous is a hearty North African main course that is the national dish of Algeria, Tunisia, and Morocco. The term couscous refers to both the stew itself and the grain that is part of the dish. Here is a quick version of couscous, flavored with turmeric and coriander. Serve with Afghan bread and a fruit salad of hulled berries, diced pineapple, and melon balls dressed with Balsamic Vinaigrette (p. 240).

¼ cup extra-virgin olive oil
1 pound boneless chicken breasts, skinned and cut in half
    (or turkey breast)
¾ cup sliced carrots
¾ cup sliced onions
½ cup water
1 teaspoon ground coriander
1 clove garlic, minced
¼ teaspoon cayenne pepper
½ teaspoon ground turmeric
1 cup drained canned chick-peas
¾ cup sliced zucchini
½ cup couscous (dry precooked semolina)
¼ cup golden raisins
1 tablespoon tub margarine
½ cup boiling water

1. Heat olive oil in heavy skillet over medium-high heat and cook chicken for 15 minutes until lightly browned on both sides.
2. Stir in carrots, onions, water, coriander, garlic, red pepper, and ¼ teaspoon of the turmeric. Bring to a boil. Reduce heat to low and simmer for 25 minutes.

3. Stir in chick-peas and zucchini and simmer for 15 minutes more.

4. Place couscous, raisins, margarine, and remaining turmeric in a medium bowl and pour boiling water over them. Stir and let stand for 5 minutes.

5. Spoon couscous into center of a serving dish and arrange chicken and vegetables around it. Pour the stew liquid over the chicken and couscous.

NUTRIENT ANALYSIS
Calories per serving: 552
Protein: 47 gm
Carbohydrates: 44 gm
Dietary fiber: 2.3 gm
Cholesterol: 94 mg
Total fat: 21.5 gm (194 cal)
Sat fat: 3.4 gm (30 cal)
Poly fat: 2.7 gm (25 cal)
Mono fat: 12 gm (107 cal)

Rapid Chicken in Wine Sauce

Jan. 21. 1996.   Good!

YIELD
4 servings

PREPARATION TIME
10 minutes

COOKING TIME
20 minutes

NUTRIENT ANALYSIS
Calories per serving: 363
Protein: 37 gm
Carbohydrates: 6.9 gm
Dietary fiber: 0.3 gm
Cholesterol: 94 mg
Total fat: 17.8 gm (160 cal)
Sat fat: 3.2 gm (29 cal)
Poly fat: 2.1 gm (19 cal)
Mono fat: 11.5 gm (104 cal)

Sauté chicken breasts in herbs, then simmer in wine and chicken broth. Serve with steamed broccoli and brown rice.

1 pound boneless chicken breasts, skinned and cut in half
    (or turkey breast)
¼ cup unbleached all-purpose flour (or 2 tablespoons
    flour and 2 tablespoons oat bran)
¼ cup mild, light flavored olive oil
1 teaspoon dried thyme leaves
1 teaspoon dried rosemary leaves
½ teaspoon dried oregano leaves
2 cloves garlic, minced
½ cup dry white wine
½ cup low-salt chicken broth
¼ cup chopped fresh parsley

1. Rinse chicken and dry on paper towels.
2. Dredge chicken in flour and sauté in 2 tablespoons olive oil. Cook over medium-high heat for 5 minutes on the first side and 3 minutes on the second side.
3. Reduce heat and add the remaining 2 tablespoons of olive oil to the skillet with thyme, rosemary, oregano, and garlic. Stir to distribute herbs evenly.
4. Add wine and chicken broth to the skillet and bring to a simmer. Cover and simmer over low heat for 10 minutes.
5. Serve garnished with parsley.

Stir-Fried Chicken with Vegetables

YIELD
4 servings

PREPARATION TIME
20 minutes

COOKING TIME
15 minutes

This stir-fried chicken recipe is just one example of the many Oriental dishes that can be prepared with olive oil. Serve it over steamed rice.

½ cup low-salt chicken broth
¼ cup dry sherry
2 tablespoons soy sauce
½ teaspoon minced fresh ginger (or ¼ teaspoon dried)
3 scallions, chopped
¼ cup extra-virgin olive oil
1 clove garlic, minced
1 pound boneless chicken breasts, skinned and cut into
*   ½-inch strips (or turkey breast)*
1 medium green bell pepper, seeded and thinly sliced
1 8-ounce can water chestnuts
½ cup sliced fresh mushrooms
½ cup dry-roasted unsalted peanuts

NUTRIENT ANALYSIS
Calories per serving: 430
Protein: 40 gm
Carbohydrates: 12 gm
Dietary fiber: 1.6 gm
Cholesterol: 94 mg
Total fat: 24 gm (212 cal)
Sat fat: 3.9 gm (35 cal)
Poly fat: 4 gm (36 cal)
Mono fat: 14.4 gm (130 cal)

1. Combine chicken broth, sherry, soy sauce, and ginger in a small bowl.
2. Stir-fry scallions in olive oil in a large skillet or wok 3 minutes until softened. Add garlic and chicken and stir-fry until chicken turns white.
3. Add green pepper, water chestnuts, mushrooms, and peanuts. Stir-fry for another minute. Pour in chicken broth mixture and cover. Steam for 5 minutes or until vegetables are crisp-tender.

VARIATION
Substitute broccoli, celery, zucchini, cauliflower, snow peas, bean sprouts, or string beans for any of the vegetables.

Paella

YIELD
6 servings

PREPARATION TIME
30 minutes

COOKING TIME
1 hour and 15 minutes

NUTRIENT ANALYSIS
Calories per serving: 643
Protein: 56 gm
Carbohydrates: 48 gm
Dietary fiber: 2.8 gm
Cholesterol: 180 mg
Total fat: 24 gm (216 cal)
Sat fat: 4.2 gm (38 cal)
Poly fat: 3 gm (27 cal)
Mono fat: 15 gm (139 cal)

There are many variations of this classic Spanish one-meal dish. This one is a combination of chicken, shrimp, clams, and vegetables baked in the oven. Serve with a salad of mixed greens and Parsley Dressing (p. 238).

1½ pounds boneless chicken breasts, skinned and cut in half (or turkey breast)
½ cup extra-virgin olive oil
3 cloves garlic, slivered
1 large green bell pepper, cut into strips
1 medium onion, chopped
3 cups low-salt chicken broth
1½ cups raw long-grain rice
1 teaspoon paprika
½ teaspoon dried oregano leaves
¼ teaspoon black pepper
¼ teaspoon crumbled saffron
½ pound raw shrimp, peeled and deveined
12 fresh littleneck clams, well rinsed and scrubbed
2 large tomatoes, chopped
1 cup frozen green peas, defrosted (or a 1-pound can of drained asparagus tips or artichoke hearts)

1. Preheat oven to 350° F. Heat olive oil in large, heavy skillet and sauté chicken pieces for 15 minutes until lightly browned. Transfer chicken to large ovenproof casserole.
2. Sauté garlic, green pepper, and onion over medium heat in remaining oil for 5 minutes. Add the chicken broth to the skillet and bring to a boil over high heat.
3. Stir in rice, paprika, oregano, black pepper, and saffron. Bring to a boil again.
4. Pour rice mixture over chicken pieces in casserole. Cover and bake for 40 minutes.
5. Add shrimp, clams, tomatoes, and peas. Cover and return to oven for 15 minutes.

SEAFOOD

FISH IN FOIL
BAKED OR BROILED FISH STEAKS
FISH FILLETS PROVENÇAL ◉
MEXICAN BAKED FISH
BAKED FISH WITH ZUCCHINI ◉
GINGER FISH FILLETS ◉
ESCABECHE
PAN-SAUTÉED FISH ◉
MARINATED SALMON
GREEK BAKED FISH WITH VEGETABLES
CITRUS-MARINATED FISH
SHRIMP WITH RED PEPPERS ◉
SCALLOPS IN GARLIC SAUCE ◉
CURRIED SCALLOPS ◉
SAUTÉED SOFTSHELL CRABS ◉

FISH

....

Fish has fewer calories than meat, and it is low in fat and extremely nutritious. An average 4 to 6 ounce serving supplies one third to one half of the adult daily protein requirements as well as B vitamins, thiamin, riboflavin, and niacin. Most fish also provide iodine, copper, and iron and, if with the bones such as canned salmon and sardines, calcium and phosphorus.

In recent years, studies have indicated that the omega-3 fatty acids found in fish may protect against heart disease by reducing blood cholesterol (particularly LDL) and triglyceride levels. Omega-3's, which are also found in high concentration in the human brain and eye, seem to inhibit the tendency of blood cells to form stroke-related artery-blocking clots. They may also help to ease headaches, premenstrual discomfort, asthma, and the inflammation of arthritis.

The highest quantities of omega-3's are found in fish such as salmon with more than 5 percent fat. Ocean fish with more than 5 percent fat include bluefish, butterfish, halibut, herring, mackerel, mullet, pompano, rainbow trout, salmon, sardines, tuna, and whitefish. When selecting fish, it's important to consider the fact that many varieties have become victims of chemical contamination as the result of dangerous pesticides, PCB's, toxic metals, and other pollutants that find their way into our inland waters. Ocean fish are currently the most untainted available.

Leaner ocean fish include cod, flounder, grouper, haddock, halibut, monkfish, ocean perch, pollack, porgies, red snapper, rockfish, scrod, sea bass, sea trout, shark, skate, sole, striped bass, swordfish, tilefish, turbot, and whiting. To gain the same number of omega-3's that are in 1½ pounds of fatter fish, you need to eat 2 to 3 pounds of these leaner fish.

Since environmental concerns and geographical location often limit the availability of specific types of fish, feel free to substitute varieties as you prepare the following recipes.

COOKING TIPS

When testing fish for doneness, insert a toothpick into the thickest part of the fish near the backbone and separate the meat from the bone. The fish is done when the flesh is opaque and no longer translucent and flakes readily. You can also test for doneness by pressing on it. If the flesh returns to its original shape after pressing it, the fish is done. Avoid overcooking fish since it tends to dry out rapidly.

When baking fish, try to use a heatproof dish that can double as a serving platter. This will prevent over-handling of the fish and you'll have one less "fishy" dish to clean.

To remove fish odors from pans after cooking fish, wash with 1 teaspoon baking soda dissolved in 1 quart water. Rinse with a small amount of vinegar, and then wash with sudsy water.

To remove fishy odors from your hands, rub with lemon juice and salt or a little vinegar before washing.

Fish in Foil

YIELD
4 servings

PREPARATION TIME
25 minutes

COOKING TIME
40 minutes

This recipe for baked fish and vegetables is a traditional *Fillets de poisson en papillote* dish, or fish baked in paper. In this version, the fish is smothered with vegetables and cooked in a wine-laced sauce sealed in an aluminum foil package. Serve with roast potato wedges with Basic Pesto (p. 264).

1½ pounds fish fillets
2 tablespoons unbleached all-purpose flour
⅛ teaspoon cayenne pepper
¼ cup extra-virgin olive oil
1 clove garlic, crushed
1 medium onion, thinly sliced
1 medium green bell pepper, seeded and thinly sliced
1 cup thinly sliced mushrooms
¼ cup dry white wine
1 large tomato or 1 cup drained canned plum tomatoes,
   chopped
1 tablespoon lemon juice
¼ cup tomato paste
¼ teaspoon dried thyme leaves
1 tablespoon minced fresh parsley

NUTRIENT ANALYSIS
Calories per serving: 422
Protein: 48 gm
Carbohydrates: 11.4 gm
Dietary fiber: 1.7 gm
Cholesterol: 70 mg
Total fat: 19 gm (170 cal)
Sat fat: 2.7 gm (24 cal)
Poly fat: 2.9 gm (26 cal)
Mono fat: 11.6 gm (104 cal)

1. Dip fish in flour and sprinkle with cayenne. Heat olive oil in large skillet over low heat and sauté garlic for 1 minute. Turn heat up to medium, add fish, and brown for about 3 minutes a side.

2. Tear off a strip of heavy aluminum foil 24 inches in length. Remove fish with a slotted spoon or wide spatula and place in the center of foil.

3. Heat oven to 425° F.

4. Sauté onions, peppers, and mushrooms in skillet in remaining oil for 5 minutes until onions and peppers are tender. Add wine, tomato, lemon juice, tomato paste, and thyme. Bring mixture to a boil and remove from heat.

5. Spoon sauce over fish and seal foil packet edges with a double fold, excluding as much air as possible. Place on a baking sheet and bake for 20 minutes.

6. Carefully cut pouch and turn back edges of foil before serving. Garnish with parsley.

Baked or Broiled Fish Steaks

YIELD
4 servings

PREPARATION TIME
10 minutes

COOKING TIME
14 minutes if broiled, 20 minutes if baked

NUTRIENT ANALYSIS
Calories per serving: 279
Protein: 30.3 gm
Carbohydrates: 0.3 gm
Dietary fiber: 0.3 gm
Cholesterol: 47 mg
Total fat: 16.9 gm (152 cal)
Sat fat: 2.4 gm (22 cal)
Poly fat: 2.2 gm (20 cal)
Mono fat: 11 gm (96 cal)

One of the easiest ways to include olive oil on a dinner menu is to use it as a coating for baked or broiled fish steaks. This basic preparation will work either way. Your fish steaks should be about 1½ inches thick. Serve with Artichokes in Mustard Sauce (p. 168).

2 medium fish steaks, 1 pound (halibut or similar fish of
*   your choice)*
¼ cup mild, light flavored olive oil
¼ teaspoon black pepper
1 teaspoon dried rosemary leaves

1. Preheat broiler (or preheat oven to 400° F.) and brush both sides of steaks with olive oil. Season with pepper and rosemary.
2. Broil for 6 minutes on each side or bake in the pre-heated oven for 15 to 20 minutes without turning until fish is no longer translucent and flakes easily.

Fish Fillets Provençal

Fish fillets are sautéed in olive oil and simmered in a tomato-onion sauce. This dish is traditionally made with cod fillets. Serve with Green Bean Salad (p. 83).

1 medium onion, chopped
5 tablespoons mild, light flavored olive oil
1 garlic clove (or 2 shallots), minced
2 large ripe tomatoes, chopped
1 teaspoon dried basil leaves
½ teaspoon dried thyme leaves
1 tablespoon minced fresh parsley
¼ teaspoon black pepper
1 pound fish fillets
¼ cup unbleached all-purpose flour

1. Sauté onion in medium skillet in olive oil 5 minutes or until tender. Add garlic and stir. Add tomatoes, basil, thyme, parsley, and pepper. Simmer for 10 minutes.
2. While sauce simmers, dredge fish in flour to coat on both sides.
3. Sauté fish in a large skillet in 2 tablespoons of olive oil until lightly browned.
4. Pour sauce over fish in skillet and simmer for 15 minutes until fish is no longer translucent and flakes easily.

YIELD
4 servings

PREPARATION TIME
10 minutes

COOKING TIME
30 minutes

NUTRIENT ANALYSIS
Calories per serving: 359
Protein: 32 gm
Carbohydrates: 11 gm
Dietary fiber: 1.8 gm
Cholesterol: 47 mg
Total fat: 20.5 gm (185 cal)
Sat fat: 2.9 gm (26 cal)
Poly fat: 2.6 gm (23 cal)
Mono fat: 13.5 gm (122 cal)

Mexican Baked Fish

YIELD
4 servings

PREPARATION TIME
10 minutes

COOKING TIME
1 hour

NUTRIENT ANALYSIS
Calories per serving: 309
Protein: 31 gm
Carbohydrates: 7.2 gm
Dietary fiber: 1.3 gm
Cholesterol: 46.7 mg
Total fat: 17 gm (153 cal)
Sat fat: 2.4 gm (22 cal)
Poly fat: 2.2 gm (20 cal)
Mono fat: 11 gm (100 cal)

Sauté fish fillets, then cover with a tomato, onion, spice, and orange juice sauce and bake. Serve with corn bread and a mixed green salad dressed with Cumin Vinaigrette (p. 240).

¼ cup extra-virgin olive oil
1 pound fish fillets
1 medium onion, minced
1 clove garlic, crushed (or 1 shallot or 2 scallions, minced)
1 large tomato, chopped
1 teaspoon dried oregano leaves
⅛ teaspoon ground cumin
⅛ teaspoon chili powder
Grated rind of 1 small orange
½ cup orange juice
¼ teaspoon black pepper

1. Preheat oven to 375° F.
2. Heat olive oil in large skillet over medium-low heat and sauté fillets for 2 minutes a side. Remove fillets with a slotted spoon and set aside.
3. Add onion, garlic, tomatoes, oregano, cumin, chili powder, and orange rind to skillet and stir well. Reduce heat to low and simmer for 20 minutes.
4. Add orange juice to skillet.
5. Oil the bottom and sides of a medium ovenproof casserole. Place half the fish on the bottom of the casserole and top with half the tomato-orange sauce. Add the rest of the fish and then the rest of the sauce. Cover and bake for 30 minutes until bubbly.

Baked Fish
with
Zucchini

Zucchini and tomatoes are included with this baked fish dish. Slice some leftover or prebaked potatoes, and sauté in olive oil while the fish cooks, and dinner will be ready!

1 medium zucchini, diced
2 medium tomatoes, diced
¼ cup mild, light flavored olive oil
1 tablespoon red wine vinegar
1 tablespoon finely minced scallions
¼ teaspoon black pepper
1 pound fish steaks, 1-inch thick

1. Preheat oven to 400° F. Sauté zucchini and tomatoes in olive oil in a skillet over medium heat for 5 minutes. Remove skillet from heat and stir in vinegar and scallions. Sprinkle with pepper.

2. Arrange fish steaks in medium oiled baking dish in one layer. Pour tomato-zucchini mixture over fish. Bake for 15 minutes or until fish is done.

YIELD
4 servings

PREPARATION TIME
10 minutes

COOKING TIME
20 minutes

NUTRIENT ANALYSIS
Calories per serving: 300
Protein: 31 gm
Carbohydrates: 5 gm
Dietary fiber: 2.4 gm
Cholesterol: 47 mg
Total fat: 17 gm (154 cal)
Sat fat: 2.4 gm (22 cal)
Poly fat: 2.3 gm (21 cal)
Mono fat: 11 gm (97 cal)

Ginger Fish Fillets

······ **Q** ···

YIELD
4 servings

PREPARATION TIME
10 minutes

COOKING TIME
25 minutes

NUTRIENT ANALYSIS
Calories per serving: 312
Protein: 32.5 gm
Carbohydrates: 4 gm
Dietary fiber: 0.1 gm
Cholesterol: 47 mg
Total fat: 17 gm (154 cal)
Sat fat: 2.5 gm (22 cal)
Poly fat: 2.3 gm (20 cal)
Mono fat: 11.1 gm (100 cal)

Serve this Chinese-inspired dish with Garden Vegetable Stir-Fry (p. 164).

1 pound fish fillets
2 tablespoons unbleached all-purpose flour
½ teaspoon minced fresh ginger
1 garlic clove (or 2 shallots), minced
¼ cup olive oil
2 tablespoons light soy sauce
2 tablespoons dry sherry
¾ cup low-salt chicken broth
2 scallions, chopped

1. Dredge fillets in flour.
2. Stir-fry ginger and garlic in oil in skillet or wok over medium heat for 3 minutes. When garlic is lightly browned, add fish and sauté for 3 minutes a side.
3. Combine soy sauce, sherry, and chicken broth. Pour over fish. Cover and cook over moderate heat for 10 minutes. Add scallions and cook, uncovered, for 5 minutes more.

Escabeche

Escabeche is a cold, flavorful fish dish that can be enjoyed as an appetizer or entrée. In Portugal, it is frequently served as a main course with hot baked potatoes. Once prepared, Escabeche is best when chilled for at least two days before serving. It can be kept in the refrigerator for three weeks and will become more delectable with each passing day. Servings given are for entrée.

½ cup extra-virgin olive oil
2 pounds mild, firm, white fish fillets, such as sea bass, swordfish, or halibut, ½-inch thick
2 medium onions, peeled and thinly sliced
2 cloves garlic (or 1 shallot or 2 scallions), minced
2 medium carrots, peeled and grated
⅔ cup wine vinegar
2 bay leaves, crumbled
½ teaspoon salt
¾ teaspoon black pepper
1 teaspoon paprika

1. Heat ¼ cup olive oil over medium heat in a large skillet and sauté fish for about 5 minutes on each side or until it turns white and flakes with a fork. Transfer fish to a medium glass bowl, cool, and break into large chunks.
2. Add the rest of the olive oil to the skillet and sauté onions and garlic for 3 to 5 minutes, until softened. Add carrots, vinegar, bay leaf, salt, pepper, and paprika. Stir and cook for 2 minutes.
3. Pour vegetable-vinegar mixture over fish and toss lightly to mix.
4. Cover and chill for at least 2 days.

YIELD
6 servings

PREPARATION TIME
20 minutes

COOKING TIME
17 minutes + at least 2 days chilling time

NUTRIENT ANALYSIS
Calories per serving: 390
Protein: 41 gm
Carbohydrates: 6.3 gm
Dietary fiber: 1.0 gm
Cholesterol: 62 mg
Total fat: 23 gm (203 cal)
Sat fat: 3.2 gm (29 cal)
Poly fat: 3 mg (27 cal)
Mono fat: 15 gm (132 cal)

Pan-Sautéed Fish

YIELD
4 servings

PREPARATION TIME
10 minutes

COOKING TIME
10 minutes

NUTRIENT ANALYSIS
Calories per serving: 375
Protein: 32 gm
Carbohydrates: 13 gm
Dietary fiber: 0.5 gm
Cholesterol: 46.7 mg
Total fat: 21 gm (193 cal)
Sat fat: 3 gm (28 cal)
Poly fat: 2.6 gm (23 cal)
Mono fat: 14 gm (129 cal)

Serve pan-sautéed fish with tomato sauce, baked new potatoes with Basic Pesto (p. 264), and a Greek Salad (p. 79). Pan-sautéed fish can be kept in a low oven for about half an hour until ready to serve.

1 pound fish fillets
¼ teaspoon black pepper
½ cup unbleached all-purpose flour (or ¼ cup flour and
    ¼ cup oat bran)
1 large clove garlic, cut in half (or 1 shallot or 2 scallions,
    sliced)
⅓ cup extra-virgin olive oil
1 teaspoon dried oregano leaves
1 lemon, quartered

1. Wash fish and pat dry. Sprinkle with pepper and dredge in flour on both sides.
2. Heat garlic in olive oil in large skillet over moderate heat. Remove garlic and sauté fish for 5 minutes or until brown and crusty to suit your taste on one side. Then turn fish and sauté for 5 minutes more or until fish flakes easily when tested with a fork. Sprinkle with oregano and squeeze lemon juice over fillets before serving.

VARIATION
For a crustier coating, dip fish first in flour, then in beaten egg whites, and finally in bread crumbs before sautéeing.

Marinated Salmon

Marinate salmon steaks, then either broil or bake them. Serve garnished with parsley and lemon slices. Serve with steamed asparagus and Lemon-Dill Rice (p. 183).

1 pound salmon fillets
½ cup extra-virgin olive oil
¼ cup orange juice
1 tablespoon wine vinegar
⅓ cup minced onion
1 teaspoon dried tarragon leaves
¼ teaspoon black pepper

1. Place salmon fillets in a large, shallow glass bowl.
2. In a small bowl, combine olive oil, orange juice, vinegar, onion, tarragon, and black pepper with a wire whisk. Pour over salmon. Marinate at room temperature for ½ hour. Turn salmon and marinate for another ½ hour.
3. Place salmon, skin-side down, on oiled broiler pan. Baste with marinade and broil for 7 to 9 minutes, 3 inches from heat.
4. Spoon remaining marinade over each serving.

VARIATION
Bake salmon at 375° F. for 30 minutes or until fish flakes when tested with a fork. Baste with marinade while baking.

YIELD
4 servings

PREPARATION TIME
10 minutes + 1 hour marinating time

COOKING TIME
9 minutes

NUTRIENT ANALYSIS
Calories per serving: 460
Protein: 31.4 gm
Carbohydrates: 2.8 gm
Dietary fiber: 0.3 gm
Cholesterol: 56 mg
Total fat: 36 gm (320 cal)
Sat fat: 5.4 gm (48.9 cal)
Poly fat: 4.8 gm (43.1 cal)
Mono fat: 23 gm (205.6 cal)

Greek Baked Fish with Vegetables

....

YIELD
6 servings

PREPARATION TIME
25 minutes

COOKING TIME
1 hour and 10 minutes

This recipe, which is a Greek favorite, will provide you with dinner in a dish. In Greece, the baked lemon slices are eaten with their rinds.

2 pounds whole fish, cleaned and cut into serving
    portions
2 tablespoons lemon juice
½ cup extra-virgin olive oil
2 cloves garlic, minced
3 medium tomatoes, chopped or 1 1-pound cans chopped
    tomatoes
2 medium onions, thinly sliced
1 green bell pepper, seeded and chopped
1 large lemon, seeded and very thinly sliced
2 tablespoons minced fresh parsley
1 10-ounce package frozen spinach, defrosted, or
    1 pound fresh spinach, washed
1 medium zucchini, sliced
2 stalks celery, chopped
¾ cup dry white wine
¾ cup tomato sauce
¼ teaspoon black pepper
3 large potatoes, peeled and sliced ½-inch thick

1. Rinse fish in cold water and pat dry on paper towels. Rub with lemon juice and 2 tablespoons of the olive oil. Return to refrigerator while preparing vegetables.
2. Heat ¼ cup olive oil in a large skillet over medium heat. Add garlic, tomatoes, onions, green pepper, lemon slices, parsley, spinach, zucchini, and celery. Stir, reduce heat, cover, and simmer for 20 minutes.
3. Preheat oven to 375° F.

4. Add wine, tomato sauce, and black pepper to skillet. Stir carefully and simmer for 5 minutes more.

5. Place fish in the center of a large baking pan and pour the vegetables over it. Top with a layer of potato slices and brush lightly with remaining olive oil.

6. Bake, uncovered, for 45 minutes or until fish is done.

NUTRIENT ANALYSIS

Calories per serving: 512
Protein: 45 gm
Carbohydrates: 26 gm
Dietary fiber: 5.2 gm
Cholesterol: 62.3 mg
Total fat: 23 gm (208 cal)
Sat fat: 3.3 gm (30 cal)
Poly fat: 3.2 gm (29 cal)
Mono fat: 14.7 gm (133 cal)

Citrus-Marinated Fish

YIELD
4 servings

PREPARATION TIME
20 minutes + 1 hour marinating time

COOKING TIME
Approximately 45 minutes

A whole white-fleshed fish of your choice is marinated in fruit juices and then simmered in a piquant tomato sauce. Serve with rice.

1 1½-pound striped bass, cleaned, head and tail removed
 or 1 pound fish fillets
Juice of 1 lemon
Juice of 1 orange
¼ teaspoon black pepper
½ cup extra-virgin olive oil
1 medium onion, chopped
1 clove garlic (or 1 shallot or 2 scallions) chopped
4 tomatoes, stems removed and cut in quarters
2 green chili peppers
⅛ teaspoon ground cinnamon
⅛ teaspoon ground cloves
1 cup water

1. Place fish in oval glass bowl or baking dish. Combine lemon juice and orange juice and pour over fish. Sprinkle with pepper. Marinate for 1 hour.
2. Puree olive oil, onion, garlic, tomatoes, chilies, cinnamon, cloves, and water in an electric blender or food processor.
3. Simmer puree in a medium saucepan over low heat for 15 minutes.
4. Select a skillet or pan that is large enough to accommodate the entire fish. If this isn't possible, cut the fish in half (and reassemble on the serving platter later when ready to serve). Place one third of the puree on the bottom of the pan. Add the fish. Top the fish with the rest of the puree.

5. Simmer the fish, over low heat, with cover slightly ajar until fish flakes when tested with a fork, about 5 to 8 minutes per pound.

NUTRIENT ANALYSIS
Calories per serving: 532
Protein: 47 gm
Carbohydrates: 12 gm
Dietary fiber: 2.7 gm
Cholesterol: 70 mg
Total fat: 32.9 gm (288 cal)
Sat fat: 4.6 gm (45 cal)
Poly fat: 4 gm (36 cal)
Mono fat: 22 gm (198 cal)

SHELLFISH

Although shellfish used to be deleted from cholesterol-aware diets, recent research related to the cholesterol-lowering properties of omega-3 fatty acids has restored them to the list of good choices. Actually, most shellfish are really quite low in cholesterol and far lower in fats than most land animals.

Shrimp
with
Red Peppers

YIELD
4 servings

PREPARATION TIME
20 minutes

COOKING TIME
10 minutes

NUTRIENT ANALYSIS
Calories per serving: 236
Protein: 24 gm
Carbohydrates: 1.2 gm
Dietary fiber: .01 gm
Cholesterol: 221.5 mg
Total fat: 14.7 (133 cal)
Sat fat: 2.3 gm (20 cal)
Poly fat: 1.6 gm (15 cal)
Mono fat: 10 gm (91 cal)

Fresh lime juice and garlic give this spicy shrimp dish a distinctive flavor. Serve it on a bed of rice.

¼ cup extra-virgin olive oil
4 large cloves garlic (or 2 shallots or 4 scallions), minced
½ teaspoon crushed dried red peppers
1 pound large fresh shrimp, shelled and deveined
2 teaspoons fresh lime juice

1. Heat olive oil over medium heat in a heavy skillet. Add garlic. Stir in peppers and shrimp as soon as garlic starts to brown, about 3 minutes. Lower heat and continue to stir.
2. Sprinkle lime juice over shrimp and continue cooking for 5 minutes.

Scallops
in
Garlic Sauce

Prepare bay scallops in a subtle Hunan-style sauce. Serve with rice and a bowl of Mandarin oranges.

3 cups broccoli florets
¼ cup extra-virgin olive oil
2 cloves garlic, minced
2 tablespoons grated fresh ginger
1 pound bay scallops
⅛ teaspoon hot chili oil

1. In a tightly covered pan, steam broccoli florets over 1 inch of water for 5 minutes or until just tender.
2. Heat olive oil over medium heat in a large skillet or wok and sauté garlic and ginger for 1 minute.
3. Add scallops and stir-fry for 3 minutes.
4. Add broccoli and sprinkle with chili oil. Simmer for 4 or 5 minutes until broccoli is heated through.

YIELD
4 servings

PREPARATION TIME
15 minutes

COOKING TIME
15 minutes

NUTRIENT ANALYSIS
Calories per serving: 242
Protein: 21 gm
Carbohydrates: 7 gm
Dietary fiber: 2.3 gm
Cholesterol: 37 mg
Total fat: 15 gm (131 cal)
Sat fat: 2 gm (18 cal)
Poly fat: 1.5 gm (14 cal)
Mono fat: 10 gm (90 cal)

Curried
Scallops

YIELD
4 servings

PREPARATION TIME
10 minutes

COOKING TIME
20 minutes

NUTRIENT ANALYSIS
Calories per serving: 248
Protein: 21 gm
Carbohydrates: 7.3 gm
Dietary fiber: 0.5 gm
Cholesterol: 37 mg
Total fat: 15 gm (135 cal)
Sat fat: 2.1 gm (18.9 cal)
Poly fat: 1.5 gm (13.5 cal)
Mono fat: 10.1 gm (91 cal)

Make this quick and easy entrée with a good curry powder. Serve with cellophane noodles and a marinated vegetable salad.

1 pound bay scallops
⅛ teaspoon black pepper
¼ cup olive oil
1 clove garlic, minced
¼ cup minced onion
1 tablespoon curry powder
½ cup low-salt chicken broth
½ cup fresh or frozen thawed peas
½ cup sliced scallions

1. Sprinkle scallops with pepper. Heat 2 tablespoons olive oil in a large skillet over medium heat and sauté for 3 minutes while stirring. Remove scallops and set aside.
2. Add remaining olive oil to skillet. Stir-fry garlic and onion for 1 minute over medium heat. Sprinkle with curry powder.
3. Add chicken broth, bring to a boil, and simmer about 10 minutes until broth is reduced by about a third. Add peas and scallions. Cook for 2 minutes. Add scallops and continue cooking for 2 more minutes.

Sautéed Softshell Crabs

Softshell crabs are crabs that have just molted. They have not hardened yet, which makes them edible, shells and all. Look for this "ready to cook" delicacy during their short season in the spring. Serve with cole slaw and Syrian Potato Salad (p. 80).

½ cup unbleached all-purpose flour (or ¼ cup oat bran
      and ¼ cup flour)
4 softshell crabs, cleaned and ready to cook
¼ cup extra-virgin olive oil
1 clove garlic, minced (or 1 shallot or 2 scallions)
2 tablespoons minced fresh parsley
⅛ teaspoon cayenne pepper
¼ teaspoon black pepper
1 lemon, quartered

1. Put flour in a flat soup plate and dredge the crabs well.
2. Heat olive oil in skillet over medium heat and sauté garlic 1 to 2 minutes until it starts to brown.
3. Add crabs and sauté 5 minutes on each side until lightly browned.
4. Serve sprinkled with parsley and peppers, and garnished with lemon quarters.

YIELD
4 servings

PREPARATION TIME
10 minutes

COOKING TIME
12 minutes

NUTRIENT ANALYSIS
Calories per serving: 293
Protein: 25 gm
Carbohydrates: 12.6 gm
Dietary fiber: 0.5 gm
Cholesterol: 113 mg
Total fat: 15.6 gm (141 cal)
Sat fat: 2.2 gm (20 cal)
Poly fat: 1.9 gm (17 cal)
Mono fat: 10.2 gm (92 cal)

MEAT

SIRLOIN STEAK WITH ONION-MUSTARD SAUCE
HUNGARIAN BEEF GOULASH
ROSEMARY BEEF STEW
PASTELON DE CARNE
CHILI CON CARNE
PASTITSIO
MOUSSAKA
BEEF AND FRUIT STEW
HUNGARIAN PORK CHOPS
VEGETABLE-PORK MEDLEY
PORK STEW WITH GREEN CHILES
SAUTÉED VEAL STRIPS ◉
BASIL-TARRAGON VEAL CHOPS
VEAL STEW MILANO
VEAL PARMIGIANA

MEAT

R ed meat has a relatively high saturated fat count when compared with poultry and fish. Since meat is a major source of saturated fat in the American diet, selecting and preparing it carefully can be a significant factor in lowering total saturated fat intake. A diet that includes too much fatty red meat can increase the risk of heart disease, contribute to obesity, and possibly be linked to some forms of cancer.

On the positive side, meat is an important source of complex protein that contains all the essential amino acid protein building blocks. It provides iron in a form that the body can utilize easily and is a source of B vitamins and minerals. When we eat more protein than we need from any source, the excess is broken down and burned for energy or stored for fat. Consequently, your goal should be to reduce your daily meat consumption to 3 or 4 ounces a day rather than cutting it out of your diet completely. Our meat recipes limit each serving to under 4 ounces.

In addition to cutting down on the amount of meat you eat, there are a number of other steps you can take to reduce the number of saturated fat calories in the meats you consume.

1. Learn how to shop for the lowest fat cuts and grades. As a result of the increased emphasis on a healthier diet, red meat consumption in the United States has decreased 15 percent in the past decade. This consumer pressure has led the meat-producing industry to develop leaner cuts of beef, lamb, and pork.

If your market carries meats that are USDA graded, look for packages that are stamped *USDA Select*. USDA grade choices are either Prime, Choice, or Select. Select contains the least fat and is also the least expensive. If your market uses their own system of labels rather than the USDA designation, ask the butcher for guidance in using these labels to make low-fat choices.

2. You need to know which cuts of meat make the healthiest choices.

BEEF: Leanest cuts are eye of round, shoulder, rump, chuck with round bone, sirloin tip roasts, flank, tenderloin, sirloin tip, extra-lean ground beef, and lean stew meat.

VEAL: All cuts of veal except the breast are lean. However, veal is higher in cholesterol than beef or pork.

LAMB: Lean cuts of lamb include leg of lamb and sirloin chops. Other fairly lean cuts are loin, shoulder, rib chops, and lamb shanks.

PORK: Relatively lean cuts are sirloin roast, loin chops, and pork tenderloin.

3. There are several low-fat cooking techniques you can use to further reduce the fat content of meat once you bring it home.

- Precook meat to get rid of excess fat before adding it to a recipe. Larger pieces of meat or meat cubes can be broiled on a rack in a broiler pan, allowing fat to drain off into the pan.
- When cooking with ground meat, brown it in a skillet by itself and pour off rendered fat before adding other ingredients.

Remember, your goal is to reduce the dangerous saturated fats found in meat and substitute the healthful monounsaturated fats found in olive oil.

Sirloin Steak with Onion-Mustard Sauce

In this quick dish, sirloin steak is sautéed in olive oil and served with an onion-mustard sauce. Serve with Spanish Rice (p. 181).

¼ cup extra-virgin flavorful olive oil
1 pound sirloin steak, cut into 4 serving pieces, excess fat trimmed
¼ teaspoon black pepper
1 large onion, thinly sliced
3 tablespoons wine vinegar
4 teaspoons Dijon mustard
¼ cup low-salt beef broth

1. In a heavy skillet, heat 2 tablespoons olive oil over medium heat. Add steak and sauté for 2 to 3 minutes on each side if you would like them medium-rare and 5 minutes on each side for well done. Remove from pan using a wide, slotted spatula. Sprinkle with pepper and set aside in a covered dish.
2. Add the remaining 2 tablespoons oil to the skillet and sauté onion slices 2 to 3 minutes until tender. Add vinegar, mustard, and broth. Stir for 2 minutes, scraping up any cooked-on bits from bottom of pan.
3. Pour onion sauce over steaks and serve.

YIELD
4 servings

PREPARATION TIME
10 minutes

COOKING TIME
15 minutes

NUTRIENT ANALYSIS
Calories per serving: 496
Protein: 31 gm
Carbohydrates: 3.8 gm
Dietary fiber: 0.7 gm
Cholesterol: 102.8 mg
Total fat: 40 gm (360 cal)
Sat fat: 12.7 gm (115 cal)
Poly fat: 2.2 gm (20 cal)
Mono fat: 22 gm (196 cal)

Hungarian Beef Goulash

YIELD

4 servings

PREPARATION TIME

15 minutes

COOKING TIME

1 hour and 55 minutes

NUTRIENT ANALYSIS

Calories per serving: 498

Protein: 39 gm

Carbohydrates: 32 gm

Dietary fiber: 2 gm

Cholesterol: 96 mg

Total fat: 23.7 gm (213 cal)

Sat fat: 5.7 gm (51 cal)

Poly fat: 1.7 gm (15 cal)

Mono fat: 14 gm (126 cal)

Goulash is a highly spiced Hungarian specialty that receives its unique flavor from the addition of paprika. Serve with a loaf of crusty French bread and some mixed greens with Citrus Dressing (p. 237).

1 pound lean round steak, cut into 1-inch cubes
¼ cup extra-virgin flavorful olive oil
1 large onion, chopped
1 cup tomato juice
½ teaspoon paprika
8 small or new potatoes, scrubbed

1. Sauté steak over medium heat in olive oil in a heavy pot. When meat is brown, about 10 minutes a side, add onions. Continue cooking 5 minutes until onions are tender.
2. Add tomato juice and paprika. Cover and simmer for 1 hour. Check frequently to see if more liquid is needed, adding additional tomato juice or water as required.
3. Add potatoes and cook, covered, for 30 minutes more.

VARIATION

Omit the potatoes. Serve the goulash with no-egg noodles.

Rosemary Beef Stew

YIELD
4 servings

PREPARATION TIME
25 minutes

COOKING TIME
1 hour and 45 minutes

NUTRIENT ANALYSIS
Calories per serving: 398
Protein: 38 gm
Carbohydrates: 9.6 gm
Dietary fiber: 1.8 gm
Cholesterol: 92 mg
Total fat: 21 gm (189 cal)
Sat fat: 4.4 gm (40 cal)
Poly fat: 1.6 gm (14 cal)
Mono fat: 12.7 gm (114 cal)

This slow-cooking, wine-accented stew is distinguished by the delicate taste of rosemary. Try serving it over slices of toasted garlic bread or egg-free noodles.

3 cups canned tomatoes or fresh, chopped
½ teaspoon dried basil leaves
¾ cup chopped celery
½ cup chopped fresh parsley
¼ teaspoon dried oregano leaves
½ teaspoon dried thyme leaves
¼ cup extra-virgin flavorful olive oil
¼ teaspoon black pepper
1 pound lean beef (top or bottom round or chuck),
    trimmed and cut into 1-inch cubes
1 clove garlic, minced
½ cup dry white wine
1 teaspoon dried rosemary leaves

1. Combine tomatoes, basil, celery, parsley, oregano, thyme, 2 tablespoons olive oil, and pepper in a large saucepan. Cover and bring to a boil over high heat. Lower heat and simmer for 30 minutes.
2. While sauce is cooking heat remaining olive oil in a large heatproof casserole. Add beef and sauté 10 to 15 minutes until browned. Add garlic and stir. Transfer meat to another dish.
3. Pour wine into the casserole and cook over high heat to reduce wine to half, stirring constantly and scraping up any bits of meat in the pan. Add meat, rosemary, and the vegetable-tomato mixture. Cover and simmer for 1½ hours or until meat is tender.

Pastelon De Carne

YIELD
6 servings

PREPARATION TIME
20 minutes

COOKING TIME
50 minutes

This cheese-topped Puerto Rican casserole dish, which combines lean ground beef and eggplant, is prepared on top of the stove and run under a hot broiler immediately before serving. Serve this filling dish with a watercress salad dressed with Parsley-Scallion Vinaigrette (p. 240).

½ pound lean ground beef
1 cup extra-virgin flavorful olive oil
1 medium onion, chopped
3 cloves garlic (or 1 shallot or 2 scallions), chopped
1 large tomato, chopped
1 8-ounce can tomato sauce
½ cup water
¼ teaspoon black pepper
⅛ teaspoon paprika
½ cup unbleached all-purpose flour
1 large eggplant (approximately 1 pound), peeled and cut into ¼-inch rounds
¼ pound reduced-fat Swiss cheese, thinly sliced

1. Brown ground beef in a skillet, stirring with a fork. Drain off any rendered fat. Remove from pan and set aside.
2. Heat ¼ cup olive oil in a large, heavy saucepan and sauté onions over low heat 5 minutes, until soft.
3. Add garlic and stir. Add ground beef, chopped tomato, tomato sauce, water, pepper, paprika, and 2 tablespoons flour. Simmer over low heat for 20 minutes, stirring as needed.
4. Dip eggplant slices in remaining flour. Heat ¾ cup olive

oil in a large skillet over moderate heat and sauté eggplant slices for 3 minutes on each side until browned.

5. Preheat broiler. Place one third of the meat sauce on bottom of a dish that can withstand the heat of the broiler. Top with half the eggplant slices, another layer of meat sauce, another layer of eggplant, the final layer of meat sauce, and the cheese slices.

6. Run under broiler for a few seconds until cheese is melted and browned.

NUTRIENT ANALYSIS
Calories per serving: 355
Protein: 17 gm
Carbohydrates: 20 gm
Dietary fiber: 3.4 gm
Cholesterol: 47.3 mg
Total fat: 23 gm (217 cal)
Sat fat: 5.6 gm (50 cal)
Poly fat: 1.6 gm (14 cal)
Mono fat: 14 gm (126 cal)

Chili Con Carne

YIELD
4 servings

PREPARATION TIME
20 minutes

COOKING TIME
1 hour and 25 minutes

This traditional chili is cooked on top of the stove. Add more chili powder to suit your taste. Serve with a mixed green salad topped with Red Onion Dressing (p. 239) and a plate of warm tortillas or corn bread.

1 pound lean ground beef
¼ cup extra-virgin flavorful olive oil
1 large onion, chopped
1 green bell pepper, chopped
1 clove garlic (or 1 shallot or 2 scallions), minced
2 tablespoons chili powder
½ teaspoon ground cumin
½ teaspoon paprika
1 bay leaf
2 tablespoons wine vinegar
4 cups water
2 cups chopped fresh or chopped and drained canned
    tomatoes
2 cups cooked red kidney or pinto beans (either canned or
    prepared at home from dried beans)

1. Brown beef in large heavy soup pot, crumbling it with a fork until well cooked. Pour off any rendered fat and drain well. Heat olive oil in soup pot and add browned beef, onion, green pepper, and garlic. Sauté until vegetables are tender.
2. Add chili powder, cumin, paprika, bay leaf, vinegar, and water. Cover and simmer for 45 minutes, stirring several times.
3. Remove bay leaf. Add tomatoes and cook for 15 minutes. Add beans and cook for an additional 15 minutes.
4. To thicken, mash some of the beans with a fork or a

potato masher. Or, if desired, add cornmeal and cook until thickened.

VARIATIONS

- Omit the water. Add 1 cup of dry white wine or light beer.
- Pour cooked chili into an ovenproof casserole, top with grated reduced-fat cheese and bake at 350° F. until cheese has melted.

NUTRIENT ANALYSIS
Calories per serving: 509
Protein: 44 gm
Carbohydrates: 29 gm
Dietary fiber: 8 gm
Cholesterol: 96 mg
Total fat: 24.5 gm (221 cal)
Sat fat: 5.7 gm (51 cal)
Poly fat: 1.7 gm (15 cal)
Mono fat: 14 gm (127 cal)

Pastitsio

....

YIELD
4 servings

PREPARATION TIME
15 minutes

COOKING TIME
1 hour and 20 minutes

Pastitsio, a Greek favorite, is a macaroni-ground beef casserole that can be baked in advance and reheated immediately before serving. If you use the optional egg yolk in the sauce, remember to count it as part of your weekly "yolk" content. Serve with Greek Salad (p. 79).

½ pound elbow macaroni
¼ cup extra-virgin flavorful olive oil
¾ pound lean ground beef
⅛ teaspoon grated nutmeg
⅛ teaspoon ground cinnamon
2 tomatoes, diced
2 tablespoons unbleached, all-purpose flour
1½ cups 1 percent milk
¼ teaspoon black pepper
4 egg whites, beaten (or 2 egg whites + 1 whole egg, beaten)
⅔ cup grated reduced-fat Parmesan cheese

1. Bring large pot of hot water to boil over high heat. Add macaroni and cook 9 to 10 minutes until al dente (tender but firm). Drain, return to pot, and toss with 1 tablespoon olive oil. Cover pot to keep warm.
2. While pasta is cooking, brown ground beef in a large skillet. Pour off any rendered fat and drain well. Set meat aside.
3. Add 1 tablespoon olive oil to the pan and sauté onion 3 to 5 minutes until tender. Add ground beef, nutmeg, cinnamon, and tomatoes. Simmer for 20 minutes.
4. In a small saucepan, heat remaining 2 tablespoons olive oil over medium heat, add flour, and cook for 1 minute while stirring with a wire whisk. Slowly add milk and

continue whisking. Let sauce come to a boil and then reduce heat. Simmer sauce for 2 minutes, stirring throughout. Add pepper.

5. Put half of the macaroni on the bottom of the casserole and top with the meat sauce. Top with half the cheese. Add the other half of the macaroni.

6. Whisk the eggs into the milk sauce and pour over the casserole. Top with remaining cheese. Bake for 30 minutes or until casserole is browned.

NUTRIENT ANALYSIS
Calories per serving: 477
Protein: 39.3 gm
Carbohydrates: 19.4 gm
Dietary fiber: 1.6 gm
Cholesterol: 85 mg
Total fat: 26.5 gm (239 cal)
Sat fat: 7.9 gm (71 cal)
Poly fat: 1.6 gm (14.4 cal)
Mono fat: 14.5 gm (131 cal)

Moussaka

YIELD

6 servings

PREPARATION TIME

20 minutes

COOKING TIME

1 hour and 30 minutes

This classic Greek dish also surfaces in a number of other Middle Eastern cuisines. In this version, fresh mashed potatoes replace the high cholesterol egg and butter bechamel sauce that is often used as a topping. Serve with Eggplant Caviar (p. 33) spread on French bread as a first course and a salad of red leaf lettuce with Parsley Dressing (p. 238).

4 small or new potatoes
¼ cup 1 percent milk
1 medium eggplant, peeled and sliced into ¼-inch slices
½ cup unbleached all-purpose flour
½ cup extra-virgin flavorful olive oil
¾ cup sliced fresh mushrooms
1 large onion, chopped
1 clove garlic (or 1 shallot or 2 scallions), crushed
1 pound lean ground lamb or use ground beef or turkey
1 cup low-salt tomato sauce
1 bay leaf
1 teaspoon dried thyme leaves
1 teaspoon dried oregano leaves
½ cup dry sherry
2 tablespoons chopped fresh parsley
¼ pound reduced-fat sharp cheese, crumbled
¼ teaspoon black pepper

1. Boil potatoes 10 to 15 minutes until tender. Peel and mash with milk.
2. Dredge eggplant slices in flour. Heat 4 tablespoons olive oil in a large skillet. Add eggplant a few slices at a time and brown well on both sides. Remove from pan and set aside.

3. Add 1 tablespoon olive oil to the skillet and sauté mushrooms 3 to 5 minutes. Add to lamb-tomato mixture.

4. Add 3 tablespoons oil to skillet and sauté onion and garlic 3 to 5 minutes until tender. Add lamb and cook for 10 minutes more. Add tomato sauce, bay leaf, thyme, oregano, sherry, and parsley. Cook until most of liquid is gone. Remove bay leaf.

5. Place a layer of sautéed eggplant in the bottom. Cover with a layer of lamb-tomato-mushroom mixture. Continue with alternate layers, ending with a top layer of the lamb mixture.

6. Spread mashed potatoes over casserole to create a top crust. Cover and bake for 30 minutes. Add cheese and bake, uncovered, for 15 minutes more.

VARIATION
Omit eggplant. Use 1 large zucchini.

NUTRIENT ANALYSIS
Calories per serving: 503
Protein: 30 gm
Carbohydrates: 26 gm
Dietary fiber: 2.5 gm
Cholesterol: 87 mg
Total fat: 30 gm (270 cal)
Sat fat: 8.3 gm (75 cal)
Poly fat: 2.3 gm (20 cal)
Mono fat: 17 gm (154 cal)

Beef
and Fruit
Stew

YIELD
4 servings

PREPARATION TIME
25 minutes

COOKING TIME
2 hours

NUTRIENT ANALYSIS
Calories per serving: 553
Protein: 39 gm
Carbohydrates: 45 gm
Dietary fiber: 7 gm
Cholesterol: 96 mg
Total fat: 25 gm (223 cal)
Sat fat: 6 gm (53 cal)
Poly fat: 1.9 gm (17 cal)
Mono fat: 14.2 gm (128 cal)

This Spanish dish combines fruits and vegetables for an unexpected taste sensation. Serve with whole wheat French bread spread with Basic Pesto (p. 264).

¼ cup extra-virgin flavorful olive oil
1 pound lean beef, cut into ¾-inch cubes
1 cup chopped onion
½ cup dry sherry
1 tablespoon tomato paste
½ teaspoon dried basil leaves
¼ teaspoon dried thyme leaves
¼ teaspoon dried oregano leaves
⅛ teaspoon ground allspice
2 cups low-salt beef broth
2 cups cubed peeled potatoes
2 cups cubed yellow squash
2 pears, cored and cubed
2 apples, cored and sliced
3 tablespoons seedless raisins
1 teaspoon minced fresh parsley

1. Heat olive oil in large, heavy soup pot and sauté the meat until browned. Remove meat and set aside. Add onions to pot and sauté 3 to 5 minutes until tender. Stir in meat, sherry, tomato paste, basil, thyme, oregano, allspice, and beef broth. Cover and simmer for 1 hour.
2. Add potatoes and squash, and cook, covered, for another 30 minutes.
3. Mix in pears, apples, and raisins and cook for 10 minutes. Garnish with parsley and serve.

Hungarian Pork Chops

Braised pork chops in a wine sauce that is given zest by the addition of mustard, thyme, and sage. Serve with Baked Vegetable Casserole (p. 158).

4 lean loin pork chops, trimmed of fat (1½ pounds before trimming and including bone)
1 small onion, chopped
¼ cup extra-virgin flavorful olive oil
1 cup low-salt chicken broth
1 cup dry white wine
¾ teaspoon unbleached all-purpose flour
1 teaspoon Dijon mustard
½ teaspoon dried thyme leaves
½ teaspoon dried sage leaves

1. Brown pork chops and onions in olive oil in a heavy skillet over medium heat. When chops have browned, add broth and wine. Cover and simmer for 1 hour.
2. Slowly sprinkle flour into sauce while stirring, cooking until smooth, about 1 minute. Add mustard, thyme, and sage. Heat thoroughly and serve.

YIELD
4 servings

PREPARATION TIME
10 minutes

COOKING TIME
1 hour and 10 minutes

NUTRIENT ANALYSIS
Calories per serving: 473
Protein: 33 gm
Carbohydrates: 2 gm
Dietary fiber: 0.3 gm
Cholesterol: 108 mg
Total fat: 31 gm (281 cal)
Sat fat: 8 gm (72 cal)
Poly fat: 3.3 gm (30 cal)
Mono fat: 18 gm (161 cal)

Vegetable-Pork Medley

YIELD
4 servings

PREPARATION TIME
35 minutes

COOKING TIME
2 hours

NUTRIENT ANALYSIS
Calories per serving: 566
Protein: 36 gm
Carbohydrates: 35 gm
Dietary fiber: 5 gm
Cholesterol: 108 mg
Total fat: 31.6 gm (284 cal)
Sat fat: 8 gm (72 cal)
Poly fat: 3.5 gm (31 cal)
Mono fat: 17.7 gm (160 cal)

This Yugoslavian dish is an unusual mix of pork, eggplant, and rice. Serve with sliced avocados, oranges, and grapefruit slices on romaine leaves with Nut Vinaigrette (p. 240).

1 pound boneless, lean pork loin
¼ cup extra-virgin flavorful olive oil
1½ cups thinly sliced onions
2 medium tomatoes, sliced
¼ teaspoon black pepper
2 cups cubed eggplant
1 cup diced green bell pepper
1 cup chopped fresh green beans
½ cup sliced carrots
½ cup raw long-grain rice
1 cup water

1. Broil pork over rack in broiling pan for 3 minutes on each side. Cut pork into 1-inch pieces and set aside.
2. Heat oven to 350° F. Heat 1 teaspoon olive oil in a medium skillet and sauté onions 3 to 5 minutes until tender.
3. Rub an ovenproof casserole with olive oil and add half the onions. Arrange half the tomato slices over onions. Sprinkle with pepper.
4. In a large bowl, combine the eggplant, pepper, beans, and carrots. Add half the eggplant mixture to casserole. Add a layer of pork and rice, then the remaining eggplant mixture. Top with the rest of the tomatoes.
5. Pour water and remaining olive oil over casserole. Cover and bake for 1 hour and 45 minutes or until meat and rice are tender.

Pork Stew
with
Green Chiles

YIELD
4 servings

PREPARATION TIME
15 to 20 minutes

COOKING TIME
1 hour and 10 minutes

NUTRIENT ANALYSIS
Calories per serving: 459
Protein: 34 gm
Carbohydrates: 11 gm
Dietary fiber: 1.5 gm
Cholesterol: 106 mg
Total fat: 31 gm (282 cal)
Sat fat: 7.9 gm (71.7 cal)
Poly fat: 3.4 gm (30 cal)
Mono fat: 17.7 gm (160 cal)

This recipe calls for mild green chiles, which are abundant in the American West and Southwest in the summer and fall. These bright green chile verde range in length from 4 to 8 inches. They are available canned, either whole or diced. While both whole and diced chiles are roasted and peeled, the diced chiles still contain seeds and are hotter. Before canning, the whole chiles are usually slit and are rinsed to remove the seeds.

Serve the stew as a main dish with warm tortillas or as a topping for roast meats or poultry in the Southwestern tradition.

¼ cup extra-virgin flavorful olive oil
1 pound lean pork loin, cut into ¾-inch cubes
3 cloves garlic (or 2 shallots or 2 scallions), minced
*14 fresh or canned whole green chiles, cut into 1-inch
    lengths (if using fresh, parch and peel before cutting)*
1 cup chopped onion
2 cups chopped canned tomatoes with liquid
¼ teaspoon dried oregano leaves
¼ teaspoon ground cumin
⅛ teaspoon ground coriander
1½ cups of water

1. Heat olive oil in large, heavy soup pot. Add pork and sauté over medium-high heat for about 10 minutes until browned.
2. Add garlic, chiles, onion, tomatoes, oregano, cumin, coriander, and water.
3. Stir, cover, and cook over medium heat for 1 hour until meat is tender.

Sautéed
Veal
Strips

YIELD
4 servings

PREPARATION TIME
10 minutes

COOKING TIME
6 minutes

NUTRIENT ANALYSIS
Calories per serving: 372
Protein: 30 gm
Carbohydrates: 2 gm
Dietary fiber: 0.2 gm
Cholesterol: 116 mg
Total fat: 25.5 gm (230 cal)
Sat fat: 7.2 gm (65 cal)
Poly fat: 1.6 gm (15 cal)
Mono fat: 15 gm (137 cal)

Cut veal cutlets into thin, delicate strips before sautéeing with bay leaves, olive oil, and then fresh lemon juice. Serve with Garden Vegetable Stir-Fry (p. 164) and steamed rice sautéed with Basic Pesto (p. 264).

3 bay leaves
¼ cup extra-virgin flavorful olive oil
1 pound veal cutlets, cut into strips ½-inch wide and 3 inches long
Juice of 1 lemon
¼ teaspoon black pepper
3 tablespoons chopped fresh parsley

1. Sauté bay leaves in oil for 1 minute. Add veal strips and cook over high heat for 3 minutes, turning several times.
2. Add lemon juice, pepper, and parsley. Toss with veal and cook for 3 to 5 minutes more.
3. Remove bay leaves and serve at once.

Basil-Tarragon Veal Chops

Marinate these veal chops for 24 hours before cooking them with herbs. Serve with Simple Vegetable Medley (p. 161).

5 tablespoons extra-virgin flavorful olive oil
½ teaspoon black pepper
1 tablespoon red wine vinegar
1 clove garlic (or 1 shallot or 2 scallions), crushed
1 tablespoon chopped fresh parsley
2 tablespoons minced scallions
4 lean loin veal chops, trimmed of fat (1½ pounds before trimming and including bone)
½ teaspoon dried basil leaves
½ teaspoon dried tarragon leaves

1. Combine 2 tablespoons olive oil, ¼ teaspoon pepper, vinegar, garlic, parsley, and scallions in a medium glass bowl.
2. Add chops, coating well with marinade. Cover bowl and refrigerate for 24 hours. Turn chops several times.
3. Remove from refrigerator and allow to return to room temperature. Preheat oven to 325° F.
4. Brown chops in remaining oil in a large skillet.
5. Place each chop on a 12-inch square of aluminum foil. Sprinkle top of each chop with half of the basil and tarragon. Turn chops over, sprinkle second side with remaining basil and tarragon. Sprinkle with remaining pepper.
6. Seal foil packages and bake for 30 minutes until tender.

YIELD
4 servings

PREPARATION TIME
10 minutes + 24 hours marinating time

COOKING TIME
35 minutes

NUTRIENT ANALYSIS
Calories per serving: 398
Protein: 31 gm
Carbohydrates: 0.7 gm
Dietary fiber: 0.1 gm
Cholesterol: 116.1 mg
Total fat: 29 gm (260 cal)
Sat fat: 7.7 gm (70 cal)
Poly fat: 1.9 gm (18 cal)
Mono fat: 17.7 gm (160 cal)

Veal Stew Milano

....

YIELD
8 servings

PREPARATION TIME
30 minutes

COOKING TIME
1 hour and 40 minutes

This colorful veal stew can be made a day in advance and reheated in a 350° F. oven for 30 minutes. It can also be frozen for several months. Serve with no-egg noodles and a mixed green salad with Honey-Dijon Vinaigrette (p. 240).

2 cloves garlic (or 1 shallot or 2 scallions), minced
2 stalks celery, finely chopped
1 large carrot, scraped and finely chopped
1 leek, cleaned and finely chopped
1 large onion, finely chopped
½ cup extra-virgin flavorful olive oil
1 28-ounce can of Italian plum tomatoes, drained and juice reserved
1 teaspoon dried basil leaves
¼ teaspoon dried thyme leaves
¼ teaspoon black pepper
¾ cup unbleached all-purpose flour
2 pounds lean boneless veal leg or shoulder, cut into 1-inch cubes
1 cup dry white wine
1¼ cups low-salt chicken broth
¼ cup minced fresh parsley
1 tablespoon grated lemon peel
1 tablespoon grated orange peel

1. In a large skillet, sauté garlic, celery, carrot, leek, and onion in ¼ cup olive oil for 10 minutes. Add tomatoes and half the reserved juice, the basil, and thyme. Cook over medium-high heat until the liquid is absorbed and sauce thickens. Transfer stew to large stovetop casserole or heavy bottomed pot.

2. Put pepper and flour into paper bag, add veal cubes, and shake until well coated. Heat remaining olive oil in skillet and brown veal; do not crowd pieces. Place browned veal on top of vegetables in casserole.

3. Add wine to pan drippings in skillet. Cook over high heat, and scrape up any browned bits from bottom. When wine is reduced by half, stir in broth and simmer for 3 minutes.

4. Pour mixture over vegetables and veal in casserole and cook on top of stove over low heat for 1 hour or until veal is tender.

5. Sprinkle parsley and lemon and orange peel over stew immediately before serving.

NUTRIENT ANALYSIS
Calories per serving: 475
Protein: 35 gm
Carbohydrates: 18 gm
Dietary fiber: 1.9 gm
Cholesterol: 116 mg
Total fat: 26 gm (236 cal)
Sat fat: 7.4 gm (67 cal)
Poly fat: 1.8 gm (17 cal)
Mono fat: 15.4 gm (139 cal)

Veal Parmigiana

YIELD
6 servings

PREPARATION TIME
15 minutes + 20 minutes chilling time

COOKING TIME
1 hour

NUTRIENT ANALYSIS
Calories per serving: 508
Protein: 35 gm
Carbohydrates: 18 gm
Dietary fiber: 1.3 gm
Cholesterol: 96 mg
Total fat: 33 gm (296 cal)
Sat fat: 10 gm (92 cal)
Poly fat: 2.2 gm (20 cal)
Mono fat: 19 gm (171 cal)

Coat veal cutlets with crumbs and chill before sautéeing in olive oil and baking with tomato-onion sauce and cheese. Serve with linguine tossed with oregano and steamed zucchini.

¼ teaspoon black pepper
2 cloves garlic (or 1 shallot or 2 scallions), minced
1½ teaspoons dried oregano leaves
½ teaspoon wine vinegar
½ cup extra-virgin flavorful olive oil
1 pound veal cutlets, cut in 6 pieces
4 egg whites, beaten
¾ cup bread crumbs (or oat bran)
1 medium onion, sliced
1 28-ounce can whole tomatoes, drained and chopped
¼ cup sliced part-skim mozzarella (2 ounces)
½ cup grated Parmesan cheese

1. In a medium glass baking dish, combine pepper, garlic, 1 teaspoon oregano, vinegar, and 1 teaspoon of the oil. Coat cutlets with mixture.

2. Dip cutlets in beaten egg whites in a small bowl. Dip in bread crumbs in a second small bowl, and chill for 20 minutes.

3. Heat remaining oil in a large skillet and sauté cutlets on both sides over moderate heat for 10 minutes until lightly browned. Place cutlets in glass baking dish.

4. Sauté onions over low heat for 10 minutes in the frying pan with oil left in pan. Add ½ teaspoon oregano and tomatoes and stir.

5. Pour tomato-onion sauce over cutlets. Top with mozzarella slices and grated Parmesan. Bake at 350° F. for 30 minutes.

VEGETABLES

ROASTED BROCCOLI AND CAULIFLOWER
BAKED VEGETABLE CASSEROLE
CARROTS IN WINE SAUCE
SAUTÉED POTATOES WITH RED PEPPER OIL
SIMPLE VEGETABLE MEDLEY
RATATOUILLE
GARDEN VEGETABLE STIR-FRY
ZUCCHINI FRITTERS
GREEN BEAN STEW
ARTICHOKES IN MUSTARD SAUCE
TOMATO DOLMA
SAUTÉED SPINACH
MEXICAN CAULIFLOWER
POTATO PANCAKES
PUFFED FRENCH "FRIED" POTATOES
LEGAL MUSHROOM OMELETTE

Roasted Broccoli and Cauliflower

YIELD
4 servings

PREPARATION TIME
10 minutes

COOKING TIME
15 minutes

Roasting broccoli and cauliflower at a high temperature makes their skin crispy and gives them a smoky flavor. You can also roast green beans, peppers, leeks, scallions, and onions. Roasted vegetables can be served at room temperature in salads sprinkled with vinaigrette dressing and sesame seeds or served warm, seasoned with pepper.

3 cups broccoli florets
2 cups cauliflower florets
¼ cup extra-virgin flavorful olive oil

1. Preheat oven to 425° F.
2. Toss vegetables and olive oil in a large bowl to completely coat them with oil and seal in their moisture.
3. Roast florets in a single layer on a baking pan for 15 minutes. Turn the vegetables once during cooking.
4. Serve at once as a side dish or let cool to room temperature for salad.

NUTRIENT ANALYSIS
Calories per serving: 166
Protein: 4.5 gm
Carbohydrates: 9 gm
Dietary fiber: 6.1 gm
Cholesterol: 0 mg
Total fat: 13.9 gm (125 cal)
Sat fat: 2 gm (18 cal)
Poly fat: 1.3 gm (12 cal)
Mono fat: 10 gm (90 cal)

Baked Vegetable Casserole

....

YIELD
4 servings

PREPARATION TIME
20 minutes

COOKING TIME
55 minutes

NUTRIENT ANALYSIS
Calories per serving: 409
Protein: 8.3 gm
Carbohydrates: 35.3 gm
Dietary fiber: 6.6 gm
Cholesterol: 0.4 mg
Total fat: 28 gm (252 cal)
Sat fat: 4 gm (36 cal)
Poly fat: 2.6 gm (23.4 cal)
Mono fat: 20 gm (180 cal)

Bake cauliflower, asparagus, artichokes, green beans, and mushrooms in a rich, flavorful olive oil sauce. Serve with Baked Fish Steaks (p. 114).

½ cup extra-virgin flavorful olive oil
1 9-ounce package frozen artichoke hearts, thawed
1 cup cauliflower florets
2 medium potatoes, peeled and thinly sliced
2 medium carrots, peeled and thinly sliced
8 fresh asparagus spears, cut into 1-inch pieces
½ cup cut green beans, in 1-inch pieces
½ cup sliced fresh mushrooms
½ cup chopped onions
1 clove garlic, minced
2 tablespoons unbleached all-purpose flour
1½ cups low-salt chicken broth
¼ teaspoon black pepper

1. Heat ¼ cup olive oil over moderate heat in a skillet. Sauté artichokes and cauliflower for 5 minutes, stirring with a wide, slotted spatula. Remove from pan to a large heatproof casserole.
2. Add potatoes and carrots to skillet and sauté for 5 minutes. Add to casserole.
3. Preheat oven to 400° F.
4. Add asparagus, beans, and mushrooms to the casserole and toss lightly to mix.
5. Pour remaining olive oil in the skillet, heat, and sauté onions and garlic for 5 minutes. Stir in flour and mix well. Add chicken broth and pepper. Stir until mixture thickens, about 5 minutes, scraping up any pieces from the bottom of the pan. Pour sauce over vegetables.

6. Cover casserole and bake for 40 minutes until vegetables are done.

Carrots in Wine Sauce

Carrots, an often taken-for-granted ingredient, move center stage when simmered in a wine sauce. Serve with Garlic Chicken (p. 96).

1½ pounds carrots, peeled and thinly sliced
¼ cup extra-virgin flavorful olive oil
1 medium onion, thinly sliced
2 tablespoons unbleached all-purpose flour
¾ cup dry white wine
¼ cup water
1 tablespoon minced fresh parsley

1. Steam carrots 6 to 7 minutes in a vegetable steamer or cook, covered, in microwave with a little water until crisp-tender.
2. In a large skillet, sauté onion in olive oil over medium heat 5 minutes or until softened. Stir in flour and gradually add wine and water.
3. When sauce is smooth, add carrots and parsley. Cover loosely and simmer for 15 minutes or until carrots are done.

YIELD
4 servings

PREPARATION TIME
15 minutes

COOKING TIME
30 minutes

NUTRIENT ANALYSIS
Calories per serving: 251
Protein: 2.5 gm
Carbohydrates: 22.5 gm
Dietary fiber: 5.4 gm
Cholesterol: 0 mg
Total fat: 14 gm (126 cal)
Sat fat: 2 gm (18 cal)
Poly fat: 1.3 gm (12 cal)
Mono fat: 9.7 gm (87 cal)

Sautéed Potatoes with Red Pepper Oil

YIELD
4 servings

PREPARATION TIME
10 minutes

COOKING TIME
30 minutes

NUTRIENT ANALYSIS
Calories per serving: 312
Protein: 3.2 gm
Carbohydrates: 35.6 gm
Dietary fiber: 2.3 gm
Cholesterol: 0 mg
Total fat: 18 gm (165 cal)
Sat fat: 2.6 gm (23 cal)
Poly fat: 1.6 gm (14 cal)
Mono fat: 13 gm (119 cal)

In this colorful dish, round red potatoes are seasoned with hot and sweet red peppers. Serve with Broiled Fish Steaks (p. 114) and green beans tossed in Basic Pesto (p. 264).

1½ pounds small red potatoes, scrubbed
1 clove garlic, chopped
⅓ cup extra-virgin flavorful olive oil
½ teaspoon crushed dried red peppers
1 medium red bell pepper, seeded and thinly sliced
1 tablespoon chopped scallion

1. In a medium saucepan, cover potatoes with water, bring to a boil, and cook for 20 minutes or until tender. Cool slightly and cut into quarters.
2. Sauté garlic in olive oil over medium heat in a large skillet for 2 minutes. Add dried red peppers and red bell pepper slices. Sauté 3 to 5 minutes until bell pepper is tender.
3. Add potatoes to skillet and stir gently to heat and to coat completely with oil.
4. Serve sprinkled with scallions.

Simple Vegetable Medley

Steam a variety of fresh vegetables and toss with a vinaigrette sauce. Serve with Chicken Pronto (p. 94).

1½ cups broccoli florets
1½ cups cauliflower florets
¾ cup cut green beans, in 1-inch pieces
2 medium carrots, peeled and thinly sliced
1 medium red bell pepper, seeded and cut into 1-inch julienne strips
½ cup sliced fresh mushrooms
½ cup olive oil
2 tablespoons red wine vinegar
¼ cup chopped scallions
¼ teaspoon dried thyme leaves

1. Steam broccoli, cauliflower, beans, and carrots in a vegetable steamer about 5 to 10 minutes, or cook covered in microwave with a little water until crisp-tender. Transfer to large serving bowl.
2. Add red pepper and mushrooms to bowl and toss to mix.
3. In a small bowl, combine oil, vinegar, scallions, and thyme with a wire whisk. Drizzle over vegetables and serve.

YIELD
4 servings

PREPARATION TIME
15 minutes

COOKING TIME
5 to 10 minutes

NUTRIENT ANALYSIS
Calories per serving: 296 mg
Protein: 3.7 gm
Carbohydrates: 12.4 gm
Dietary fiber: 5.2 gm
Cholesterol: 0 mg
Total fat: 27.5 gm (247 cal)
Sat fat: 3.9 gm (35 cal)
Poly fat: 2.5 gm (22.5 cal)
Mono fat: 20 gm (180 cal)

Ratatouille

YIELD
6 servings

PREPARATION TIME
20 minutes

COOKING TIME
Approximately 1 hour

There are numerous approaches to making this classic dish, which originated in the south of France. The word ratatouille means poor man's stew. Make Ratatouille a day ahead to allow flavors to blend, and serve it either hot, at room temperature, or cold. This simple version will keep in your refrigerator for five days.

½ cup extra-virgin flavorful olive oil
1 medium onion, finely chopped
1 clove garlic, minced
½ teaspoon dried basil leaves
½ teaspoon dried oregano leaves
½ teaspoon dried thyme leaves
½ teaspoon dried rosemary leaves
1 pound ripe tomatoes or 1 20-ounce can tomatoes,
*   chopped and with juice*
¼ teaspoon black pepper
¼ teaspoon cayenne pepper
2 medium zucchini, sliced ¼-inch thick
1 green bell pepper, seeded and thinly sliced
1 red bell pepper, seeded and thinly sliced
1 medium eggplant, approximately 1 pound, peeled and
*   diced*
2 tablespoons minced fresh parsley

1. Heat olive oil in a large, heavy pot. Sauté onion for 3 to 5 minutes until softened. Add garlic, basil, oregano, thyme, and rosemary and sauté briefly.
2. Stir in tomatoes and simmer over low heat, uncovered, for 15 minutes. Add black pepper and cayenne.
3. Add zucchini, green and red peppers, eggplant, and parsley to the sauce. Cover and simmer for 30 minutes.

Stir once, and simmer another 10 minutes if necessary until vegetables are tender. Avoid extra stirring, if possible, to retain shape of vegetables.

4. Cool and refrigerate in a glass or ceramic container overnight. Serve cold or at room temperature, garnished with lemon wedges; or reheat over low flame in a covered saucepan, stirring frequently.

VARIATIONS

- Serve garnished with chopped scallions, Parmesan cheese, olives, or lemon wedges.
- Omit eggplant. Use three zucchini instead of two.

NUTRIENT ANALYSIS

Calories per serving: 220
Protein: 2.3 gm
Carbohydrates: 13.7 gm
Dietary fiber: 5 gm
Cholesterol: 0 mg
Total fat: 19 gm (168 cal)
Sat fat: 2.7 gm (24 cal)
Poly fat: 1.8 gm (16 cal)
Mono fat: 13 gm (120 cal)

Garden Vegetable Stir-Fry

....

YIELD
4 servings

PREPARATION TIME
20 minutes

COOKING TIME
18 minutes

Combine broccoli, string beans, cabbage, mushrooms, and onions for this classic Oriental dish, which breaks with tradition by using olive oil. Serve over steamed rice or lo mein noodles.

¾ cup broccoli florets
¾ cup cut green beans in 1-inch pieces, ends trimmed
¼ cup mild, light flavored olive oil
1 clove garlic, minced
¾ cup cabbage, diced
1 medium onion, diced
¾ cup sliced fresh mushrooms
½ cup low-salt chicken broth
1 tablespoon light soy sauce

1. Steam broccoli florets and string beans in a vegetable steamer or cook, covered, in microwave with a little water 5 to 10 minutes until crisp-tender.
2. Heat oil in a skillet or wok over medium heat. Add garlic and cook 1 minute while stirring. Add string beans, cabbage, and onions. Stir-fry over medium-high heat for 2 minutes.
3. Add broccoli and mushrooms. Stir-fry for 2 minutes more.
4. Add broth and soy sauce and stir until heated.
5. Reduce heat to medium, cover, and cook 2 to 3 minutes. Serve at once.

VARIATIONS

The following combinations can also be used for basic stir-fried vegetables. Always add toughest vegetables first, such as carrots, and more tender ones last.

- Use 1 cup fresh mushrooms, sliced; ½ cup bamboo shoots or water chestnuts, sliced; and 1 pound spinach leaves.
- Use ½ pound bean sprouts, blanched; ½ pound asparagus, cut into 1-inch sections; and 1 celery stalk, chopped.
- Use 2 green peppers, seeded and cut in strips; 2 tomatoes, peeled and cubed; and ½ pound bean sprouts.
- Use 2 carrots, cut in thin diagonal slices; 2 stalks celery, cut in thin diagonal slices; and ¼ pound leeks, thinly sliced.

NUTRIENT ANALYSIS
Calories per serving: 155
Protein: 2.7 gm
Carbohydrates: 6.4 gm
Dietary fiber: 1.9 gm
Cholesterol: 0.125 mg
Total fat: 13.9 gm (125 cal)
Sat fat: 2 gm (19 cal)
Poly fat: 1.3 gm (12 cal)
Mono fat: 10 gm (90 cal)

Zucchini Fritters

YIELD
4 servings

PREPARATION TIME
20 minutes

COOKING TIME
10 minutes

NUTRIENT ANALYSIS
Calories per serving: 138
Protein: 3.9 gm
Carbohydrates: 2.6 gm
Dietary fiber: 2.4 gm
Cholesterol: 6.6 mg
Total fat: 12.8 gm (115 cal)
Sat fat: 3 gm (28 cal)
Poly fat: 1 gm (9 cal)
Mono fat: 8.2 gm (74 cal)

Zucchini dishes are a great favorite throughout the Mediterranean region. Rich in vitamin A, these fritters from Provence are accented with Parmesan cheese and basil. Serve with broiled chicken or lamb chops.

2 medium-sized zucchini
3 tablespoons mild, light flavored olive oil
1 clove garlic, minced
1/3 cup grated Parmesan cheese
1/4 teaspoon dried basil leaves

1. Coarsely grate zucchini and press in a strainer to remove excess liquid.
2. Combine zucchini, 2 tablespoons olive oil, garlic, cheese, and basil in a bowl.
3. Shape into 3-inch fritters or patties and brown on both sides in remaining olive oil in a skillet or griddle. Serve hot.

Green Bean Stew

In this colorful dish, fresh green beans are simmered in a tomato sauce. Serve with Scallops in Garlic Sauce (p. 127).

¼ cup extra-virgin flavorful olive oil
½ cup chopped onion
1 clove garlic, minced
3 cups fresh cut green beans, in 1-inch pieces
3 medium tomatoes, chopped
2 tablespoons minced fresh parsley

1. Steam green beans 7 to 10 minutes in a vegetable steamer or cook, covered, in microwave with a little water until crisp-tender.
2. Sauté onion and garlic in olive oil in a large skillet 5 minutes or until tender. Stir in green beans, tomatoes, and parsley. Bring to a boil, reduce heat, and simmer for 15 minutes.

VARIATION
Substitute lima beans for all or part of the green beans.

YIELD
4 servings

PREPARATION TIME
15 minutes

COOKING TIME
30 minutes

NUTRIENT ANALYSIS
Calories per serving: 179
Protein: 2.9 gm
Carbohydrates: 13 gm
Dietary fiber: 3.7 gm
Cholesterol: 0 mg
Total fat: 14 gm (126 cal)
Sat fat: 2 gm (18 cal)
Poly fat: 1.4 gm (13 cal)
Mono fat: 10 gm (90 cal)

Artichokes in Mustard Sauce

.... ⊙ ....

YIELD
4 servings

PREPARATION TIME
10 minutes

COOKING TIME
20 minutes

NUTRIENT ANALYSIS
Calories per serving: 200
Protein: 4 gm
Carbohydrates: 20 gm
Dietary fiber: 5.7 gm
Cholesterol: 0 mg
Total fat: 14 gm (124 cal)
Sat fat: 2 gm (18 cal)
Poly fat: 1.3 gm (12 cal)
Mono fat: 10 gm (90 cal)

Serve frozen artichokes in a tangy mustard sauce. Serve with Linguine with Oil and Garlic (p. 188).

2 9-ounce packages frozen artichokes
¼ cup extra-virgin flavorful olive oil
1½ teaspoon dry mustard
¼ teaspoon black pepper
½ teaspoon paprika
⅛ teaspoon dried oregano leaves
¼ cup vinegar
Juice of 1 lemon

1. Follow package cooking directions on frozen artichokes, reducing water by half and adding oil to the artichokes and cooking water.
2. Combine mustard, pepper, paprika, oregano, vinegar, and lemon juice in a small saucepan. Drain the cooking liquid from the artichokes into the mustard sauce and bring to a boil.
3. Spoon sauce over artichokes just before serving or serve separately in a small pitcher.

Tomato Dolma

Rice, pine nuts, dill, and mint are combined in this vegetarian version of stuffed vegetables, a Turkish favorite. Served lukewarm or cold, with Greek Lentil Soup (p. 56) and Syrian flat bread.

6 large ripe tomatoes
½ cup extra-virgin flavorful olive oil
1 medium onion, peeled and grated
½ cup raw long-grain rice
3 tablespoons pine nuts
¼ teaspoon black pepper
1 cup water
1 teaspoon dried dill leaves
1 teaspoon dried mint leaves
2 tablespoons minced fresh parsley

1. Cut off tops of tomatoes and set aside. Carefully scoop out pulp, and turn tomatoes upside down to drain. Chop pulp from 5 tomatoes (save the rest for another recipe or discard).
2. Heat ¼ cup olive oil in a large skillet and sauté onions 5 minutes until tender. Add rice and stir. Add pine nuts, pepper, tomato pulp, and ¼ cup water. Simmer 5 minutes.
3. Stir in dill, mint, and parsley. Preheat oven to 375° F.
4. Fill tomatoes halfway and cover with reserved tops. Arrange in a large ovenproof casserole. Add ¾ cup boiling water and ¼ cup olive oil. Cover and bake for 40 minutes or until stuffing is cooked.

YIELD
6 servings

PREPARATION TIME
20 minutes

COOKING TIME
55 minutes

NUTRIENT ANALYSIS
Calories per serving: 248
Protein: 2.4 gm
Carbohydrates: 19.5 gm
Dietary fiber: 2.7 gm
Cholesterol: 0 mg
Total fat: 18.5 gm (167 cal)
Sat fat: 2.6 gm (23 cal)
Poly fat: 1.8 gm (15 cal)
Mono fat: 13 gm (120 cal)

Sautéed
Spinach

YIELD
4 servings

PREPARATION TIME
15 minutes

COOKING TIME
15 minutes

NUTRIENT ANALYSIS
Calories per serving: 230
Protein: 9.2 gm
Carbohydrates: 9 gm
Dietary fiber: 7.1 gm
Cholesterol: 5 mg
Total fat: 19.6 gm (177 cal)
Sat fat: 3.8 gm (39 cal)
Poly fat: 1.8 gm (16 cal)
Mono fat: 13 gm (117 cal)

Steam and sauté fresh spinach in garlic-flavored oil, then season with nutmeg and Parmesan cheese. Serve with Sirloin Steak with Onion-Mustard Sauce (p. 135).

2 pounds fresh spinach, well washed and trimmed
5 tablespoons extra-virgin flavorful olive oil
3 cloves garlic, whole
¼ teaspoon ground nutmeg
¼ teaspoon black pepper
¼ cup grated Parmesan cheese

1. Place spinach in heavy saucepan without water and cook, tightly covered, over low heat for 5 minutes or until wilted. Drain and press to remove excess liquid.
2. Heat oil in large skillet and add garlic. Sauté until lightly browned. Remove garlic and discard.
3. Add spinach, nutmeg, and pepper to skillet and toss in oil over medium heat for 3 to 5 minutes until well coated.
4. Transfer to serving dish and sprinkle with cheese immediately before serving.

Mexican Cauliflower

B̲ake steamed cauliflower in a tomato sauce with spices and top with bread crumbs and cheese. Serve with sautéed turkey cutlets.

1 medium cauliflower, washed and separated into florets
¼ cup extra-virgin flavorful olive oil
1 small onion, finely chopped
¼ cup chopped green bell pepper
1 8-ounce can tomatoes, chopped
1 tablespoon chili powder
⅛ teaspoon ground cloves
1 tablespoon ground cinnamon
¼ teaspoon black pepper
8 pitted black olives, rinsed
¼ cup bread crumbs
2 tablespoons grated reduced-fat Cheddar cheese

1. Steam cauliflower for 5 minutes in a vegetable steamer or cook, covered, in microwave with a little water until crisp-tender.
2. Heat olive oil over medium heat in a large skillet. Sauté onion and green pepper for 5 minutes until tender.
3. Stir in tomatoes and cook for 3 minutes. Add chili powder, cloves, cinnamon, black pepper, and olives. Cook for 2 minutes.
4. Preheat oven to 375° F.
5. Lightly oil a medium baking dish and place cauliflower in it. Pour tomato sauce over cauliflower.
6. Combine bread crumbs and cheese and sprinkle over sauce. Bake for about 10 minutes until crumbs and cheese have browned.

YIELD
4 servings

PREPARATION TIME
10 minutes

COOKING TIME
25 minutes

NUTRIENT ANALYSIS
Calories per serving: 200
Protein: 4.2 gm
Carbohydrates: 14.0 gm
Dietary fiber: 3.3 gm
Cholesterol: 1.1 mg
Total fat: 16 gm (143 cal)
Sat fat: 2.4 gm (22 cal)
Poly fat: 1.3 gm (12 cal)
Mono fat: 11 gm (98 cal)

Potato Pancakes

YIELD

4 servings (2 cakes each)

PREPARATION TIME

20 minutes

COOKING TIME

15 minutes

NUTRIENT ANALYSIS

Calories per serving: 360
Protein: 11.6 gm
Carbohydrates: 23 gm
Dietary fiber: 1.5 gm
Cholesterol: 18 mg
Total fat: 25 gm (228 cal)
Sat fat: 6.4 gm (58 cal)
Poly fat: 2 gm (18 cal)
Mono fat: 16.3 gm (147 cal)

These wonderful little pancakes are a combination of potatoes, cheese, and onions. Serve with Split Pea Soup (p. 51).

2 cups peeled grated raw potatoes
½ cup minced onion
6 tablespoons extra-virgin flavorful olive oil
¼ cup grated reduced-fat Cheddar cheese (or other grated cheese)
2 egg whites, lightly beaten
¼ teaspoon black pepper

1. Soak grated potatoes in cold water for 5 minutes. Drain and dry on paper towels.
2. Sauté onion in 2 tablespoons olive oil in a large skillet 3 to 5 minutes until tender.
3. Combine the sautéed onion with the potatoes, cheese, egg whites, and pepper in a large bowl.
4. Heat the remaining 4 tablespoons olive oil in skillet. Place ¼ cup of the potato mixture at a time in skillet and use a wide slotted spatula to flatten into a small cake. Sauté until brown, turn, and then sauté on the other side. Serve hot plain, with tomato ketchup or with unsweetened applesauce.

Puffed French "Fried" Potatoes

....

These potatoes are a crispy, lower calorie alternative to deep fried French fries. Serve with Sautéed Softshell Crabs (p. 129).

2 pounds potatoes
¼ cup extra-virgin flavorful olive oil
¼ teaspoon fresh ground pepper

1. Preheat oven to 400° F.
2. Peel and wash potatoes. Cut potatoes lengthwise in ½-inch slices. Cut again into strips.
3. Divide potatoes between two baking sheets, drizzle with olive oil, and toss to coat well. Spread out potatoes on baking sheet and sprinkle with pepper.
4. Bake for 20 minutes. Remove pans from oven and let cool for 5 minutes.
5. Return pans to oven for 10 minutes more until lightly browned and puffed. Serve hot.

YIELD
4 servings

PREPARATION TIME
15 minutes

COOKING TIME
30 minutes

NUTRIENT ANALYSIS
Calories per serving: 315
Protein: 3.9 gm
Carbohydrates: 45.4 gm
Dietary fiber: 2.5 gm
Cholesterol: 0 mg
Total fat: 14 gm (123 cal)
Sat fat: 2 gm (18 cal)
Poly fat: 1.2 gm (11 cal)
Mono fat: 9.9 gm (90 cal)

Legal Mushroom Omelette

YIELD
1 serving

PREPARATION TIME
5 minutes

COOKING TIME
1 minute

Light, fluffy omelettes are one of the quickest and most impressive dishes you can make, and they are healthful if made with less yolk and more whites. It is worth getting an egg separator for this and other recipes.

1 tablespoon chopped mushrooms
2 teaspoons mild, light flavored olive oil
2 egg whites
⅓ egg yolk (cut yolk with a sharp knife and discard extra)
Dash of pepper, dried basil leaves, and dried marjoram leaves (or use fresh herbs, if available)
½ small clove garlic (or ½ shallot or 1 scallion), minced
Dash of salt (optional)
1 teaspoon grated Parmesan cheese

1. In a small skillet, sauté mushrooms for 2 to 3 minutes in 1 teaspoon olive oil until tender. Set aside.
2. Beat egg whites, yolk, pepper, basil, marjoram, and garlic well in a small bowl with a fork or a wire whisk.
3. Heat 1 teaspoon olive oil in a 7-inch nonstick skillet over medium-high heat. Sprinkle a dash of salt in the pan, if desired. When hot, add the egg all at once.
4. Immediately tip the pan so uncooked egg runs to the edges of the pan. Use a wooden spatula to quickly lift the edges of the omelette and let the egg run under. The egg will cook and puff up in about 30 seconds.
5. Sprinkle the mushrooms and Parmesan cheese in a row in the center of the omelette.
6. Fold one third of the omelette over, tip pan in same direction, and fold omelette over on itself once again (use spatula to help with last fold).

7. Let omelette sit in pan for a minute to heat filling before turning out. Slide onto a warmed plate and serve hot.

NOTE
To make two omelettes, beat 4 egg whites and ⅔ yolk in a small bowl. Pour out half of the mixture into skillet, and make first omelette. Then reheat pan and make second one, using another teaspoon of olive oil.

VARIATIONS
Instead of mushrooms, basil, marjoram, garlic, and Parmesan cheese, try the following fillings:

- 1 tablespoon chopped, cooked spinach; 1 teaspoon minced fresh parsley; and ½ small garlic clove, minced.
- 1 tablespoon chopped, cooked asparagus and ¼ teaspoon cayenne pepper.
- 1 tablespoon chopped, sautéed green bell pepper; 1 teaspoon tomato sauce; and ¼ teaspoon chili powder.
- 1 tablespoon chopped, sautéed zucchini; ¼ teaspoon dried basil; and 1 tablespoon part-skim grated mozzarella cheese.

NUTRIENT ANALYSIS
Calories per serving: 164
Protein: 10.4 gm
Carbohydrates: 1.76 gm
Dietary fiber: 0.7 gm
Cholesterol: 95.5 mg
Total fat: 12.77 gm (110 cal)
Sat fat: 3.3 gm (27 cal)
Poly fat: 1.05 gm (9 cal)
Mono fat: 7.9 gm (71 cal)

GRAINS,
BEANS, AND
PASTA

TABBOULEH
RISOTTO
SPANISH RICE
SPINACH AND RICE
LEMON-DILL RICE
BLACK BEANS
STEWED NAVY BEANS
NEW YEAR'S DAY BLACK-EYED PEAS
LINGUINE WITH OIL AND GARLIC
SHELL PASTA WITH FISH FILLETS AND ZUCCHINI
PASTA WITH SHRIMP
LINGUINE WITH CLAM SAUCE
TUNA LINGUINE
PASTA WITH CHICKEN AND PEPPERS
PASTA WITH SPINACH-CHEESE SAUCE

Tabbouleh

This Near Eastern standard is a "wheat salad," which is made from cracked bulgur wheat. Tabbouleh is a very nutritious food that tastes best when made with fresh tomatoes, parsley, and mint. Syrians and Lebanese scoop up Tabbouleh with grape, lettuce, or cabbage leaves for a healthful dip. Serve with grilled chicken cutlets (p. 220).

1 cup medium-fine bulgur (a precooked cracked wheat)
1½ cups cold water
½ cup extra-virgin flavorful olive oil
1 small onion, finely chopped
3 scallions, finely chopped
2 large ripe tomatoes, chopped
8 fresh mint leaves, chopped
1 cup fresh parsley, chopped
¼ teaspoon black pepper
⅓ cup fresh lemon juice

1. Put bulgur wheat in a large bowl. Add water and olive oil and stir. Soak for 30 minutes.
2. Add remaining ingredients and toss to combine well. Serve at room temperature.

VARIATION
Tabbouleh can be made ahead of time, chilled, and served when ready. Refrigerate for 2 hours or more before serving.

YIELD
6 servings

PREPARATION TIME
15 minutes + 30 minutes marinating time

NUTRIENT ANALYSIS
Calories per serving: 219.6
Protein: 2.2 gm
Carbohydrates: 12.1 gm
Dietary fiber: 1.4 gm
Cholesterol: 0 mg
Total fat: 18.8 gm (169 cal)
Sat fat: 2.6 gm (23.4 cal)
Poly fat: 1.5 gm (14.4 cal)
Mono fat: 13.2 gm (118.8 cal)

Risotto

YIELD
5 servings

PREPARATION TIME
10 minutes

COOKING TIME
Approximately 25 minutes

NUTRIENT ANALYSIS
Calories per serving: 383
Protein: 9.2 gm
Carbohydrates: 42 gm
Dietary fiber: 0.9 gm
Cholesterol: 5.8 mg
Total fat: 19 gm (171 cal)
Sat fat: 3.8 gm (34 cal)
Poly fat: 1.6 (14 cal)
Mono fat: 13 gm (117 cal)

Risotto is a special Italian rice dish with a fine, rich flavor. To make it authentic, find Italian Arborio rice in the gourmet section of your supermarket or specialty grocery. Risotto requires constant stirring, so save this recipe for a day when you're feeling patient. Present it with a cruet of olive oil. Serve with Citrus-Herb Baked Chicken (p. 100).

3 cups low-salt chicken broth (additional broth may be
    needed)
1 medium onion, chopped
6 tablespoons extra-virgin flavorful olive oil
1⅓ cups raw Italian Arborio rice
⅓ cup grated Parmesan cheese
¼ teaspoon black pepper

1. In a medium saucepan, heat chicken broth to a simmer over medium heat.

2. While broth is heating, sauté onion in olive oil in a large heatproof casserole for 3 to 5 minutes until soft. Add rice and stir to coat with oil.

3. Add ½ cup broth and stir with a wooden spoon until the broth has been absorbed. Continue this pattern with rest of broth, adding it ½ cup at a time and stirring until it is absorbed by the rice. When you have used all the broth, test the rice to see if it is still too chewy. If so, add more hot broth or hot water until it reaches the desired consistency.

4. Remove from heat and stir in cheese and black pepper.

Spanish Rice

Sauté rice, onions, and green pepper in olive oil, then simmer in chicken broth and tomato sauce. Serve with Mexican Baked Fish (p. 116) and steamed green beans.

1 medium onion, finely chopped
½ cup green bell pepper, finely chopped
¼ cup mild, light flavored olive oil
1 cup raw long-grain rice
2 cups low-salt chicken broth
1 cup tomato sauce
½ teaspoon ground cumin
¼ teaspoon black pepper
¼ teaspoon salt (optional)

1. Sauté onion and green pepper in olive oil over medium heat in heavy skillet 5 minutes or until tender.
2. Add rice, stirring until it turns a whitish gold, about 3 to 5 minutes.
3. Add chicken broth, tomato sauce, cumin, black pepper, and salt (if desired). Bring to a boil, reduce heat to low, and simmer, uncovered, for 20 minutes or until rice is done and liquid is absorbed.

YIELD
4 servings

PREPARATION TIME
10 minutes

COOKING TIME
25 minutes

NUTRIENT ANALYSIS
Calories per serving: 345
Protein: 7 gm
Carbohydrates: 45.8 gm
Dietary fiber: 1.3 gm
Cholesterol: 0.5 mg
Total fat: 14.6 gm (132 cal)
Sat fat: 2.2 gm (20 cal)
Poly fat: 1.3 gm (12 cal)
Mono fat: 10.3 gm (92 cal)

Spinach and Rice

....

YIELD
4 servings

PREPARATION TIME
15 minutes

COOKING TIME
35 minutes

NUTRIENT ANALYSIS
Calories per serving: 290
Protein: 4.9 gm
Carbohydrates: 23.4 gm
Dietary fiber: 3.8 gm
Cholesterol: 0 mg
Total fat: 20.8 gm (187 cal)
Sat fat: 3 gm (27 cal)
Poly fat: 1.8 gm (17 cal)
Mono fat: 15 gm (134 cal)

Serve this Greek-inspired dish with Citrus-Marinated Striped Bass (p. 124) and fruit salad.

6 tablespoons extra-virgin flavorful olive oil
1 medium onion, chopped
1 pound fresh spinach, well washed, drained, and
    chopped or 1 10-ounce package of frozen chopped
    spinach, defrosted
½ cup raw long-grain rice
1 tablespoon tomato paste
1½ cups water
¼ teaspoon black pepper
¼ teaspoon dried dill leaves

1. Heat olive oil in a large, heavy saucepan over medium heat and sauté onions for 5 minutes or until lightly browned.

2. Stir in spinach, cover, and simmer for about 5 minutes or until spinach wilts.

3. Add all remaining ingredients and stir well.

4. Cover and reduce heat to low. Simmer for 25 minutes or until rice is tender.

Lemon-Dill Rice

....

This rice has a refreshing lemon-dill flavor. Serve with Sautéed Veal Strips (p. 150) and steamed squash.

¼ cup extra-virgin flavorful olive oil
1 cup chopped onion
1 cup raw long-grain rice
½ cup dry white wine
Grated rind of ½ lemon
1½ cups low-salt chicken broth
½ teaspoon dried dill leaves
¼ teaspoon black pepper
Juice of 1 lemon
2 tablespoons chopped fresh parsley

1. Heat olive oil over medium heat in a large skillet and sauté onion for 5 minutes until tender. And rice and sauté for 2 minutes.
2. Stir in wine, lemon rind, broth, and dill. Cover and reduce heat to low. Simmer for 25 minutes or until rice is tender and liquid is absorbed.
3. Stir in pepper and lemon juice immediately before serving. Garnish with parsley.

YIELD
4 servings

PREPARATION TIME
15 minutes

COOKING TIME
30 minutes

NUTRIENT ANALYSIS
Calories per serving: 342
Protein: 5.4 gm
Carbohydrates: 42 gm
Dietary fiber: 1.3 gm
Cholesterol: 0.4 mg
Total fat: 14.3 gm (129.5 cal)
Sat fat: 2.1 gm (19 cal)
Poly fat: 1.3 gm (11 cal)
Mono fat: 10 gm (92 cal)

Black Beans

YIELD

4 servings

PREPARATION TIME

15 minutes + overnight or 1-hour soaking time

COOKING TIME

1 hour and 50 minutes

NUTRIENT ANALYSIS

Calories per serving: 252
Protein: 5.5 gm
Carbohydrates: 16 gm
Dietary fiber: 2.9 gm
Cholesterol: 0 mg
Total fat: 18 gm (165 cal)
Sat fat: 2.6 gm (24 cal)
Poly fat: 1.7 gm (15 cal)
Mono fat: 13.2 gm (119 cal)

For full-flavored black beans, simmer them in a melange of ingredients including onions, chili peppers, sherry, and oregano. Serve as a side dish with Spicy Mexican Chicken (p. 97).

½ pound dried black beans, sorted and rinsed
⅓ cup extra-virgin flavorful olive oil
3 cloves garlic (or 1 shallot or 3 scallions), chopped
3 green chilies, seeded and chopped
¾ cup chopped red or Bermuda onion
¼ teaspoon black pepper
¼ teaspoon dried oregano leaves
¼ teaspoon ground cumin
½ teaspoon sugar
2 tablespoons dry sherry
1½ tablespoons wine vinegar

1. Soak beans overnight; or cover with 2½ cups cold water, boil for 2 minutes, and let stand for 1 hour. Drain.
2. Put beans and 4 cups of water in a heavy soup pot. Bring to a boil over high heat. Reduce heat, cover, and simmer over moderate heat for 45 minutes.
3. While beans are cooking, heat olive oil in a skillet over medium heat and sauté garlic, chilies, and ½ cup onions for 5 minutes until tender. Remove from heat.
4. Remove 1 cup of cooked black beans from the kettle with a slotted spoon. Add them to skillet and mash with garlic, onions, and chilies. Then pour this mixture back into the pot.
5. Add pepper, oregano, cumin, sugar, sherry, and vinegar. Stir, cover, and cook for 1 hour until beans are soft.
6. Serve sprinkled with remaining ¼ cup chopped onions.

Stewed
Navy
Beans

Prepare navy beans with olive oil, onion, garlic, tomato sauce, carrots, and celery. Serve for supper with grilled low-skim mozzarella cheese sandwiches on Garlic Bread (p. 275) and a mixed vegetable salad dressed with Pickle Vinaigrette (p. 241).

½ pound dried navy beans, sorted and rinsed
½ cup extra-virgin flavorful olive oil
1 large onion, chopped
1 clove garlic, chopped
½ cup tomato sauce
1 medium carrot, thinly sliced
1 stalk celery, thinly sliced
¼ teaspoon black pepper
¼ cup chopped fresh parsley
1 teaspoon dried basil leaves
4 cups boiling water

1. Soak beans overnight; or cover with 2½ cups cold water, boil for 2 minutes, and let stand for 1 hour. Drain.
2. Heat olive oil in large soup pot and sauté onions and garlic for 7 to 10 minutes over medium heat until lightly browned. Add tomato sauce, carrot, celery, black pepper, parsley, and basil. Sauté for 10 more minutes.
3. Add beans and boiling water. Lower heat, cover, and simmer for 45 minutes or until beans are tender.

YIELD
4 servings

PREPARATION TIME
15 minutes + overnight or
1-hour soaking time

COOKING TIME
1 hour and 5 minutes

NUTRIENT ANALYSIS
Calories per serving: 215
Protein: 5.6 gm
Carbohydrates: 18.1 gm
Dietary fiber: 3.8 gm
Cholesterol: 0 mg
Total fat: 13.9 gm (125 cal)
Sat fat: 1.9 gm (17 cal)
Poly fat: 1.2 gm (10.6 cal)
Mono fat: 9.9 gm (89 cal)

New Year's Day
Black-Eyed
Peas

YIELD
4 servings

PREPARATION TIME
10 minutes

COOKING TIME
1 hour + chilling time

NUTRIENT ANALYSIS
Calories per serving: 228
Protein: 4.9 gm
Carbohydrates: 12.5 gm
Dietary fiber: 4.1 gm
Cholesterol: 0 mg
Total fat: 18.4 gm (166 cal)
Sat fat: 2.7 gm (24 cal)
Poly fat: 1.5 gm (14 cal)
Mono fat: 13.2 gm (119 cal)

There is a tradition in the southern United States that black-eyed peas must be eaten on New Year's Eve or New Year's Day for good luck. The idea was to get a dollar in the new year for each pea you ate, but with inflation that's not the same luck as it once was.

The dish, in both the hot and cold version, actually tastes best the second day and can be refrigerated for a week. Serve as a side dish with Cuban Sauce (p. 249).

½ pound dried black-eyed peas, sorted and rinsed
4 cups water
1 small onion, chopped
1 garlic clove, minced
½ teaspoon black pepper
1 large bay leaf
⅛ teaspoon dried thyme leaves
2 tablespoons wine vinegar
⅓ cup extra-virgin olive oil

1. Place black-eyed peas and water in medium pot and bring to a boil over high heat.
2. Reduce heat and stir in onion, garlic, pepper, bay leaf, thyme, vinegar, and olive oil. Cover and simmer for 1 hour or until peas are tender. Remove bay leaf and serve with rice.

VARIATION
For a cold salad, cook the peas and bay leaf alone in water. When tender, drain and add onion, garlic, black pepper, and thyme. In a small bowl, combine vinegar and olive oil with a wire whisk. Pour over peas, stir, and refrigerate at least two hours before serving.

PASTA

· ·

COOKING PASTA

Cook pasta in a large pot of boiling water, allowing about 1 quart of water for every ¼ pound of pasta. Slip pasta into the boiling water, a small amount at a time, so that the water keeps boiling. Stir with a fork immediately to be sure it doesn't stick together.

Fresh pasta cooks very quickly, often in 2 or 3 minutes; dried pasta takes between 7 and 12 minutes. Refer to individual package directions.

Taste pasta frequently to check for doneness. Stop cooking when it is al dente, tender but not mushy. Drain at once in a colander and toss with a tablespoon of olive oil to keep it from sticking together.

Time your sauce so that it is ready as the pasta finishes cooking to avoid having the pasta become soft and gluey while waiting. If you are using pasta in salad, rinse it in cold water after draining.

Linguine with Oil and Garlic

YIELD
4 servings

PREPARATION TIME
10 minutes

COOKING TIME
20 minutes

NUTRIENT ANALYSIS
Calories per serving: 373
Protein: 5 gm
Carbohydrates: 28 gm
Dietary fiber: 0.7 gm
Cholesterol: 0 mg
Total fat: 28 gm (251 cal)
Sat fat: 3.8 gm (35 cal)
Poly fat: 2.3 gm (21 cal)
Mono fat: 20 gm (179 cal)

Basic pasta is the best setting for a really flavorful olive oil. Serve with Broccoli Salad (p. 75) and Herb Bread (p. 276).

10 cloves garlic, minced
½ cup extra-virgin flavorful olive oil
¾ pound linguine
¼ teaspoon black pepper
¼ teaspoon salt (if desired)

1. Sauté garlic in 2 tablespoons olive oil until lightly browned. Remove from heat.
2. In a large pot with 4 quarts boiling water, cook linguine for 8 to 12 minutes or according to package directions until tender.
3. Drain in a colander and return to pot. Toss with garlic and its oil, remaining olive oil, pepper, and salt (if desired).

Shell Pasta with Fish Fillets and Zucchini

Pair the white fish of your choice with zucchini in a simmered tomato sauce and serve over shell pasta. Serve with a salad of grapefruit and orange sections, green pepper, and pineapple dressed with Basic Vinaigrette (p. 240).

4 tablespoons extra-virgin flavorful olive oil
2 tablespoons chopped onion
1 clove garlic, minced
1/8 teaspoon cayenne pepper
3 cups chopped fresh or drained canned tomatoes
1 teaspoon dried oregano leaves
1 teaspoon dried basil leaves
1 medium zucchini, diced
3/4 pound shell pasta
3/4 pound white fish fillets, cut into 1-inch pieces
1/4 cup chopped fresh parsley

1. Heat 3 tablespoons olive oil in large skillet and sauté onion over medium heat 5 minutes or until tender. Add garlic and cayenne and sauté 2 more minutes.
2. Add tomatoes, oregano, and basil. Stir and simmer for 10 minutes.
3. Add zucchini and simmer for 5 minutes more.
4. While sauce simmers, cook pasta, according to package directions, in 3 quarts of boiling water until al dente.
5. Stir fish into sauce and simmer for 5 minutes more. Drain pasta and toss with 1 tablespoon oil. Serve sauce over shell pasta and garnish with parsley.

YIELD
4 servings

PREPARATION TIME
20 minutes

COOKING TIME
25 minutes

NUTRIENT ANALYSIS
Calories per serving: 341
Protein: 27.5 gm
Carbohydrates: 28 gm
Dietary fiber: 3.9 gm
Cholesterol: 35 mg
Total fat: 13.6 gm (123 cal)
Sat fat: 1.8 gm (17 cal)
Poly fat: 1.8 gm (17 cal)
Mono fat: 8.3 gm (75 cal)

Pasta
with
Shrimp

YIELD

4 servings

PREPARATION TIME

25 minutes

COOKING TIME

15 minutes

NUTRIENT ANALYSIS

Calories per serving: 438
Protein: 27 gm
Carbohydrates: 25 gm
Dietary fiber: 2.4 gm
Cholesterol: 221 mg
Total fat: 25 gm (231 cal)
Sat fat: 3.7 gm (33 cal)
Poly fat: 2.6 gm (24 cal)
Mono fat: 17.6 gm (158 cal)

Season sautéed shrimp and vegetables with lemon and basil, then serve as a topping for thin spaghetti. Serve with whole-wheat bread sticks and a bowl of peach slices.

¾ pound vermicelli (thin spaghetti)
1 clove garlic, minced
½ teaspoon grated lemon rind
7 tablespoons extra-virgin flavorful olive oil
1 medium carrot, sliced
1 medium zucchini, trimmed and thinly sliced
1 medium red bell pepper, seeded and cut into thin strips
1 pound medium shrimp, shelled and deveined
1 tablespoon lemon juice
⅛ teaspoon black pepper
1 teaspoon dried basil leaves
1 tablespoon minced fresh parsley

1. Cook pasta according to package directions in 3 quarts of water until al dente.
2. While pasta is cooking, sauté garlic and lemon rind over medium heat in 6 tablespoons olive oil in skillet for 1 minute. Add carrot, zucchini, red peppers, and shrimp. Cook and stir for 3 to 4 minutes until shrimp turns pink.
3. Sprinkle with lemon juice, black pepper, basil, and parsley.
4. Drain pasta and toss with remaining tablespoon olive oil. Serve pasta with shrimp and vegetable sauce on top.

Linguine
with
Clam Sauce

Stir a few tablespoons of the pesto of your choice from p. 264 into this delicious pasta dish immediately before serving. Serve with a tossed raw vegetable salad dressed with Olive Vinaigrette (p. 241).

¾ pound linguine
½ cup extra-virgin flavorful olive oil
2 cloves garlic, minced
⅓ cup diced onion
⅓ cup chopped green bell pepper
⅓ cup shredded carrots
2 cups diced tomatoes
¼ cup reserved clam juice from can
1 cup canned minced clams with juice
6 tablespoons chopped fresh parsley
1 teaspoon dried thyme leaves
¼ teaspoon black pepper

1. For linguine, put 3 quarts water in a large pot over high heat.
2. While water is coming to a boil prepare sauce. Heat all but 1 tablespoon of olive oil in a large skillet over medium heat and sauté garlic, onion, green pepper, and carrots for 5 minutes or until vegetables are crisp-tender.
3. Add tomatoes, clam juice, clams, parsley, thyme, and black pepper. Stir and simmer for 10 minutes.
4. While vegetables are simmering, cook linguine, according to package directions, in boiling water until al dente. Drain and toss with remaining 1 tablespoon olive oil. Serve with clam sauce.

YIELD
4 servings

PREPARATION TIME
15 minutes

COOKING TIME
20 minutes

NUTRIENT ANALYSIS
Calories per serving: 457
Protein: 15 gm
Carbohydrates: 29 gm
Dietary fiber: 3 gm
Cholesterol: 28.5 mg
Total fat: 32 gm (288 cal)
Sat fat: 4.4 gm (40 cal)
Poly fat: 2.9 gm (26 cal)
Mono fat: 22.4 gm (202 cal)

Tuna Linguine

YIELD
4 servings

PREPARATION TIME
10 minutes

COOKING TIME
13 minutes

NUTRIENT ANALYSIS
Calories per serving: 374
Protein: 17 gm
Carbohydrates: 28 gm
Dietary fiber: 0.7 gm
Cholesterol: 18.9 mg
Total fat: 22 gm (198 cal)
Sat fat: 3.2 gm (29 cal)
Poly fat: 2.1 gm (19 cal)
Mono fat: 15.2 gm (137 cal)

A speedy, delicious way to eat a serving of protein, complex carbohydrates, and monounsaturates when you feel too exhausted to do much more than boil water. Serve with Israeli Salad (p. 78) and Italian bread.

1 6½-ounce can white albacore tuna, packed in water
6 tablespoons extra-virgin flavorful olive oil
Juice of 1 lemon
½ cup chopped fresh parsley
¼ teaspoon black pepper
¼ teaspoon salt (if desired)
¾ pound linguine (or any pasta)

1. Drain tuna. In a small bowl, break tuna into pieces and add oil. Combine with lemon juice, parsley, pepper, and salt (if desired).
2. Cook pasta in 4 quarts boiling water for 8 to 9 minutes or according to package directions until al dente. Drain.
3. Toss with tuna sauce to combine well. Serve.

Pasta with Chicken and Peppers

....

This combination of chicken, red and green peppers, and tomatoes is served with tubular pasta. Top with fresh grated Parmesan cheese. Serve with a salad of fresh or canned pears and watercress with Mint Vinaigrette (p. 241).

¾ *pound tubular pasta, such as penne*
5 tablespoons extra-virgin flavorful olive oil
1 large boneless chicken breast, skinned and cut into
    julienne strips (1 pound)
1 medium onion, chopped
1 medium red bell pepper, cut into julienne strips
1 medium green bell pepper, cut into julienne strips
1 clove garlic, minced
⅛ *teaspoon cayenne pepper*
2 large tomatoes, chopped

1. For pasta, put 3 quarts water in a large pot over high heat.

2. While water is coming to a boil prepare sauce. Heat 2 tablespoons olive oil over medium heat in a large skillet. Sauté chicken until it turns white. Remove chicken and set aside.

3. Add 2 tablespoons olive oil to skillet and sauté onion and peppers until tender.

4. Return chicken to pan and add garlic and cayenne. Cook for 3 minutes, stirring constantly.

5. Add tomatoes and simmer for 10 minutes.

6. While chicken is simmering, cook pasta, according to package instructions, until al dente. Drain and toss with remaining tablespoon olive oil. Serve with chicken and peppers.

YIELD
4 servings

PREPARATION TIME
15 minutes

COOKING TIME
25 minutes

NUTRIENT ANALYSIS
Calories per serving: 422
Protein: 32 gm
Carbohydrates: 26 gm
Dietary fiber: 2.7 gm
Cholesterol: 75 mg
Total fat: 20 gm (188 cal)
Sat fat: 3.4 gm (30 cal)
Poly fat: 2.3 gm (21 cal)
Mono fat: 13.6 gm (123 cal)

Pasta with Spinach-Cheese Sauce

.... ⊙ ....

YIELD
4 servings

PREPARATION TIME
15 minutes

COOKING TIME
15 minutes

NUTRIENT ANALYSIS
Calories per serving: 274
Protein: 11.6 gm
Carbohydrates: 25 gm
Dietary fiber: 2.5 gm
Cholesterol: 2.5 mg
Total fat: 14.9 gm (134 cal)
Sat fat: 2.3 gm (21 cal)
Poly fat: 1.2 gm (11 cal)
Mono fat: 10.1 gm (91 cal)

Puree wilted spinach, onion, and ricotta or cottage cheese to create this smooth, rich pasta sauce. Serve with sliced tomatoes and a bowl of grated Parmesan cheese.

¼ cup extra-virgin flavorful olive oil
1 medium onion, chopped
1 clove garlic, chopped
3 cups chopped fresh spinach, well washed and drained
1 cup low-fat ricotta or cottage cheese
½ cup chopped fresh parsley
1 teaspoon dried basil leaves
1 teaspoon lemon juice
¼ teaspoon black pepper
¼ teaspoon ground nutmeg
¾ pound spaghetti

1. Heat 3 tablespoons olive oil in large skillet over medium heat and sauté onion and garlic until onion is tender.
2. Add chopped spinach to skillet and cook 3 to 5 minutes until spinach wilts.
3. Place wilted spinach, onions, and garlic in blender container with cheese, parsley, basil, lemon juice, pepper, and nutmeg. Blend until pureed. Leave in blender, covered, to keep sauce warm.
4. Cook pasta in 3 quarts boiling water, according to package directions, until al dente. Toss with remaining tablespoon olive oil.
5. Add ¼ cup hot water from pasta to sauce in blender and blend again. Serve over pasta.

MICROWAVE
RECIPES

HOT BEAN DIP
EGGPLANT SALAD SPREAD
CHICKEN WITH GREEN PEPPERS ◉
TURKEY CUTLETS ◉
FISH STEAKS IN VEGETABLE SAUCE
BAKED LOIN PORK CHOPS ◉
STUFFED PEPPERS ◉
LINGUINE WITH RED CLAM SAUCE
EGGPLANT WITH TOMATOES AND PENNE ◉
QUICK MICROWAVE TOMATO SAUCE ◉
TRI-COLORED PEPPER BAKE ◉
ZUCCHINI-YELLOW SQUASH CASSEROLE ◉
CAULIFLOWER AND GREEN BEANS VINAIGRETTE ◉
MUSHROOMS IN OIL-GARLIC SAUCE ◉
SPINACH WITH OIL AND GARLIC ◉
NEW POTATOES AND BROCCOLI ◉
BAKED NEW POTATOES WITH PAPRIKA ◉
LEMON SCALLOPED POTATOES ◉

OLIVE OIL AND YOUR MICROWAVE

Olive oil is used mainly for flavoring in microwave cooking. We have included a wide variety of dishes that can be made in the microwave with olive oil. Try substituting olive oil for other vegetable oils in your own favorite microwave recipes.

The recipes that follow are meant to be cooked in a full-size microwave oven. Directions indicate heat settings as 100 percent HIGH, which is "10" on some ovens or 50 percent MEDIUM, which is "5" on some ovens. Since there are no industry standards for temperature dials, you may have to interpret these settings for your particular microwave and select the closest option. Rotation directions can be ignored for microwaves equipped with carousels.

Hot
Bean
Dip

YIELD
4 servings

PREPARATION TIME
10 minutes

COOKING TIME
7 minutes

NUTRIENT ANALYSIS
Calories per serving: 382
Protein: 22 gm
Carbohydrates: 33.6 gm
Dietary fiber: 12.5 gm
Cholesterol: 17.9 mg
Total fat: 18.6 gm (167 cal)
Sat fat: 5.4 gm (49 cal)
Poly fat: 1.4 gm (13 cal)
Mono fat: 11.3 gm (102 cal)

S erve this tangy chili-flavored dip with salt-free corn chips or crisp vegetable crudités.

4 cups canned kidney or pinto beans, drained, with ⅓ cup reserved liquid
¼ cup extra-virgin flavorful olive oil
1 cup grated reduced-fat Cheddar cheese
1 tablespoon minced onion
1 tablespoon chili powder
¼ teaspoon paprika

1. Combine beans, olive oil, and ⅓ cup bean liquid in a 2-quart microwave-safe bowl. Cover with microwave-safe plastic wrap. Heat at 100 percent HIGH for 4 minutes.
2. Remove from oven and mash bean mixture with fork or potato masher until smooth.
3. Stir in cheese, onion, chili powder, and paprika. Cover again and heat microwave at 100 percent HIGH for approximately 3 minutes or until cheese melts.
4. Remove from microwave and serve warm.

Eggplant Salad Spread

Serve this smooth and tangy spread with crackers or pita bread wedges.

1 large eggplant
½ cup chopped onion
½ cup minced celery
1 clove garlic, minced
1 teaspoon dried oregano leaves
¼ teaspoon black pepper
¼ cup extra-virgin flavorful olive oil
2 tablespoons wine vinegar
2 tablespoon pine nuts (optional)

1. Place eggplant on paper plate, prick with a fork and cook, uncovered, at 100 percent HIGH for 12 minutes. Remove and cool.
2. Cut eggplant in half and scoop out pulp, placing it in a blender or food processor.
3. Add onions, celery, garlic, oregano, and pepper and process at medium speed until well blended.
4. Place in a medium bowl and stir in olive oil and wine vinegar. Sprinkle with pine nuts.
5. Cover and chill for several hours, stirring occasionally. Serve chilled or at room temperature.

YIELD
4 servings

PREPARATION TIME
10 minutes + several hours chilling time

COOKING TIME
12 minutes

NUTRIENT ANALYSIS
Calories per serving: 173
Protein: 1.4 gm
Carbohydrates: 9.8 gm
Dietary fiber: 3.2 gm
Cholesterol: 0 mg
Total fat: 15.4 gm (139 cal)
Sat fat: 2 gm (19 cal)
Poly fat: 1.7 gm (15 cal)
Mono fat: 11 gm (99 cal)

Chicken
with
Green Peppers

················· ● ···

YIELD
4 servings

PREPARATION TIME
10 minutes

COOKING TIME
12 minutes

NUTRIENT ANALYSIS
Calories per serving: 350
Protein: 37 gm
Carbohydrates: 10.3 gm
Dietary fiber: 3.3 gm
Cholesterol: 94 mg
Total fat: 17.9 gm (161 cal)
Sat fat: 3.2 gm (29 cal)
Poly fat: 2.2 gm (20 cal)
Mono fat: 11.5 gm (103 cal)

Chicken and green peppers are cooked with tomatoes, onions, and olive oil in this easy to prepare recipe. Serve with Baked New Potatoes with Paprika (p. 214).

¼ cup mild, light flavored olive oil
1 large onion, chopped
2 medium green bell peppers, seeded and cut into strips
4 large tomatoes, cut in quarters
¼ teaspoon black pepper
1 pound boneless chicken breasts, skinned and cut in half
*   to make 4 pieces*

1. Heat oil in an uncovered baking dish for 2 minutes at 100 percent HIGH. Add onions, cover with microwave-safe plastic wrap, and cook for 2 minutes more at 100 percent HIGH.
2. Take baking dish out of oven. Put green peppers, tomatoes, and black pepper in a bowl. Pour oil-onion mixture over vegetables and stir to coat.
3. Return vegetables to the center of the baking dish. Surround with four chicken pieces. Cover tightly and cook at 100 percent HIGH for 10 minutes.
4. Remove from oven. Uncover carefully and check to be sure chicken is done. Return to microwave another minute or two to complete cooking, if necessary.

Turkey Cutlets

Turkey cutlets are breaded and prepared in the micro-wave in this simple recipe. Serve with Quick Micro-wave Tomato Sauce (p. 207) and Zucchini-Yellow Squash Casserole (p. 209).

4 turkey cutlets (1 pound), cut in half
2 tablespoons mild, light flavored olive oil
2 egg whites, slightly beaten
¾ cup fine bread crumbs (or half bread crumbs and half
  oat bran)
¼ cup grated Parmesan cheese
⅛ teaspoon black pepper
2 cups Quick Microwave Tomato Sauce (p. 207) or
  canned sauce

1. Pound turkey cutlet halves between two pieces of wax paper until they are ¼-inch thick.
2. Beat olive oil into egg whites in a shallow dish or soup plate.
3. Combine bread crumbs, Parmesan cheese, and pepper in a second shallow dish.
4. Dip each turkey cutlet into oil-egg mixture and then into crumb mixture. Place in 1 layer on microwave-safe baking dish. Cover tightly with microwave-safe plastic wrap and cook at 100 percent HIGH for 6 minutes.
5. Rotate dish and reposition turkey pieces so all sides cook. Cook for 5 minutes more.
6. Remove from oven. Uncover carefully and check to be sure turkey is done. Return to microwave to complete cooking, another minute or two, if necessary.
7. Serve with Quick Microwave Tomato Sauce.

YIELD
4 servings

PREPARATION TIME
10 minutes

COOKING TIME
12 minutes

NUTRIENT ANALYSIS
Calories per serving: 480
Protein: 33 gm
Carbohydrates: 21.6 gm
Dietary fiber: 0.4 gm
Cholesterol: 64 mg
Total fat: 26.4 gm (238 cal)
Sat fat: 5.2 gm (47 cal)
Poly fat: 2.6 gm (23 cal)
Mono fat: 16 gm (144 cal)

Fish Steaks in Vegetable Sauce

....

YIELD
4 servings

PREPARATION TIME
15 minutes

COOKING TIME
25 minutes

NUTRIENT ANALYSIS
Calories per serving: 342
Protein: 31.8 gm
Carbohydrates: 9 gm
Dietary fiber: 2.8 gm
Cholesterol: 47 mg
Total fat: 17 gm (155 cal)
Sat fat: 2.5 gm (22 cal)
Poly fat: 2.4 gm (21 cal)
Mono fat: 11 gm (99 cal)

Use your microwave to steam the vegetables and poach the fish in this tasty dish. Serve with pasta.

¼ cup extra-virgin flavorful olive oil
1 clove garlic (or 2 shallots or scallions), chopped
1 medium onion, finely chopped
2 small zucchini, chopped
1 small carrot, scrubbed and finely chopped
½ cup chopped fresh or drained canned tomatoes
½ cup dry white wine
1 teaspoon dried dill leaves
¼ teaspoon salt (optional)
4 fish steaks (1 pound), about ¾-inch thick

1. Place olive oil in a 2-quart, microwave-safe bowl. Add garlic and onion, cover with microwave-safe wrap, and cook for 2 minutes on 100 percent HIGH.
2. Add zucchini, carrot, tomatoes, wine, dill, and salt (if desired). Cover and cook on 100 percent HIGH for 10 minutes, stirring several times.
3. Place fish in vegetable sauce with thicker sides pointing toward the outside edges of the bowl. Cook on 100 percent HIGH for 10 minutes, without covering. Rotate dish halfway through cooking time and reposition fish so all sides cook evenly. Fish is done when it flakes easily with a fork and is no longer translucent.

Baked Loin Pork Chops

Bake lean loin pork chops in an herb-tomato sauce. Serve with New Potatoes and Broccoli (p. 213).

4 ½-inch-thick loin chops (1 pound), trimmed of fat
¼ cup mild light flavored olive oil
2 cloves garlic, chopped
¼ teaspoon dried oregano leaves
¼ teaspoon dried basil leaves
¼ teaspoon black pepper
1 green bell pepper, seeded and diced
¾ cup chopped fresh or drained canned tomatoes

1. Place pork chops in a large microwave-safe baking dish with the fleshy parts of the chop pointing toward the outsides of the dish. Cover with microwave-safe plastic wrap and cook on 100 percent HIGH for 14 minutes. Turn chops over and rearrange after 7 minutes. Rotate dish several times while cooking. Remove from microwave. Cut into pork chops near the bone to make sure there are no pink juices. Return and microwave for 2 minutes more if not completely cooked. When done, remove from microwave and set aside.
2. Combine oil and garlic in a 2-quart microwave-safe dish. Cook on 100 percent HIGH for 45 seconds. Add oregano, basil, black pepper, green pepper, and tomatoes. Cook for 5 minutes, stirring several times. Remove from oven.
3. Pour sauce over pork chops in baking dish and cover with microwave-safe plastic wrap. Microwave on 100 percent for 3 minutes.

YIELD
4 servings

PREPARATION TIME
10 minutes

COOKING TIME
25 minutes

NUTRIENT ANALYSIS
Calories per serving: 425
Protein: 32.3 gm
Carbohydrates: 3.6 gm
Dietary fiber: 0.6 gm
Cholesterol: 108 mg
Total fat: 31 gm (280 cal)
Sat fat: 7.9 gm (71 cal)
Poly fat: 3.3 gm (30 cal)
Mono fat: 17.7 gm (160 cal)

Stuffed Peppers

YIELD
4 servings

PREPARATION TIME
15 minutes

COOKING TIME
30 minutes

NUTRIENT ANALYSIS
Calories per serving: 263
Protein: 4 gm
Carbohydrates: 31.7 gm
Dietary fiber: 2.6 gm
Cholesterol: 0 mg
Total fat: 14.4 gm (130 cal)
Sat fat: 2.4 gm (22 cal)
Poly fat: 1.8 gm (16 cal)
Mono fat: 10.3 gm (92 cal)

Stuff red peppers with a mixture of ground turkey, rice, tomatoes, onions, and basil. Serve with Spinach with Oil and Garlic (p. 212).

4 medium red bell peppers
¼ cup mild, light flavored olive oil
1 medium onion, finely chopped
⅔ cup ground turkey
2 cups chopped canned tomatoes, drained
½ cup raw long-grain rice
½ teaspoon salt (optional)
1 teaspoon dried basil leaves
¼ teaspoon black pepper
½ cup water
2 tablespoons tomato paste

1. Cut tops off of peppers and reserve. Carefully scoop out pepper cores and seeds.
2. Heat olive oil in a large heatproof dish, uncovered, for 2 minutes at 100 percent HIGH. Add onion and turkey. Stir. Cook for 5 minutes, uncovered, at 100 percent HIGH.
3. Add tomatoes, rice, salt (if desired), basil, and black pepper and mix well.
4. Stuff cored peppers with turkey mixture and put tops back on peppers. Sit stuffed peppers in a microwave-safe baking dish.
5. Combine water and tomato paste. Pour over and around peppers and tightly cover baking dish. Microwave at 100 percent HIGH for 20 minutes. Remove from oven, uncover, and let stand for 5 more minutes.

Linguine with Red Clam Sauce

....

Prepare clam sauce in the microwave while your pasta is cooking on the stove. Serve with Broccoli Salad (p. 75).

¼ cup mild, light flavored olive oil
3 cloves garlic, chopped
1 small onion, chopped fine
½ cup chopped fresh parsley
¼ cup dry white wine
2 cups chopped fresh or drained canned tomatoes
¼ teaspoon dried oregano leaves
⅛ teaspoon black pepper
24 littleneck clams, well scrubbed
¾ pound linguine

1. Heat 3 tablespoons olive oil in a 1-quart microwave-safe dish at 100 percent HIGH for 1 minute. Add garlic and onion and cook for 2 minutes more.
2. Combine olive oil mixture with parsley, wine, tomatoes, oregano, and pepper in a microwave-safe glass baking dish. Cover with microwave-safe wrap and cook at 100 percent HIGH for 5 minutes, stirring once. Add clams and tightly re-cover dish. Microwave at 100 percent HIGH for 7 to 12 minutes or until clams open.
3. Cook linguine, according to package directions, in 3 quarts of water until al dente. Drain and toss with the remaining tablespoon olive oil.
4. Serve the linguine with the clam sauce.

VARIATION

Omit littleneck clams. Use 12 ounces of canned clams. Microwave on 100 percent HIGH for 3 minutes after adding clams to sauce.

YIELD
4 servings

PREPARATION TIME
15 minutes

COOKING TIME
25 minutes

NUTRIENT ANALYSIS
Calories per serving: 324
Protein: 11.2 gm
Carbohydrates: 35 gm
Dietary fiber: 2.2 gm
Cholesterol: 14.5 mg
Total fat: 15 gm (136 cal)
Sat fat: 2 gm (18 cal)
Poly fat: 1.4 gm (13 cal)
Mono fat: 10 gm (90 cal)

Eggplant with Tomatoes and Penne

YIELD
4 servings

PREPARATION TIME
10 minutes

COOKING TIME
7 minutes

NUTRIENT ANALYSIS
Calories per serving: 225
Protein: 4.6 gm
Carbohydrates: 21.7 gm
Dietary fiber: 4.2 gm
Cholesterol: 0 mg
Total fat: 15.5 gm (14 cal)
Sat fat: 2.1 gm (19 cal)
Poly fat: 1.5 gm (14 cal)
Mono fat: 10.7 gm (97 cal)

Microwave eggplant in an olive-tomato sauce and serve with tubular pasta. Garnish with grated Parmesan cheese. Serve a salad of chicory, escarole, cherry tomatoes, and cucumber slices topped with Red Onion Dressing (p. 239).

¼ *cup extra-virgin flavorful olive oil*
2 *cloves garlic, minced*
4 *cups canned plum tomatoes*
2 *tablespoons chopped black olives*
½ *teaspoon dried oregano leaves*
¼ *teaspoon black pepper*
½ *teaspoon salt (optional)*
1 *medium eggplant, peeled and diced*
¾ *pound penne or other tubular pasta*

1. Heat olive oil and garlic in a 2-quart, microwave-safe dish at 100 percent HIGH for 1 minute.
2. Add tomatoes, olives, oregano, pepper, and salt (if desired) and mix well. Microwave at 100 percent HIGH, uncovered, for 3 minutes. Stir several times.
3. Add eggplant and stir to coat with tomato mixture. Cover and cook at 100 percent HIGH for 3 minutes. Stir several times.
4. Cook penne, according to package directions, in 3 quarts of water until al dente. Drain and toss with 1 tablespoon olive oil. Serve with eggplant-tomato sauce.

Quick
Microwave
Tomato Sauce

T his all-purpose sauce can be served "as is" or can be used as a base for a meat sauce with addition of lean ground beef or ground turkey.

1/4 cup extra-virgin flavorful olive oil
1 clove garlic (or 2 shallots or scallions), chopped
1 small onion, chopped
1/4 cup dry white wine
2 cups drained canned plum tomatoes
1 tablespoon tomato paste
1/4 teaspoon black pepper
1/4 teaspoon salt (optional)
1 teaspoon dried basil leaves

1. Combine oil, garlic, and onion in a 3-quart microwave-safe bowl. Cover with microwave-safe wrap and cook for 2 minutes at 100 percent HIGH.
2. Add wine, tomatoes, tomato paste, pepper, and basil. Cover and cook at 100 percent HIGH for 5 minutes. Uncover and cook at MEDIUM 50 percent for 15 minutes. Let stand for 7 minutes before serving.

YIELD
4 cups

PREPARATION TIME
9 minutes

NUTRIENT ANALYSIS
Calories per serving: 176
Protein: 1.5 gm
Carbohydrates: 7.4 gm
Dietary fiber: 1.2 gm
Cholesterol: 0 mg
Total fat: 13.9 gm (125 cal)
Sat fat: 2 gm (18 cal)
Poly fat: 1.3 gm (12 cal)
Mono fat: 10 gm (90 cal)

Tri-Colored Pepper Bake

.... ⊙ ....

YIELD
4 servings

PREPARATION TIME
15 minutes

COOKING TIME
8 minutes

NUTRIENT ANALYSIS
Calories per serving: 151
Protein: 1.2 gm
Carbohydrates: 6.9 gm
Dietary fiber: 1.8 gm
Cholesterol: 0 mg
Total fat: 14 gm (26 cal)
Sat fat: 2 gm (18 cal)
Poly fat: 1.4 gm (13 cal)
Mono fat: 10 gm (90 cal)

Bake red, green, and yellow peppers in an olive oil sauce. Served with Linguine with Red Clam Sauce (p. 205).

3 medium red bell peppers, seeded and cut into strips
1 medium yellow bell pepper, seeded and cut into strips
2 medium green bell peppers, seeded and cut into strips
¼ cup mild, light flavored olive oil
1 clove garlic, minced
½ teaspoon dried oregano leaves
¼ teaspoon salt (optional)
⅛ teaspoon black pepper
½ cup chopped fresh parsley

1. Place red peppers in bottom of a 2-quart microwave-safe dish. Top with yellow and green peppers.
2. Combine olive oil, garlic, oregano, salt (if desired), and black pepper with a wire whisk. Pour over peppers. Tightly cover dish with microwave-safe plastic wrap. Microwave on 100 percent HIGH for 6 to 8 minutes.
3. Remove from oven and pierce plastic with knife tip to release steam. Remove plastic wrap with care. Garnish with parsley before serving.

Zucchini-Yellow Squash Casserole

Top zucchini, yellow squash, onions, and tomatoes with Parmesan cheese. Serve with microwaved turkey burgers for a quick supper.

¼ cup extra-virgin flavorful olive oil
1 medium onion, minced
1 clove garlic, minced
½ teaspoon dried basil leaves
1 medium yellow squash
1 medium zucchini
4 medium ripe tomatoes, chopped
½ cup grated Parmesan cheese
1 teaspoon fresh lemon juice

1. Place oil, onion, garlic, and basil in a microwave-safe baking dish and cook at 100 percent for 4 minutes. Remove from microwave.
2. Stir in yellow squash, zucchini, and tomatoes, coating well with oil.
3. Cover with microwave-safe plastic wrap and cook at 100 percent HIGH for 8 minutes. Remove from oven.
4. Carefully remove wrap and sprinkle with Parmesan cheese. Return to microwave, uncovered, for 5 minutes at 100 percent HIGH. Serve hot or at room temperature, drizzled with lemon juice.

YIELD
4 servings

PREPARATION TIME
15 minutes

COOKING TIME
17 minutes

NUTRIENT ANALYSIS
Calories per serving: 236
Protein: 7.8 gm
Carbohydrates: 13.4 gm
Dietary fiber: 5.6 gm
Cholesterol: 9.9 mg
Total fat: 18 gm (162 cal)
Sat fat: 4.4 gm (40 cal)
Poly fat: 1.5 gm (14 cal)
Mono fat: 11 gm (99 cal)

Cauliflower and Green Beans Vinaigrette

YIELD
4 servings

PREPARATION TIME
15 minutes

COOKING TIME
10 minutes

NUTRIENT ANALYSIS
Calories per serving: 153
Protein: 2.2 gm
Carbohydrates: 7.5 gm
Dietary fiber: 2.6 gm
Cholesterol: 0 mg
Total fat: 13.8 gm (124 cal)
Sat fat: 2 gm (18 cal)
Poly fat: 1.2 gm (11 cal)
Mono fat: 10 gm (90 cal)

Toss fresh cauliflower and green beans in an oil and vinegar dressing and serve at room temperature. Serve with Tuna Linguine (p. 192).

½ pound cauliflower florets
½ pound green beans, ends trimmed and cut into 1-inch pieces
¼ cup extra-virgin flavorful olive oil
2 tablespoons wine vinegar
¼ teaspoon salt (optional)
¼ teaspoon black pepper

1. Place cauliflower florets in a single layer in a microwave-safe baking dish with ¼ cup water. Cover with microwave-safe plastic wrap. Cook at 100 percent HIGH for 4 minutes. Allow to stand for 3 minutes.
2. Place beans in a microwave-safe baking dish with ¼ cup water. Cover and cook on 100 percent HIGH for 6 minutes, stirring once. Allow to stand for 2 minutes.
3. Drain cauliflower and beans and toss together in a salad bowl.
4. Shake oil, vinegar, salt (if desired), and pepper in a small jar or with a wire whisk to combine well. Pour over vegetables and serve.

Mushrooms in Oil-Garlic Sauce

Microwave mushrooms in oil and garlic, then sprinkle with parsley. Serve these hot, sprinkled with Parmesan cheese or at room temperature as part of an appetizer tray.

¼ cup extra-virgin flavorful olive oil
2 cloves garlic, minced
1 pound fresh mushrooms, washed, towel dried, and
    thinly sliced
3 tablespoons minced fresh parsley
¼ teaspoon salt (optional)
¼ teaspoon black pepper

1. Place oil and garlic in a 2-quart, microwave-safe bowl. Cover with microwave-safe plastic wrap and cook on HIGH 100 percent for 2 minutes.
2. Stir in mushrooms. Re-cover and cook on 100 percent HIGH for 5 minutes, stirring twice.
3. Remove from microwave and sprinkle with parsley, salt (if desired), and pepper.

YIELD
4 servings

PREPARATION TIME
15 minutes

COOKING TIME
8 minutes

NUTRIENT ANALYSIS
Calories per serving: 152
Protein: 2.5 gm
Carbohydrates: 6 gm
Dietary fiber: 2.2 gm
Cholesterol: 0 mg
Total fat: 14 gm (126 cal)
Sat fat: 2 gm (18 cal)
Poly fat: 1.3 gm (12 cal)
Mono fat: 10 gm (90 cal)

Spinach with Oil and Garlic

YIELD
4 servings

PREPARATION TIME
5 minutes

COOKING TIME
11 minutes

NUTRIENT ANALYSIS
Calories per serving: 161
Protein: 4.6 gm
Carbohydrates: 8.1 gm
Dietary fiber: 3.0 gm
Cholesterol: 0 mg
Total fat: 13.8 gm (124 cal)
Sat fat: 1.9 gm (18 cal)
Poly fat: 1.3 gm (11 cal)
Mono fat: 10 gm (90 cal)

Use this cooking method with other leafy vegetables.

¼ cup olive oil
2 cloves garlic, minced
2 10-ounce boxes frozen spinach
¼ teaspoon salt (optional)
¼ teaspoon black pepper

Combine olive oil and garlic in a 4-quart, microwave-safe casserole. Cook for 1 minute. Add frozen spinach. Cover with microwave-safe plastic wrap and cook on 100 percent HIGH for 10 minutes, stirring several times. Add salt (if desired) and pepper and serve.

New Potatoes and Broccoli

Toss colorful red potatoes and broccoli with onion and celery in a garlic-oil sauce. Serve with microwave baked flounder fillets.

1½ pounds red potatoes, peeled and cut into 1-inch cubes
⅓ cup water
1 pound broccoli, cut into 1-inch florets
5 tablespoons extra-virgin flavorful olive oil
1 clove garlic (or 2 shallots or scallions), chopped
¼ cup wine vinegar
¼ teaspoon black pepper
¼ teaspoon salt (optional)
½ cup thinly sliced celery
½ cup chopped red onion

1. Combine potatoes and water in 3-quart, microwave-safe casserole. Cover with microwave-safe plastic wrap and cook at 100 percent HIGH for 10 minutes. Stir once.

2. Layer broccoli on top of potatoes in casserole. Re-cover. Microwave at 100 percent HIGH for 3 minutes. Re-move casserole and drain vegetables.

3. Place oil and garlic in the empty casserole, cover, and return to microwave. Microwave at 100 percent HIGH for 1½ minutes. Remove from microwave and stir in vinegar, pepper, salt (if desired), potatoes, broccoli, celery, and red onion.

YIELD
5 servings

PREPARATION TIME
20 minutes

COOKING TIME
15 minutes

NUTRIENT ANALYSIS
Calories per serving: 271
Protein: 5.4 gm
Carbohydrates: 35 gm
Dietary fiber: 5.6 gm
Cholesterol: 0 mg
Total fat: 14 gm (126 cal)
Sat fat: 2 gm (18 cal)
Poly fat: 1.3 gm (12 cal)
Mono fat: 10 gm (90 cal)

Baked New Potatoes with Paprika

YIELD
4 servings

PREPARATION TIME
10 minutes

COOKING TIME
15 minutes

NUTRIENT ANALYSIS
Calories per serving: 299
Protein: 3.7 gm
Carbohydrates: 41.8 gm
Dietary fiber: 3.4 gm
Cholesterol: 0 mg
Total fat: 13.8 gm (124 cal)
Sat fat: 2 gm (18 cal)
Poly fat: 1.2 gm (11 cal)
Mono fat: 10 gm (90 cal)

Bake new potatoes with garlic, oil, and paprika. Serve with a cold salad, meat or ground turkey loaf, and fresh green beans steamed in the microwave.

12 small new potatoes, scrubbed
5 cloves garlic, chopped
¼ cup mild, light flavored olive oil
¼ teaspoon paprika
¼ teaspoon salt (optional)

1. Place potatoes, garlic, olive oil, paprika, and salt (if desired) in a 2-quart, microwave-safe dish. Toss potatoes to coat well with oil mixture. Tightly cover dish.
2. Microwave at 100 percent HIGH for 10 minutes if potatoes are small, 15 if they are large. Rearrange potatoes in dish once during cooking period.
3. Remove from oven. Uncover and serve.

Lemon Scalloped Potatoes

M icrowave sliced potatoes in a lemon-oil sauce and season with lemon peel, Parmesan cheese, and oregano. Serve with microwaved boneless chicken breasts and green salad with Parsley-Scallion Vinaigrette (p. 241).

¼ cup mild, light flavored olive oil
1 tablespoon lemon juice
3 large potatoes, scrubbed and thinly sliced
2 teaspoons freshly grated lemon peel
3 tablespoons grated Parmesan cheese
½ teaspoon dried oregano leaves
¼ teaspoon salt (optional)

1. Arrange potato slices in a large microwave-safe baking dish. Sprinkle with olive oil and lemon juice.
2. Combine lemon peel, Parmesan cheese, oregano, and salt (if desired). Sprinkle over potatoes.
3. Tightly cover dish with microwave-safe plastic wrap. Cook on 100 percent HIGH for 12 minutes. Remove from oven and carefully remove wrap.
4. Return to oven and cook uncovered at 100 percent HIGH for 5 minutes.

YIELD
4 servings

PREPARATION TIME
15 minutes

COOKING TIME
15 minutes

NUTRIENT ANALYSIS
Calories per serving: 229
Protein: 3.7 gm
Carbohydrates: 21 gm
Dietary fiber: 1.1 gm
Cholesterol: 3.7 mg
Total fat: 15 gm (135 cal)
Sat fat: 2.8 gm (26 cal)
Poly fat: 1.2 gm (11 cal)
Mono fat: 10.3 gm (93 cal)

GRILLING

SPICY CHICKEN
LEMON-BARBECUED CHICKEN
GRILLED TURKEY CUTLETS IN CITRUS MARINADE
GRILLED FISH IN A BASKET
FOIL-WRAPPED WHOLE FISH
ZESTY BARBECUED FISH
GARLIC SHRIMP
SCAMPI IN FOIL
GRILLED SCALLOPS
SHISH KABOB
GRILLED POTATOES AND PESTO
GRILLED GARLIC BREAD

GRILLING TIPS

Warm weather cooking often finds us standing in front of our barbecues, where olive oil is an ideal ingredient for all of our favorite dishes.

In recent years, the pleasure of grilling has been clouded by reports that burnt meats may create carcinogens. When the fat in meat drips onto the coals, the combustion causes potentially harmful smoke to rise and be absorbed on the surface of the meat. To make grilling safer, you can take a few simple preventive measures.

1. First, grill foods at lower temperatures. This will require raising your barbecue grill farther away from the heat source.

2. If you use wood when you barbecue, use maple or hickory or similar hardwoods and avoid soft woods such as pine. Avoid wood from pesticide treated areas.

3. Do not use pine cones as fuel and limit mesquite use to a few scattered chips to avoid high levels of benzopyrene.

4. Keep fat from dripping onto your heat source and producing smoke. Put a metal drip pan or piece of heavy duty aluminum foil in the center of your bed of charcoal underneath your grilling food. Keep coals to one side and food to the other.

Proper circulation, which is very important, is easier to obtain with a kettle style barbecue than with a small hibachi. Barbecue in a well-vented location where any smoke that does form can drift away instead of accumulating on your food. Also experiment with cooking on foil on your grill as we do in some of the following recipes to prevent food from coming into contact with the flame.

In keeping with your low cholesterol diet guidelines, don't overemphasize red meat in your barbecue menus. Fish is a good choice since it appears to form few mutagens and also contains fats that may protect against cancer.

When you do barbecue meat, use lower-fat cuts of beef so that fat doesn't drip on coals and cause flareups. To further reduce fat content, precook the meat in a microwave at HIGH for 30 to 90 seconds before grilling and discard any juice that collects. Don't eat liquid drippings and cut away any charred portions.

Don't grill frozen meat since the outside chars while the inside remains frozen.

You may also wish to consider barbecuing over a gas grill because they are more convenient to use and do not require the use of charcoal or wood products. They also provide even heat, which is helpful when you are grilling for longer time periods at lower temperatures. Neither gas nor electric grills are thought to be significantly safer than charcoal grills since chemicals form when fat drips on any heat source. However, the Swedes have invented a vertical grill, which is reported to be very effective in reducing the risks from chemicals.

Most grilled foods are also delicious if cooked in advance and served at room temperature or slightly chilled. They are excellent in salads, also.

In case of rain, or during the colder months, these recipes will work equally well using your indoor broiler.

POULTRY

Poultry generally requires a longer, slower cooking time than meat or fish on the grill. If possible, cook on a covered grill using medium heat and baste frequently. Chicken pieces require about 15 minutes on each side, while boned chicken and turkey cutlets need about 8 minutes a side.

FISH

Moderately fat (with healthful omega-3 oils), full-flavored fish, such as salmon, trout, mackerel, and bluefish, are suggested for grilling as opposed to more delicately flavored fish such as sole. Avoid over-grilling fish so as not to change its texture and taste. It is done when it flakes with a fork.

SHELLFISH

Shrimp and scallops are also simple to grill and can be prepared with a wide variety of marinades to provide flavor excitement.

Spicy
Chicken

The lemon juice in this marinade helps to tenderize, preserve, and flavor the chicken. Serve with bowls of cherry tomatoes, fresh pineapple chunks, chutney, banana, unsalted peanuts, and light soy sauce for dipping.

½ cup extra-virgin olive oil
½ cup lemon juice
2 teaspoons crushed dried red peppers
¼ teaspoon black pepper
2 whole chicken breasts, cut in half (1 pound)

1. Using a wire whisk, combine olive oil, lemon juice, red pepper flakes, and black pepper in a large glass bowl.
2. Add chicken breasts, stir, and cover bowl. Marinate in refrigerator for 2 hours, turning breasts every half hour.
3. Barbecue over medium heat for 15 minutes. Turn and barbecue for 15 minutes on the other side until meat is cooked.

YIELD
4 servings

PREPARATION TIME
15 minutes + 2 hours for marinating

COOKING TIME
30 minutes

NUTRIENT ANALYSIS
Calories per serving: 432
Protein: 35 gm
Carbohydrates: 3.4 gm
Dietary fiber: 0.3 gm
Cholesterol: 94 mg
Total fat: 30 gm (270 cal)
Sat fat: 5 gm (45 cal)
Poly fat: 3 gm (27 cal)
Mono fat: 21 gm (189 cal)

Lemon-Barbecued Chicken

YIELD
4 servings

PREPARATION TIME
15 minutes

COOKING TIME
35 to 45 minutes

NUTRIENT ANALYSIS
Calories per serving: 429
Protein: 35 gm
Carbohydrates: 2.3 gm
Dietary fiber: 0.05 gm
Cholesterol: 94 mg
Total fat: 30 gm (278 cal)
Sat fat: 5 gm (45 cal)
Poly fat: 3.2 gm (29 cal)
Mono fat: 21 gm (192 cal)

Baste chicken with a lemon and olive oil sauce flavored with brown sugar, dry mustard, thyme, rosemary, and tarragon. Serve with Ratatouille (p. 162) and crusty French rolls.

½ cup extra-virgin olive oil
¼ cup lemon juice
½ cup water
1 teaspoon brown sugar
1 teaspoon dry mustard
¼ teaspoon dried thyme leaves
¼ teaspoon dried rosemary leaves
¼ teaspoon dried tarragon leaves
2 whole chicken breasts, cut in half, rinsed, and patted
  dry (1 pound)

1. For barbecue sauce, combine olive oil, lemon juice, water, brown sugar, mustard, thyme, rosemary, and tarragon in a small saucepan. Heat to boiling point, lower heat, and keep warm.

2. Brush chicken with barbecue sauce. Place chicken over medium heat on grill and broil slowly, turning frequently for 35 to 45 minutes. Begin to baste with barbecue sauce after chicken browns and continue doing so until finished grilling.

Grilled Turkey Cutlets in Citrus Marinade

Turkey cutlets are quick and easy to grill. For a change of pace, marinate them in this citrus sauce. Serve with Green Bean Salad (p. 83) and baked potatoes in foil.

½ cup orange juice
2 tablespoons light soy sauce
1 teaspoon chopped fresh gingerroot
2 cloves garlic, minced
1 small onion, minced
1 teaspoon honey
1 teaspoon Dijon mustard
¼ cup extra-virgin olive oil
1 pound ½-inch-thick turkey cutlets

1. Combine orange juice, soy sauce, gingerroot, garlic, onion, honey, mustard, and olive oil in a large glass bowl.
2. Marinate turkey cutlets in olive oil mixture for 2 hours in refrigerator.
3. Grill over medium heat for 3 to 5 minutes per side until done to your taste.
4. Bring remaining marinade to a boil, pour over turkey slices, and serve.

YIELD
4 servings

PREPARATION TIME
*15 minutes + 2 hours
marinating time*

COOKING TIME
6 to 10 minutes

NUTRIENT ANALYSIS
Calories per serving: 333
Protein: 35 gm
Carbohydrates: 7.2 gm
Dietary fiber: 0.6 gm
Cholesterol: 79 mg
Total fat: 17.6 gm (158 cal)
Sat fat: 3.1 gm (28 cal)
Poly fat: 2.1 gm (19 cal)
Mono fat: 10.7 gm (94 cal)

Grilled Fish
in a
Basket

YIELD
4 servings

PREPARATION TIME
25 minutes

COOKING TIME
15 minutes

NUTRIENT ANALYSIS
Calories per serving: 359
Protein: 45 gm
Carbohydrates: 0.7 gm
Dietary fiber: 0.02 gm
Cholesterol: 70 mg
Total fat: 18 gm (166 cal)
Sat fat: 2.2 gm (20 cal)
Poly fat: 2.7 gm (24 cal)
Mono fat: 11.6 gm (104 cal)

Since fish fall apart easily and can be difficult to turn when grilling, a good solution is to split the fish lengthwise and barbecue it open faced in a wire basket. Try this method, which produces a crispy-skinned fish, with striped bass, bluefish, or salmon. Serve with corn roasted in foil and grilled tomatoes with Basic Pesto (p. 264).

¼ cup extra-virgin olive oil
1½ pounds whole fish, cleaned, head and tail removed
2 tablespoons lemon juice
¼ teaspoon dried thyme leaves
¼ teaspoon dried rosemary leaves
¼ teaspoon black pepper

1. Rub a folding wire basket with a little olive oil. Split the fish and place it in the basket.
2. In a small glass bowl, combine olive oil, lemon juice, thyme, rosemary, and pepper.
3. Brush fish with olive oil mixture. Broil for approximately 15 minutes over medium flame, turning frequently and basting with the olive oil mixture several times. Remove from grill when done to your taste.
4. When removing fish from basket, place basket over a plate. Loosen fish from the wires on the top half of the basket. Open basket and carefully turn it over onto a serving platter. Gently loosen fish from any sticking basket wires.

Foil-Wrapped Whole Fish

An alternative method of grilling whole fish is to wrap them in foil. In this recipe, whole fresh fish is wrapped in foil with olive oil, onions, and a medley of herbs. The result is moist and flavorful. Serve with grilled whole onions and baked potatoes in foil. Use minced fresh herbs if available.

¼ cup extra-virgin olive oil
1 medium onion, sliced
1½ pounds fish, cleaned, head and tail removed
¼ teaspoon black pepper
½ teaspoon chopped fresh parsley
¼ teaspoon dried tarragon leaves
¼ teaspoon dried dill leaves
¼ teaspoon dried thyme leaves
¼ teaspoon dried rosemary leaves

1. Pour half the olive oil in the center of a large piece of heavy-duty aluminum foil. Sprinkle half the onions over the olive oil.
2. Place fish on top of onions.
3. Pour the rest of the onions and olive oil over fish. Sprinkle with herbs.
4. Bring foil around fish, sealing top and ends with a double fold.
5. Place on grill over medium heat. Cook for 25 minutes, turning foil packet several times. Serve fish with juices spooned over each serving.

YIELD
4 servings

PREPARATION TIME
10 minutes

COOKING TIME
25 minutes

NUTRIENT ANALYSIS
Calories per serving: 367
Protein: 46 gm
Carbohydrates: 2.2 gm
Dietary fiber: 0.5 gm
Cholesterol: 70 mg
Total fat: 18.6 gm (167 cal)
Sat fat: 2.6 gm (23 cal)
Poly fat: 2.8 gm (25 cal)
Mono fat: 11.6 gm (104 cal)

Zesty Barbecued Fish

YIELD
4 servings

PREPARATION TIME
10 minutes

COOKING TIME
10 to 15 minutes

NUTRIENT ANALYSIS
Calories per serving: 402
Protein: 30 gm
Carbohydrates: 2.7 gm
Dietary fiber: 0.4 gm
Cholesterol: 46.7 mg
Total fat: 30 gm (270 cal)
Sat fat: 4.3 gm (38 cal)
Poly fat: 3.4 gm (30 cal)
Mono fat: 21 gm (189 cal)

A third method of grilling fish, in addition to foil wrapping and basket grilling, works well for fillets. Try this with firm mackerel, bluefish, or striped bass. This spicy barbecue sauce also works well with chicken. Serve with grilled eggplant and grilled fresh pineapple slices.

½ *cup extra-virgin olive oil*
¼ *cup wine vinegar*
½ *teaspoon dry mustard*
1 *teaspoon brown sugar*
1½ *cups water*
1 *teaspoon chili powder*
¼ *teaspoon Tabasco sauce*
¼ *teaspoon black pepper*
½ *teaspoon paprika*
½ *clove garlic, minced*
½ *medium onion, minced*
¼ *teaspoon cayenne pepper*
4 *fish fillets (1 pound)*

1. Combine olive oil, vinegar, dry mustard, brown sugar, water, chili powder, Tabasco sauce, black pepper, paprika, garlic, onion, and cayenne in a large saucepan. Bring to a boil and cook for 10 minutes.
2. Transfer the saucepan to the side of your grill. Thread each fish fillet over a long fork, piercing it in two places to hold it securely.
3. Dip the fillets in the sauce and grill over medium heat. Baste the fish with the sauce every 2 minutes and grill until done. Carefully remove from grill with a wide spatula and serve with remaining sauce.

Garlic
Shrimp

Marinate shrimp in garlic, wine, olive oil, soy sauce, and spices before grilling. Serve with sliced carrots, celery, and green pepper grilled in foil packets and cold rice pilaf.

½ cup dry white wine
½ cup extra-virgin olive oil
½ cup light soy sauce
2 teaspoons dried tarragon leaves
¼ teaspoon cayenne pepper
3 cloves garlic, minced
1½ pounds large raw shrimp, shelled and deveined
1 large lemon, cut in wedges

1. With a wire whisk, combine wine, olive oil, soy sauce, tarragon, cayenne pepper, and garlic in a large glass bowl.
2. Toss the shrimp in the marinade until well coated.
3. Cover the bowl and marinate in the refrigerator for 2 hours.
4. Remove shrimp from marinade and grill over medium heat for 5 to 7 minutes on each side, until tender. Brush with remaining marinade several times. Serve with lemon wedges.

YIELD
6 servings

PREPARATION TIME
25 minutes + 2 hours marinating time

COOKING TIME
10 to 15 minutes

NUTRIENT ANALYSIS
Calories per serving: 305.3
Protein: 26.4 gm
Carbohydrates: 2.6 gm
Dietary fiber: 0.1 gm
Cholesterol: 221.5 mg
Total fat: 19.2 gm (173 cal)
Sat fat: 2.9 gm (26 cal)
Poly fat: 2 gm (18 cal)
Mono fat: 13.4 gm (121 cal)

Scampi
in Foil

YIELD
4 servings

PREPARATION TIME
20 minutes

COOKING TIME
12 to 15 minutes

NUTRIENT ANALYSIS
Calories per serving: 353
Protein: 23 gm
Carbohydrates: 0.7 gm
Dietary fiber: 0.02 gm
Cholesterol: 221 mg
Total fat: 28 gm (253 cal)
Sat fat: 4.2 gm (37 cal)
Poly fat: 2.8 gm (25 cal)
Mono fat: 20 gm (180 cal)

Wrapping shrimp in foil packets is another quick and easy way to prepare shrimp on your barbecue. Serve with sliced zucchini and tomatoes baked in foil packets and grilled Garlic Bread (p. 275).

1 clove garlic, minced
½ cup extra-virgin olive oil
¼ teaspoon dried rosemary leaves
¼ teaspoon dried basil leaves
1½ tablespoons lemon juice
¼ teaspoon black pepper
1 pound raw medium shrimp, shelled and deveined

1. With a wire whisk, combine garlic, olive oil, rosemary, basil, lemon juice, and pepper.
2. Pour olive oil mixture over shrimp. Toss and divide shrimp into four portions. Place each portion on a square of heavy-duty aluminum foil.
3. Bring foil up over shrimp and twist ends together to seal.
4. Place on grill over medium heat and grill for 12 to 15 minutes until shrimp is pink and cooked.

Grilled Scallops

Sea scallops have a special flavor after being marinated in olive oil and lime juice and then grilled. Serve with potato slices and dill baked in foil and skewered mushrooms, green peppers, and cherry tomatoes.

2 tablespoons minced scallions
1 clove garlic, minced
2 tablespoons fresh lime juice
¼ cup extra-virgin olive oil
¼ teaspoon black pepper
1 pound scallops

1. Combine scallions, garlic, lime juice, olive oil, and black pepper in a large glass bowl.
2. Add scallops to bowl and marinate for 30 minutes.
3. Thread scallops on four skewers and grill over medium heat for 8 minutes or until done to your taste. Turn several times during cooking and baste with remaining marinade.

VARIATION
Marinate scallops in a ginger-honey marinade. Combine 3 tablespoons lemon juice, ¼ cup olive oil, 1 tablespoon honey, 1 tablespoon soy sauce, and 1 clove garlic, minced. Marinate for 3 hours in the refrigerator before grilling. Dip scallops in ¼ cup toasted sesame seeds before serving.

YIELD
4 servings

PREPARATION TIME
10 minutes + 30 minutes marinating time

COOKING TIME
Approximately 8 minutes

NUTRIENT ANALYSIS
Calories per serving: 249
Protein: 26 gm
Carbohydrates: 3 gm
Dietary fiber: 0.04 gm
Cholesterol: 60 mg
Total fat: 15 gm (135 cal)
Sat fat: 1.9 gm (17 cal)
Poly fat: 1.4 gm (12 cal)
Mono fat: 9.9 gm (89 cal)

Shish Kabob

YIELD
4 servings

PREPARATION TIME
*15 minutes + 3 hours
marinating time*

COOKING TIME
10 minutes

NUTRIENT ANALYSIS
Calories per serving: 519
Protein: 50 gm
Carbohydrates: 10 gm
Dietary fiber: 2.3 gm
Cholesterol: 167
Total fat: 31 gm (286 cal)
Sat fat: 9.4 gm (85 cal)
Poly fat: 2.3 gm (20.9 cal)
Mono fat: 16.4 gm (147 cal)

Marinated, skewered lamb dishes appear in many cuisines from the lamb brochettes of Provence to the shish kabob of Turkey. This version can be cooked over an outdoor barbecue or broiled in your oven. Serve with Lemon-Dill Rice (p. 183).

*1½ pounds boneless lamb shoulder or leg, cut into 1-inch
    cubes*
1 onion, cut in quarters
2 green bell peppers, seeded and cut into 1-inch pieces
2 tomatoes, cut in quarters
¼ cup extra-virgin flavorful olive oil
⅓ cup lemon juice
1 teaspoon black pepper
2 cloves garlic (or 1 shallot or 2 scallions), mashed
½ teaspoon dried thyme leaves
½ teaspoon dried oregano leaves

1. Place meat, onion, peppers, and tomatoes in a medium glass bowl.
2. Make marinade by combining olive oil, lemon juice, pepper, garlic, thyme, and oregano in a small bowl. Pour over lamb and vegetables. Cover and marinate for 3 hours in a cool place.
3. Thread meat and vegetables on skewers, alternating meat with vegetables. Grill over medium heat, basting with remaining marinade, for 12 minutes or until cooked to your liking.

SPANISH KABOBS
Omit marinade. Use ¼ cup olive oil; 1 small onion, chopped; 2 cloves garlic, minced; 1 tablespoon minced fresh parsley; 1 teaspoon paprika; ¼ teaspoon cayenne

pepper; ¼ teaspoon dried oregano leaves; and ¼ teaspoon ground cumin.

TERIYAKI KABOBS

Marinate 1 pound lean sirloin steak, cut in strips ¼-inch thick and 1-inch wide in a ½ cup light soy sauce, 1 teaspoon brown sugar, ¼ cup extra-virgin flavorful olive oil, 1 tablespoon minced gingerroot, ¼ teaspoon black pepper, and 2 cloves garlic, minced in a glass bowl for 2 hours in the refrigerator. Thread steak strips on four skewers, accordian style. Place a water chestnut on the end of each skewer. Broil over medium heat for 12 minutes or until done, turning often and basting with marinade.

LAMB-EGGPLANT KABOBS

Marinate 1½ pounds of lean lamb leg or shoulder, trimmed and cut in 1-inch cubes in ½ cup extra-virgin flavorful olive oil, ⅓ cup lemon juice, 1 clove garlic minced, 1 teaspoon dried rosemary leaves, 1 teaspoon dried thyme leaves, and ¼ teaspoon black pepper in a glass bowl overnight in the refrigerator. When ready to grill, peel the eggplant and cut it into 1-inch pieces. Alternately thread lamb and eggplant cubes onto skewers. Brush with leftover marinade and barbecue over medium heat for 10 minutes. Brush with marinade and cook for 10 more minutes or until lamb is cooked to your liking.

FISH KABOBS

Marinate 1 pound firm, meaty fish steaks or fillets, cut in 1-inch pieces in ½ cup extra-virgin olive oil, ¼ cup wine vinegar, 1 clove garlic minced, ¼ teaspoon dried oregano

(continued)

in a glass bowl in the refrigerator for 30 minutes. Thread fish chunks on skewers alternating with 1 large onion, cut in 1-inch cubes; 1 medium green bell pepper, seeded and cut in 1-inch pieces; 12 cherry tomatoes; and 1 small zucchini, cut in 1-inch slices. Grill kabobs for approximately 5 minutes on each side, basting with remaining marinade.

MIXED VEGETABLE KABOBS

Steam 1 medium zucchini, cut in ¾-inch slices and 1 medium yellow squash cut in ¾-inch slices for 3 minutes. Steam 8 small onions for 10 minutes. Cool onions and peel. Add 1 small eggplant, cut in ¾-inch slices; 1 medium red bell pepper, seeded and cut in 8 pieces; and 8 large mushrooms. Marinate in 1 tablespoon lemon juice, 1 tablespoon wine vinegar, 1 clove garlic, minced, 1 teaspoon dried basil leaves, ¼ teaspoon dried thyme leaves, 1 tablespoon chopped fresh parsley, 1 teaspoon Dijon mustard, ¼ cup extra-virgin olive oil, and ¼ teaspoon black pepper in a glass bowl 4 hours in the refrigerator. Stir frequently. Thread vegetables alternately on four skewers and grill over medium heat for 10 minutes on each side or until done to suit your taste. Baste frequently with remaining marinade.

VEGETABLE-FRENCH BREAD KABOBS

Soak 1 loaf French bread, cut in 1-inch cubes in ½ cup extra-virgin flavorful olive oil. Alternately thread barbecue skewers with a cube of bread, a large fresh mushroom, a 1-inch cube of low-skim mozzarella cheese, a cube of bread, a cherry tomato, a cube of cheese, a cube of bread, a 1-inch square piece of green bell pepper, a cube of cheese, and a final cube of bread. Barbecue skewers over moderate heat for 10 minutes until bread is toasted and cheese melts. Eat at once.

Grilled Potatoes and Pesto

Grill red potatoes with Parmesan cheese and the pesto of your choice in foil packets. Serve with grilled turkey burgers and Dilled Lentil Salad (p. 82).

1½ pounds red potatoes, scrubbed and cut in half
¼ cup pesto (any from p. 264)
1 tablespoon grated Parmesan cheese

1. Boil potatoes in a large pan of water for 10 minutes over medium heat. Drain and cool.
2. Cut four 10-inch pieces of heavy-duty aluminum foil. Place a quarter of the potatoes on each piece of foil. Spoon 1 tablespoon pesto on each potato packet. Sprinkle with Parmesan cheese and wrap packets securely.
3. Grill foil packets over medium heat for 10 minutes.

YIELD
4 servings

PREPARATION TIME
10 minutes

COOKING TIME
20 minutes

NUTRIENT ANALYSIS
Calories per serving: 272
Protein: 3.6 gm
Carbohydrates: 34.1 gm
Dietary fiber: 1.9 gm
Cholesterol: 1.2 mg
Total fat: 14 gm (127 cal)
Sat fat: 2.3 gm (21 cal)
Poly fat: 1.2 gm (11 cal)
Mono fat: 10 gm (90 cal)

Grilled Garlic Bread

.... ⊙ ....

YIELD

4 servings, 3 slices each

PREPARATION TIME

5 minutes

NUTRIENT ANALYSIS

Calories per serving: 278
Protein: 0.1 gm
Carbohydrates: 32 gm
Dietary fiber: 0 gm
Cholesterol: 0 mg
Total fat: 14 gm (126 cal)
Sat fat: 1.9 gm (17 cal)
Poly fat: 1.3 gm (12 cal)
Mono fat: 10 gm (90 cal)

Traditional garlic bread tastes better than ever when prepared on your outdoor grill! Serve with a platter of ripe tomato slices and cubes of low-skim mozzarella.

1 medium-sized loaf French bread, cut into ½-inch slices
2 cloves garlic, cut in half
¼ cup extra-virgin flavorful olive oil
¼ teaspoon black pepper

1. Toast the bread slices on the grill over moderate heat until the marks from the grill appear on the surface of the bread.
2. Remove from grill and rub while hot with whole garlic cloves.
3. Drizzle with olive oil, sprinkle with pepper, and serve.

ON THE
SIDE

DRESSINGS
SAUCES
MARINADES
PESTOS
ROUILLES
FLAVORED OILS
SUN-DRIED TOMATOES

CITRUS DRESSING ⊙
PARSLEY DRESSING ⊙
RED ONION DRESSING ⊙
BASIC VINAIGRETTE ⊙
TOMATO DRESSING ⊙
ONE EGG BLENDER MAYONNAISE ⊙
CHILI PEPPER BARBECUE SAUCE ⊙
ROMESCO SAUCE
WINE BASTING SAUCE
CAYENNE SAUCE ⊙
CUBAN SAUCE ⊙
GREEK OIL AND LEMON SAUCE ⊙
BASIC TOMATO SAUCE (CANNED TOMATOES)
BASIC TOMATO SAUCE (FRESH TOMATOES)
SPICY TOMATO SAUCE WITH WINE
VEGETABLE-PESTO SAUCE
BASIC MARINADE ⊙
TERIYAKI SAUCE ⊙
HAWAIIAN MARINADE ⊙
SESAME MARINADE FOR FISH ⊙
MEXICAN MARINADE FOR BEEF ⊙
WINE MARINADE FOR LAMB ⊙
PINE NUT PARMESAN PESTO ⊙
BASIC ROUILLE ⊙
EASY BLENDER ROUILLE ⊙
FLAVORED OLIVE OIL
SUN-DRIED TOMATOES

Citrus Dressing

This tangy dressing spiced with ginger works well with fruit or poultry salads.

⅓ cup orange juice
1 tablespoon lemon juice
2 teaspoons minced, peeled fresh gingerroot
3 scallions, thinly sliced
2 tablespoons wine vinegar
¼ teaspoon black pepper
½ cup mild, light flavored olive oil

1. In a medium bowl, mix orange juice, lemon juice, gingerroot, scallions, vinegar, and pepper with a fork or wire whisk.
2. Slowly add oil, whisking until dressing has thickened. Serve at room temperature.

VARIATION
Omit gingerroot. Add 1 tablespoon minced fresh dill and pour over red potato salad.

YIELD
8 servings (2 tablespoons each)

PREPARATION TIME
10 minutes

NUTRIENT ANALYSIS
Calories per serving: 132
Protein: 0.23 gm
Carbohydrates: 4.1 gm
Dietary fiber: 0.2 gm
Cholesterol: 0 mg
Total fat: 13.5 gm (122 cal)
Sat fat: 1.9 gm (17 cal)
Poly fat: 1.1 gm (9.9 cal)
Mono fat: 9.3 gm (84 cal)

Parsley
Dressing

YIELD
14 servings
(2 tablespoons each)

PREPARATION TIME
10 minutes

NUTRIENT ANALYSIS
Calories per serving: 107
Protein: 0.3 gm
Carbohydrates: 1.4 gm
Dietary fiber: 0.4 gm
Cholesterol: 0 mg
Total fat: 11.7 gm (104 cal)
Sat fat: 1.7 gm (15 cal)
Poly fat: 1 gm (9 cal)
Mono fat: 9 gm (81 cal)

This smooth, tangy dressing can be used on green salads, poultry, fish, or seafood salads.

2 cups packed parsley leaves
1 cup chives, cut into 1-inch pieces
1 clove garlic
2 tablespoons Dijon mustard
¾ cup extra-virgin flavorful olive oil
¼ cup wine vinegar
3 tablespoons lemon juice
¼ teaspoon black pepper

1. Puree the parsley, chives, and garlic in a blender or food processor.
2. Add mustard, olive oil, vinegar, lemon juice, and black pepper. Blend until smooth.

Red
Onion
Dressing

Mild red onions, wine vinegar, and dry mustard give this dressing a zesty flavor that works particularly well with mixed green salads.

1 cup extra-virgin flavorful olive oil
¼ cup lemon juice
¼ cup wine vinegar
½ teaspoon dry mustard
1 teaspoon finely chopped red onion
½ teaspoon dried oregano leaves
½ teaspoon dried thyme leaves
2 cloves garlic, minced

1. Combine all ingredients in a tightly covered jar and shake energetically until ingredients are well blended.
2. Store at room temperature for 2 or 3 hours before using.

YIELD
12 servings
(2 tablespoons each)

PREPARATION TIME
10 minutes

NUTRIENT ANALYSIS
Calories per serving: 161
Protein: 0.1 gm
Carbohydrates: 1 gm
Dietary fiber: 0 gm
Cholesterol: 0 mg
Total fat: 18 gm (162 cal)
Sat fat: 2.6 gm (23 cal)
Poly fat: 1.5 gm (14 cal)
Mono fat: 13.3 gm (120 cal)

Basic Vinaigrette

YIELD
10 servings
(2 tablespoons each)

PREPARATION TIME
10 minutes

NUTRIENT ANALYSIS
Calories per serving: 191
Protein: 0 gm
Carbohydrates: 0.5 gm
Dietary fiber: 0 gm
Cholesterol: 0 mg
Total fat: 22 gm (190 cal)
Sat fat: 3.1 gm (28 cal)
Poly fat: 1.8 gm (16 cal)
Mono fat: 15.9 gm (143 cal)

Basic vinaigrette dressing can be adapted to highlight a wide variety of salad recipes and provide a unique menu accent. Try serving Cumin Vinaigrette with a meal with a Mexican accent or Sesame Vinaigrette when you're serving Oriental dishes.

⅓ cup wine or cider vinegar
¼ teaspoon salt (optional)
¼ teaspoon black pepper
1 cup extra-virgin flavorful olive oil

1. Mix vinegar, salt, and pepper with a fork or wire whisk.
2. Slowly whisk in oil until well blended.

VARIATIONS
• Herb Vinaigrette: Add 1 teaspoon each dried mustard, basil, tarragon.
• Anchovy Vinaigrette: Add 2 ounces of chopped anchovy fillets.
• Avocado Vinaigrette: Add ¼ cup mashed avocado and ½ teaspoon Worcestershire sauce.
• Balsamic Vinaigrette: Omit wine vinegar. Use balsamic vinegar. Add 1 tablespoon of minced shallots and ¼ teaspoon dried marjoram leaves.
• Chive Vinaigrette: Add 2 teaspoons minced fresh chives.
• Cranberry Vinaigrette: Add 2 tablespoons of chopped raw cranberries.
• Creamy Dijon Vinaigrette: Add 2 teaspoons Dijon mustard and ½ tablespoon of mayonnaise.
• Cumin Vinaigrette: Add ½ teaspoon ground cumin.
• Curry Vinaigrette: Add 2 teaspoons curry powder and 1 tablespoon finely chopped scallions.

- Dijon Vinaigrette: Add 2 teaspoons Dijon mustard.
- Honey-Dijon Vinaigrette: Add 1 tablespoon of Dijon mustard and 2 tablespoons of honey.
- Mint Vinaigrette: Add 2 tablespoons chopped fresh mint.
- Olive Vinaigrette: Add ¼ cup chopped black or green olives.
- Orange Vinaigrette: Omit wine vinegar. Use champagne vinegar. Add 2 teaspoons grated orange rind and 3 tablespoons of fresh orange juice.
- Nut Vinaigrette: Add ¼ cup finely chopped almonds or walnuts.
- Parmesan Vinaigrette: Add 1 tablespoon of Parmesan cheese.
- Parsley-Scallion Vinaigrette: Add 1 tablespoon chopped fresh parsley and 1 finely chopped scallion.
- Pickle Vinaigrette: Add 1 tablespoon minced fresh parsley, 2 tablespoons minced dill pickle, 1 tablespoon minced green bell pepper, and 1 teaspoon grated onion.
- Raspberry Vinaigrette: Omit wine vinegar. Use raspberry vinegar.
- Rosy Vinaigrette: Add 1 tablespoon ketchup, ¼ teaspoon dried tarragon leaves, ¼ teaspoon dry mustard, ¼ teaspoon paprika.
- Sesame Vinaigrette: Omit wine vinegar. Use rice vinegar. Add 2 cloves minced garlic and 2 tablespoons of toasted sesame seeds.

Tomato Dressing

YIELD
8 servings

PREPARATION TIME
10 minutes

NUTRIENT ANALYSIS
Calories per serving: 55
Protein: 0.3 gm
Carbohydrates: 1.7 gm
Dietary fiber: 0.6 gm
Cholesterol: 0 mg
Total fat: 5.5 gm (50 cal)
Sat fat: 0.8 gm (7 cal)
Poly fat: 0.5 gm (4 cal)
Mono fat: 4 gm (36 cal)

This quick and easy blender dressing is made from fresh tomatoes. Try it with a salad of romaine lettuce, scallions, and cucumbers.

3 medium ripe fresh tomatoes
¼ cup extra-virgin flavorful olive oil
1 clove garlic, minced
¼ teaspoon cayenne pepper

1. Cut tomatoes into quarters.
2. Place tomatoes, olive oil, garlic, and cayenne pepper in a blender container. Blend until smooth.

One Egg Blender Mayonnaise

YIELD
8 servings (2 tablespoons each)

PREPARATION TIME
10 minutes

Although it isn't possible to make authentic mayonnaise without egg yolks, this version reduces the cholesterol by only using one yolk. Remember to include the yolk in your weekly allowance!

1. Mix mustard, lemon juice, and egg in an electric blender. Let sit for 3 minutes.
2. Add olive oil slowly in a very thin stream. Push down around edges with a rubber spatula.
3. Refrigerate for an hour before serving.

VARIATION

Omit whole-grain mustard. Use ¼ teaspoon dry mustard, 1 minced garlic clove, and ¼ teaspoon black pepper.

NUTRIENT ANALYSIS
Calories per serving: 187
Protein: 0.3 gm
Carbohydrates: 0.02 gm
Dietary fiber: 0.0 gm
Cholesterol: 34 mg
Total fat: 21 gm (189 cal)
Sat fat: 3.1 gm (28 cal)
Poly fat: 1.8 gm (16 cal)
Mono fat: 15 gm (135 cal)

SAUCES

One of the easiest and quickest ways to add olive oil to your diet is by using sauces and marinades that include it. Although many of the recipes in other chapters incorporate sauces, we have added a collection of sauces and marinades for you to mix and match with your favorite foods. For the best taste, use extra-virgin flavorful olive oil.

Chili Pepper Barbecue Sauce

Like many of our barbecue traditions, this spicy sauce comes from south of the Rio Grande. Use as a basting sauce for grilling or roasting meat and poultry.

½ cup extra-virgin flavorful olive oil
1 medium onion, chopped
1 clove garlic, minced
1 small fresh chili pepper, minced
2 tablespoons chili powder
2 large ripe tomatoes, cut up
¼ cup wine vinegar
¼ cup water
½ teaspoon salt (optional)

1. Heat 1 tablespoon olive oil in a skillet. Sauté onions for 5 minutes until softened.
2. Add garlic, chili pepper, chili powder, and tomatoes and simmer until sauce starts to thicken.
3. Add vinegar, water, and salt (if desired). Cook for 8 minutes, stirring constantly. Use immediately or refrigerate for later use.

YIELD
8 ¼-cup servings or 2 cups of sauce

PREPARATION TIME
10 minutes

COOKING TIME
15 minutes

NUTRIENT ANALYSIS
Calories per serving: 136
Protein: 0.7 gm
Carbohydrates: 3.6 gm
Dietary fiber: 0.6 gm
Cholesterol: 0 mg
Total fat: 14 gm (124 cal)
Sat fat: 1.9 gm (17 cal)
Poly fat: 1.2 gm (11 cal)
Mono fat: 10 gm (90 cal)

Romesco Sauce

....

YIELD
*7 ¼-cup servings or
1¾ cups of sauce*

PREPARATION TIME
*10 minutes + overnight
soaking time*

NUTRIENT ANALYSIS
Calories per serving: 302
Protein: 4.4 gm
Carbohydrates: 19.7 gm
Dietary fiber: 0.7 gm
Cholesterol: 0 mg
Total fat: 25.7 gm (231 cal)
Sat fat: 3.6 gm (32 cal)
Poly fat: 2.5 gm (23 cal)
Mono fat: 18 gm (165 cal)

Romesco Sauce originated on the northern Mediterranean coast of Spain and is noted for its fiery qualities. Try serving it with cod, shellfish, or vegetables. It can be kept in the refrigerator for several weeks.

2 small dried red chili peppers
¼ cup blanched slivered almonds
1 tomato, peeled, seeded, and finely chopped
3 cloves garlic, peeled
¾ cup extra-virgin flavorful olive oil
¼ cup red wine vinegar

1. Soak peppers for several hours or overnight in a small quantity of cold water.
2. Heat oven to 350° F. Toast almonds on a baking sheet for 10 minutes.
3. Process peppers, tomato, almonds, and garlic in a blender or food processor until well blended.
4. Add olive oil to blender or food processor container in a steady stream with the machine on. When sauce starts to become thick, add vinegar and blend until smooth.

Wine Basting Sauce

This sauce can be adapted for use with fish, poultry, or meat by varying the type of wine and choice of herbs.

2 cloves garlic (or 2 shallots or 2 scallions), minced
1 cup dry white wine or red wine
¼ cup lemon juice
1 cup extra-virgin flavorful olive oil
1 teaspoon black pepper
1 teaspoon dried thyme, basil, or oregano leaves

1. Simmer all ingredients over low heat for 30 minutes in a small covered saucepan.
2. Use warm or cold sauce to baste fish, meat, or poultry. Can be refrigerated up to one week.

YIELD
9 ¼-cup servings or 2¼ cups
sauce

PREPARATION TIME
10 minutes

COOKING TIME
30 minutes

NUTRIENT ANALYSIS
Calories per serving: 236
Protein: 0.1 gm
Carbohydrates: 1.1 gm
Dietary fiber: 0.07 gm
Cholesterol: 0 mg
Total fat: 24 gm (216 cal)
Sat fat: 3.4 gm (31 cal)
Poly fat: 2.03 gm (18 cal)
Mono fat: 17.7 gm (159 cal)

Cayenne
Sauce

YIELD
4 ½-cup servings or
2 cups of sauce

PREPARATION TIME
10 minutes

COOKING TIME
20 minutes

NUTRIENT ANALYSIS
Calories per serving: 144
Protein: 1.6 gm
Carbohydrates: 5.5 gm
Dietary fiber: 2 gm
Cholesterol: 0 mg
Total fat: 13.8 gm (124 cal)
Sat fat: 2 gm (18 cal)
Poly fat: 1.2 gm (11 cal)
Mono fat: 10 gm (90 cal)

This sauce is made with canned tomatoes and can be served with pasta or vegetables.

¼ cup extra-virgin flavorful olive oil
1 1-pound can plum tomatoes, drained and chopped
1 clove garlic (or 2 shallots or 2 scallions), minced
½ teaspoon dried tarragon leaves
⅛ teaspoon cayenne pepper
1½ tablespoons minced fresh parsley
¼ teaspoon black pepper

1. Heat oil in a medium, nonaluminum saucepan over moderate heat.
2. Add all remaining ingredients. Cover and simmer over low heat for 20 minutes, stirring occasionally with a wooden spoon.

Cuban Sauce

This sauce is traditionally eaten with black beans, and it also tastes wonderful with meat, poultry, or seafood.

4 medium red bell peppers, quartered, seeded, and cored
¼ cup extra-virgin flavorful olive oil
2 garlic cloves (or 2 shallots or 2 scallions), minced
¾ cup canned drained and chopped plum tomatoes
¼ teaspoon sugar
¼ teaspoon black pepper
⅛ teaspoon cayenne pepper
¼ teaspoon dried oregano leaves
1 tablespoon red wine vinegar

1. Heat broiler. Put peppers on a baking sheet and rub well with some olive oil (reserve remaining oil).
2. Place peppers under broiler, 3 inches from heat, turning frequently until all sides are blackened and charred.
3. Let peppers cool. Peel with a sharp paring knife.
4. Process peppers in a blender or food processor with garlic and tomatoes until smooth. Add sugar, black and red pepper, and oregano.
5. Simmer in a saucepan over low heat, adding remaining olive oil. Simmer for 20 minutes or until thickened, stirring occasionally with a wooden spoon.
6. Pour in vinegar immediately before serving. Eat warm or at room temperature.

YIELD
4 servings

PREPARATION TIME
10 minutes

COOKING TIME
20 minutes

NUTRIENT ANALYSIS
Calories per serving: 151.9
Protein: 1.2 gm
Carbohydrates: 7.6 gm
Dietary fiber: 1.8 gm
Cholesterol: 0 mg
Total fat: 14 gm (126 cal)
Sat fat: 2 gm (18 cal)
Poly fat: 1.4 gm (13 cal)
Mono fat: 10 gm (90 cal)

Greek Oil and Lemon Sauce

YIELD
*4 1/8-cup servings or
1/2 cup of sauce*

PREPARATION TIME
10 minutes

NUTRIENT ANALYSIS
Calories per serving: 241
Protein: 0.07 gm
Carbohydrates: 0.8 gm
Dietary fiber: 0.09 gm
Cholesterol: 0 mg
Total fat: 27 gm (243 cal)
Sat fat: 3.8 gm (34 cal)
Poly fat: 2.3 gm (20 cal)
Mono fat: 20 gm (180 cal)

This versatile sauce can be used in place of mayonnaise over broiled or poached fish, poured over salads, and as a dressing for steamed vegetables. It can also be used to baste fish that is being grilled outdoors or cooked under a broiler to prevent it from drying out.

1/2 cup extra-virgin flavorful olive oil
2 tablespoons lemon juice
1/4 teaspoon black pepper
1 tablespoon chopped fresh parsley

1. Process oil, lemon juice, and pepper in blender container.
2. Add parsley and process until well blended.

Basic Tomato Sauce (Canned Tomatoes)

....

Use this all-purpose sauce on pasta, meat, fish, or vegetable dishes.

1 cup chopped onion
1 clove garlic, minced
5 tablespoons extra-virgin flavorful olive oil
½ cup chopped fresh parsley
¼ cup chopped fresh basil (or 1 tablespoon dried basil leaves)
¾ cup tomato paste
2½ cups canned plum tomatoes, including liquid
½ teaspoon sugar
⅛ teaspoon salt
⅛ teaspoon black pepper

1. Sauté onion and garlic in oil in a heavy, nonaluminum saucepan for 3 minutes.
2. Add all remaining ingredients and stir with a wooden spoon.
3. Bring sauce to a boil and reduce heat to low. Simmer for 1 hour, stirring occasionally. Use immediately or refrigerate and use as needed.

YIELD
5 1-cup servings

PREPARATION TIME
10 minutes

COOKING TIME
1 hour

NUTRIENT ANALYSIS
Calories per serving: 200
Protein: 3.7 gm
Carbohydrates: 18 gm
Dietary fiber: 1.6 gm
Cholesterol: 0 mg
Total fat: 14 gm (130 cal)
Sat fat: 2 gm (19 cal)
Poly fat: 1.4 gm (13 cal)
Mono fat: 10 gm (90 cal)

Basic Tomato Sauce (Fresh Tomatoes)

YIELD
*4 ¾-cup
servings*

PREPARATION TIME
15 minutes

COOKING TIME
50 minutes

NUTRIENT ANALYSIS
Calories per serving: 205
Protein: 3.7 gm
Carbohydrates: 18.9 gm
Dietary fiber: 6.5 gm
Cholesterol: 0 mg
Total fat: 14 gm (130 cal)
Sat fat: 2 gm (18 cal)
Poly fat: 1.5 gm (14 cal)
Mono fat: 10 gm (90 cal)

This simple, thick tomato sauce freezes well and can be served on pasta or used as a base for soups and stews.

3 pounds ripe fresh plum tomatoes
1 large onion, finely chopped
¼ cup extra-virgin flavorful olive oil
¼ teaspoon black pepper
¼ teaspoon sugar
1 teaspoon dried oregano leaves
1 tablespoon dried basil leaves

1. Immerse tomatoes in boiling water for 1 minute. Remove from water, plunge into cold water, and peel off skins, using a sharp paring knife.
2. In a heavy, nonaluminum saucepan, sauté onion 3 to 5 minutes in oil until tender. Stir with a wooden spoon.
3. Add tomatoes, pepper, sugar, oregano, and basil. Cover and simmer over low heat for 45 minutes, stirring occasionally.
4. If not using immediately, cool and pour into a jar and cover with ¼ inch of olive oil. Will keep in refrigerator for one week.

VARIATIONS
• For a hotter sauce, add fresh, grated horseradish or horseradish sauce to taste.
• For a thinner sauce, cook only for 20 minutes.

Spicy Tomato Sauce with Wine

....

Try serving this all-purpose tomato sauce as a topping for roast potatoes.

1/4 cup extra-virgin flavorful olive oil
2 tablespoons minced onion
1 clove garlic, minced
3 medium ripe tomatoes, chopped
1 tablespoon tomato paste
1/2 cup dry white wine
2 tablespoons water
1 tablespoon minced fresh parsley
1/4 teaspoon cayenne pepper
Dash of Tabasco sauce
1 bay leaf
1/8 teaspoon sugar
1/4 teaspoon black pepper

1. Heat oil in a skillet and sauté onion and garlic for 3 to 5 minutes until softened. Add tomatoes and stir-fry for two minutes or more.
2. Add remaining ingredients and stir. Cover and simmer for 30 minutes. Strain sauce before serving.

YIELD
4 1/2-cup servings

PREPARATION TIME
20 minutes

COOKING TIME
35 minutes

NUTRIENT ANALYSIS
Calories per serving: 144
Protein: 1.1 gm
Carbohydrates: 5.6 gm
Dietary fiber: 1.7 gm
Cholesterol: 0 mg
Total fat: 14 gm (124 cal)
Sat fat: 2 gm (18 cal)
Poly fat: 1.2 gm (11 cal)
Mono fat: 10 gm (90 cal)

Vegetable-Pesto Sauce

....

YIELD
4 1¼-cup servings

PREPARATION TIME
20 minutes

COOKING TIME
25 to 30 minutes

NUTRIENT ANALYSIS
Calories per serving: 275
Protein: 1.9 gm
Carbohydrates: 7 gm
Dietary fiber: 2.5 gm
Cholesterol: 0.1 mg
Total fat: 27 gm (248 cal)
Sat fat: 4 gm (27 cal)
Poly fat: 2.5 gm (23 cal)
Mono fat: 20 gm (180 cal)

This sauce makes an excellent meal when served with pasta and grated cheese.

¼ cup extra-virgin flavorful olive oil
1 cup julienne sliced red bell peppers
1 cup julienne sliced zucchini
1 cup julienne sliced yellow squash
½ cup diced eggplant
⅓ cup minced red or Bermuda onion
¼ cup pesto (any from p. 264)
½ cup low-salt chicken broth
¼ teaspoon black pepper
¼ teaspoon crushed dried red peppers

1. Heat oil in skillet over moderate heat. Add peppers, zucchini, yellow squash, and eggplant. Stir and sauté for 5 minutes.
2. Add onion and cook for 3 more minutes.
3. Stir in Pesto and chicken broth. Cook about 15 minutes until sauce is reduced by ⅓.

MARINADES

M arinades can be mixed with a wooden spoon, shaken in a jar, or mixed in a blender. They can be prepared fresh or in advance and stored in a jar in the refrigerator, overnight or longer.

Wash, wipe, and dry foods before marinating; do not marinate frozen foods since they will dilute the marinade as they thaw. Place foods to be marinated in glass, ceramic, enamel, or stainless steel containers. Avoid plastic, cast-iron, aluminum, or copper containers.

Foods to be marinated less than an hour can be left out at room temperature in a covered container. For longer marinating times, cover and store foods in the refrigerator. While delicate fish may require only an hour to marinate, tough meat may require as much as two days.

If food is not completely immersed in marinade, remember to turn it several times. Marinating tenderizes food and may consequently reduce cooking time by as much as one third.

Basic Marinade

YIELD
4 ½-cup servings, 1 cup
marinade

PREPARATION TIME
10 minutes

NUTRIENT ANALYSIS
Calories per serving: 360
Protein: 0 gm
Carbohydrates: 0.9 gm
Dietary fiber: 0.03 gm
Cholesterol: 0 mg
Total fat: 40.5 gm (365 cal)
Sat fat: 5.8 gm (52 cal)
Poly fat: 3.5 gm (31 cal)
Mono fat: 30 gm (0.27 cal)

Use this herb marinade for marinating and basting 1 pound of chicken, fish, or meat.

2 tablespoons wine vinegar
1 clove garlic (or ½ shallot or 2 scallions), minced
1 tablespoon Dijon mustard
¼ teaspoon dried parsley leaves
¼ teaspoon dried thyme leaves
¼ teaspoon dried marjoram leaves
¾ cup extra-virgin flavorful olive oil
¼ teaspoon black pepper

1. In a small bowl, mix vinegar with garlic, mustard, parsley, thyme, and marjoram.
2. Whisk in olive oil and black pepper.

Teriyaki Sauce

Teriyaki Sauce can be used as a marinade for chicken, fish, and lean beef strips or flank steak. Place chicken, fish, or beef in a glass dish and pour marinade over it. To marinate chicken or beef, cover and refrigerate overnight. To marinate fish, cover and refrigerate for 1 hour. Also use Teriyaki Sauce as a basting sauce while cooking poultry and seafood.

¼ cup extra-virgin flavorful olive oil
¼ cup light soy sauce
¼ cup pineapple juice
2 tablespoons wine vinegar
1 teaspoon ground ginger
2 tablespoons chopped scallions
1 clove garlic, minced
1 tablespoon dry sherry

1. Combine ingredients in a jar and shake energetically until well combined.
2. Pour over chicken or fish.

YIELD
4 ½-cup servings, 2 cups sauce

PREPARATION TIME
10 minutes + marinating time

NUTRIENT ANALYSIS
Calories per serving: 145
Protein: 2 gm
Carbohydrates: 4.4 gm
Dietary fiber: 0.05 gm
Cholesterol: 0 mg
Total fat: 13.5 gm (122 cal)
Sat fat: 1.9 gm (17 cal)
Poly fat: 1.2 gm (11 cal)
Mono fat: 9.9 gm (90 cal)

Hawaiian
Marinade

YIELD

8 ½-cup servings,
2 cups marinade

PREPARATION TIME

10 minutes

NUTRIENT ANALYSIS

Calories per serving: 49
Protein: 0.9 gm
Carbohydrates: 4.3 gm
Dietary fiber: 0.5 gm
Cholesterol: 0 mg
Total fat: 3.4 gm (30 cal)
Sat fat: 0.5 gm (4 cal)
Poly fat: 0.3 gm (3 cal)
Mono fat: 2.5 gm (23 cal)

This marinade gives a Polynesian flavor to chicken, fish, or ribs.

1 16-ounce can of juice-pack crushed pineapple
½ cup light soy sauce
¼ cup extra-virgin olive oil
¼ teaspoon ground ginger

1. In a glass bowl, mix pineapple and soy sauce with a fork or wire whisk.
2. Whisk in the olive oil and ginger.

Sesame Marinade for Fish

Use this marinade for fish fillets or kabobs.

¼ cup extra-virgin flavorful olive oil
⅓ cup lemon juice
1 tablespoon grated lemon rind
1 tablespoon light soy sauce
1 teaspoon honey
2 tablespoons toasted sesame seeds
2 tablespoons chopped fresh parsley

1. Combine olive oil, lemon juice, lemon peel, soy sauce, and honey with a fork or wire whisk.
2. Whisk in sesame seeds and parsley.

YIELD
4 servings, ¾ cup marinade

PREPARATION TIME
10 minutes

NUTRIENT ANALYSIS
Calories per serving: 156
Protein: 1.5 gm
Carbohydrates: 3.9 gm
Dietary fiber: 0.05 gm
Cholesterol: 0 mg
Total fat: 15.7 gm (141 cal)
Sat fat: 1.9 gm (17 cal)
Poly fat: 1.1 gm (10 cal)
Mono fat: 10 gm (90 cal)

Mexican Marinade for Beef

YIELD
4 servings, 1 cup marinade

PREPARATION TIME
10 minutes

NUTRIENT ANALYSIS
Calories per serving: 132
Protein: 0.3 gm
Carbohydrates: 3.2 gm
Dietary fiber: 0.3 gm
Cholesterol: 0 mg
Total fat: 13.5 gm (122 cal)
Sat fat: 1.9 gm (17 cal)
Poly fat: 1.2 gm (10 cal)
Mono fat: 10 gm (90 cal)

This spicy marinade can be poured over lean steak. Marinate steak overnight and broil.

¼ *cup extra-virgin flavorful olive oil*
¼ *cup orange juice*
¼ *cup tomato juice*
¼ *cup lime juice*
1 teaspoon paprika
1 teaspoon dried ground cumin
1 teaspoon dried oregano leaves
½ *teaspoon crushed dried red peppers*
1 clove garlic, minced

1. Combine olive oil, orange juice, tomato juice, and lime juice with a fork or wire whisk.
2. Whisk in remaining ingredients.

Wine Marinade for Lamb

.... Q ....

Marinate lamb for dishes such as Souvlakia overnight in this lemon-and-wine–flavored marinade.

¼ cup extra-virgin flavorful olive oil
½ cup lemon juice
¼ cup dry white wine
¼ teaspoon dried thyme leaves
¼ teaspoon dried rosemary leaves
¼ teaspoon dried oregano leaves
1 bay leaf
2 cloves garlic, minced
¼ teaspoon black pepper

1. Combine olive oil, lemon juice, and white wine with a fork or wire whisk.
2. Whisk in remaining ingredients.

YIELD
4 servings, 1 cup marinade

PREPARATION TIME
10 minutes

NUTRIENT ANALYSIS
Calories per serving: 138
Protein: 0.2 gm
Carbohydrates: 2.6 gm
Dietary fiber: 0.1 gm
Cholesterol: 0 mg
Total fat: 13.5 gm (122 cal)
Sat fat: 1.9 gm (69 cal)
Poly fat: 1.2 gm (11 cal)
Mono fat: 10 gm (90 cal)

PESTOS AND ROUILLES

....

PESTO SAUCES

Pesto sauce, an Italian creation, is a thick sauce or paste of herbs, garlic, cheese, nuts, and olive oil. Pesto means pounded, and the ingredients in pesto are pounded or blended until they become a sauce. Learning to make and enjoy pesto sauces is an easy, delicious, and practical way to incorporate olive oil into your diet. While classic pesto sauce is made with fresh basil, other fresh herbs are often used as well. When fresh herbs are seasonally unavailable, dried herbs can be substituted. Vegetables such as spinach, curly parsley, flat Italian parsley, coriander, Chinese parsley (cilantro), and watercress can also become pesto bases.

Prepared pestos can be purchased, but because they are so flavorful and simple to make, we highly recommend making your own.

TIPS ON MAKING AND USING PESTOS

- Pesto can be made by hand using a mortar and pestle or in your food processor or blender. Our recipes suggest using a blender, but they will work equally well with the mortar and pestle method.
- You can keep homemade pesto in the refrigerator for 3 or 4 weeks. Pack it into a small plastic container and cover it with a thin layer of olive oil. Then tightly cover to prevent discoloring or spoiling. When you are ready to use it, you may notice some slight discoloration on the surface, but this won't harm the flavor. Stir the discolored top layer into the rest of the pesto in the container and remove what you need. Add some more olive oil to the remaining pesto in the container, re-cover, and return to the refrigerator. If you make pesto without cheese for storing and add when serving, it will keep even longer.
- Frozen pesto can be kept for 9 months. It's a good idea to freeze it in small quantities to make it easy to thaw the specific amount you need for each recipe.
- You can freeze pesto in ½ cup or 1 cup plastic containers that have tight lids. You don't need to add the layer of olive oil on top. For smaller portions, freeze pesto by the tablespoon on baking sheets covered with

wax paper. When the pesto ovals are frozen, transfer them to a plastic bag and fasten the top with a twist-tie to store.

- If you have fresh basil available and no time to spend in the kitchen making pesto, there's a quick alternative way to freeze it. Chop the basil and place a tablespoon of chopped basil in each compartment of an ice cube tray. Then add enough olive oil to fill the trays three-fourths full. Freeze the cubes and store the frozen basil-oil blocks in a plastic bag for later use.

QUICK TIPS FOR USING PESTOS

1. Stuff large mushrooms with pesto, top with bread crumbs, and place under broiler until bread crumbs are browned.
2. Use pesto as a spread for bread or baked potatoes.
3. Add pesto to soups or stews. Add to sautéed or steamed vegetable combinations.
4. Baste poultry or meat with pesto that has been thinned with basting juices and a small quantity of oil or wine.
5. Add a few tablespoons of pesto to a bread recipe to create flavorful, pungent herb breads.
6. Toss your favorite cooked pasta with pesto, a little 1 percent milk, and some grated Parmesan cheese.
7. Use as a base for pasta sauce or for flavoring for dishes such as calzone or lasagne.
8. Sauté leftover seafood or poultry, steamed vegetables, and cooked rice in olive oil mixed with pesto.
9. Use as an omelette filling for omelettes made with a reduced quantity of egg yolks or egg substitute.
10. Stir a tablespoon into your favorite salad dressing.
11. Top seafood or poultry with pesto before broiling.

Pine Nut
Parmesan
Pesto

YIELD
4 servings, 1 cup pesto

PREPARATION TIME
15 minutes

NUTRIENT ANALYSIS
Calories per serving: 339
Protein: 5 gm
Carbohydrates: 21.5 gm
Dietary fiber: 0.05 gm
Cholesterol: 0 mg
Total fat: 28.3 gm (256 cal)
Sat fat: 3.8 gm (34.5 cal)
Poly fat: 2.3 gm (20.3 cal)
Mono fat: 19.8 gm (179 cal)

2 cups packed fresh basil leaves
2 cloves garlic
½ cup grated Parmesan cheese
2 tablespoons grated Romano cheese
¼ cup pine nuts or walnuts
½ cup extra-virgin flavorful olive oil
Freshly ground pepper

1. Combine basil, garlic, cheeses, and nuts in a food processor or blender and process on medium-high or puree setting to mix. Turn machine off, scrape sides down with a rubber spatula, and process until well blended.
2. With machine running, slowly add olive oil in a trickle. Season with pepper to taste and process until smooth.
3. Allow pesto to stand 5 to 10 minutes before serving to allow the flavors to blend.

VARIATIONS
• Basil Parsley Pesto: Omit cheese and nuts. Increase basil to 2½ cups. Add ½ cup of fresh parsley and an additional 2 garlic cloves.
• Mint Pesto: Omit 1 cup of basil leaves. Add 1 cup of fresh mint leaves.
• Oregano Parsley Pesto: Omit basil leaves and Romano cheese. Add 1 cup fresh oregano leaves and 1½ cups fresh parsley leaves.
• Parsley Thyme Pesto: Omit basil leaves. Add 1½ cups of fresh parsley and 2 tablespoons of dried thyme leaves or 1½ cups of fresh parsley, 1 teaspoon of dried thyme leaves, 2 teaspoons of dried rosemary leaves, and 1 teaspoon of dried oregano leaves.

Basic
Rouille

Rouille is a thick, fiery Mediterranean red pepper sauce that adds a new flavor dimension to soups and stews. Traditionally diners help themselves to the rouille and swirls it into his bowl. Since rouille is very spicy, it should be added in ½ teaspoonfuls. It can be added to vegetable or bean soups for a memorable taste sensation.

1 hot red pepper (fresh or dried)
2 cloves garlic
1 tablespoon bread crumbs, soaked in water and pressed
    out
¼ cup extra-virgin flavorful olive oil

1. Pound red pepper and garlic in a mortar until pulverized.
2. Add bread crumbs and slowly pour in olive oil. Mix until well blended.

YIELD
¼ cup, 4 servings

PREPARATION TIME
15 minutes

NUTRIENT ANALYSIS
Calories per serving: 127
Protein: 0.3 gm
Carbohydrates: 1.6 gm
Dietary fiber: 0 gm
Cholesterol: 0 mg
Total fat: 13.5 gm (122 cal)
Sat fat: 1.9 gm (16.5 cal)
Poly fat: 1.2 gm (10 cal)
Mono fat: 10 gm (89.5 cal)

Easy Blender Rouille

YIELD
24 tablespoon-sized servings

PREPARATION TIME
15 minutes

COOKING TIME
5 minutes

NUTRIENT ANALYSIS
Calories per tablespoon: 34
Protein: 0.2 gm
Carbohydrates: 0.9 gm
Dietary fiber: 0.03 gm
Cholesterol: 0 mg
Total fat: 3.4 gm (30 cal)
Sat fat: 0.5 gm (4.5 cal)
Poly fat: 0.3 gm (2.7 cal)
Mono fat: 2.5 gm (23 cal)

This is a rouille that features the added flavors of sweet peppers and basil. It can be refrigerated for 2 or 3 weeks or frozen indefinitely.

2 small dried red peppers or 1 teaspoon Tabasco sauce
½ green bell pepper, seeded and chopped
1 tablespoon dried basil leaves
3 cloves garlic, minced
1 thick slice of white bread, crust removed, dipped in water, and pressed out
¼ teaspoon black pepper
6 tablespoons extra-virgin flavorful olive oil

1. If using dried peppers, blanch in boiled water removed from heat for 5 minutes. Drain.
2. Place hot peppers, or Tabasco, bell pepper, basil, garlic, black pepper, and bread in food processor or blender on medium-high or puree setting and process to mix. Turn machine off, scrape sides down with a rubber spatula, and process until well blended.
3. With machine running, slowly add olive oil in a trickle and process until a smooth mixture results.

FLAVORED OLIVE OILS

Flavored olive oils can be used in making pesto, mayonnaise, and salad dressings; as a marinade for grilled foods; in soups and stews; and as a condiment with cold seafood, poultry, and vegetables.

Flavored olive oils can be purchased commercially or you can create your own at home with any combination of fresh herbs such as basil, parsley, mint, tarragon, rosemary, and thyme. Do not let raw garlic marinate as it can spoil easily.

DIRECTIONS FOR MAKING HERB-FLAVORED OLIVE OIL
1. Wash and dry well 1 cup of fresh herb leaves and stems.
2. Place the herbs in a 1½-cup jar or bottle with a tight fitting lid.
3. Fill jar or bottle with olive oil of your choice. Close tightly.
4. Store for 3 weeks in a cool, dark place.
5. Strain oil into another jar or bottle. Add several sprigs of herbs to the oil before closing tightly. Store in the refrigerator.

Also experiment with combinations of herbs as well as with lemon wedges and cloves.

DIRECTIONS FOR MAKING
GARLIC-PEPPER-TOMATO-FLAVORED OIL
1. Place 15 sun-dried tomatoes in a bowl and cover with warm water for 15 minutes. Drain on paper towels.
2. Place half of a small crumbled red chili pepper in a small mason jar. Add 1 clove of garlic, 1 bay leaf, and 2 peppercorns. Add half the soaked tomatoes and cover with ¼ cup of olive oil.
3. Add rest of chili pepper, 1 clove of garlic, 1 bay leaf, and 2 peppercorns. Fill jar with olive oil.
4. Cover and let sit in a cool, dark location for at least 24 hours. Will keep 3 to 4 weeks. Do not keep raw garlic stored in oil longer.

SUN-DRIED TOMATOES

In Italy, ripe plum tomatoes are dried in the hot sun. When dried, they look like shriveled red chili peppers and are wonderfully flavorful since the drying process intensifies their natural sweetness and flavor.

Sun-dried tomatoes should be used to give an extra flavor punch to a recipe instead of as a main ingredient. For example, a tablespoon or two will flavor a pasta dish for four. They can be used without additional cooking in garlicky pasta sauces, pizza, pasta salads, and with strongly flavored vegetables like broccoli or chicory. They work well in stir-fries with chicken, beef, and shrimp or in rice, pasta, and grain salads.

Sun-dried tomatoes are sold either loose in packages or packed in oil and are quite expensive. You can make them yourself by drying the tomatoes and varying the flavorings to suit your taste, using any combination of herbs that pleases you.

If you live in a sunny, dry climate you can dry tomatoes outdoors. Otherwise, an oven will do a fine job.

TO DRY PLUM TOMATOES IN THE OVEN:

1. Select perfect, ripe fresh Italian plum tomatoes.
2. Cut each tomato in half and open like a book. Cut out the seeds, trim the stems, and cut out any blemishes.
3. Preheat the oven to 220° F. Place the tomatoes on racks on baking sheets. Sprinkle tomatoes lightly with salt. Bake for 7 hours. Rotate baking sheets in the oven during baking time and remove smaller tomatoes as they dry.
4. Cool tomatoes and fold them closed.

TO DRY SMALLER CHERRY TOMATOES FOR PASTAS, PIZZAS, SAUCES, OR GARNISHES:

1. Preheat oven to 450° F. for 20 minutes.
2. Cut fresh red or yellow cherry tomatoes in half. Grease a cookie sheet with olive oil and place the tomatoes on the sheet, cut-sides up. If desired, sprinkle with herbs.

3. Place tomatoes in oven. Turn oven down to 250° F. Leave for 2 hours or until dried to your taste.

STORING DRIED TOMATOES

After tomatoes have been dried, you can store them in an herb-flavored oil. To do this, pack dried tomatoes tightly in ½-pint jars with a layer of fresh herbs in between two layers of tomatoes. Cover with olive oil. Run a knife around the tomatoes to help air escape. Seal jars and store at room temperature for several months for best flavor.

After you've finished the tomatoes, you can reuse the remaining tomato-flavored oil in pasta salads and for sautéeing fresh vegetables.

BREADS
AND
DESSERTS

OLIVE BREAD
GARLIC BREAD
HERB BREAD
SCONES WITH HERBS AND PARMESAN
BANANA OAT BRAN MUFFINS
BLUEBERRY MUFFINS
ORANGE FRENCH TOAST
PANCAKES AND WAFFLES
SESAME-ALMOND COOKIES
ORANGE-WALNUT COOKIES
RUM RAISIN ORANGE CAKE
CHUNKY APPLE CAKE
ORANGE FLAT CAKE
CARROT CAKE
BISCUITS FOR SHORTCAKE

BREADS

....

Olive oil enhances and adds to the aromatic joy of baking bread from scratch. The flours and herbs added to these breads taste even better when baked with olive oil. And the loaves are fine textured and easy to cut. Almost all recipes can be adapted to include olive oil. Use the more flavorful oils with savory breads such as the two herb and olive breads that follow and the milder, lighter flavored oils with plain or sweeter breads.

Olive Bread

YIELD

5 servings (3 slices each)

PREPARATION TIME

40 minutes + 2 hours rising time

COOKING TIME

1 hour

NUTRIENT ANALYSIS

Calories per serving: 138 cal
Protein: 2.7 gm
Carbohydrates: 13.4 gm
Dietary fiber: 1.0 gm
Cholesterol: 0 mg
Total fat: 9.7 gm (87 cal)
Sat fat: 1.2 gm (11 cal)
Poly fat: 0.6 gm (6 cal)
Mono fat: 6.4 gm (58 cal)

This bread is made with olive oil and is full of whole olives as well. It's the perfect touch for a meal featuring an entrée like Chicken Verde (p. 95) and is excellent sliced and spread with humus or baba gannouj spread.

1 package active dried yeast
1 cup warm water (110° F.)
½ teaspoon brown sugar
2 cups unbleached all-purpose flour
1 cup rye flour
½ teaspoon salt
5 tablespoons extra-virgin flavorful olive oil
1 medium onion, minced
1 16-ounce can pitted black or green olives, or a
   combination, rinsed and drained

1. Sprinkle yeast over warm water in a small bowl. Add sugar, stir, and set aside until yeast starts to bubble.
2. Sift all-purpose flour, rye flour, and salt into a large bowl. Make a well in the center of flour mixture and pour in yeast and 2 tablespoons oil. Stir to make a stiff dough. Knead on a floured surface until smooth, about 15 minutes.
3. Wash and oil the bowl with 1 tablespoon olive oil. Return dough ball to bowl and turn to coat with oil. Cover and let rise in a warm place until double in bulk, about 1 hour.
4. In a small skillet, sauté onion in 2 tablespoons olive oil 5 minutes over medium heat until soft. Cool.
5. Punch dough down and knead again on a well-floured surface. Work onions and whole olives into dough as you knead.
6. Oil a baking tray or a 9-inch loaf pan.
7. Shape dough into a ball and place on prepared tray or pan. Cover and let rise again in a warm place for 1 hour.

8. Preheat oven to 400° F. Place loaf in oven and bake for 1 hour until lightly browned. Cool on wire rack.

Garlic Bread

Here's a quick way to make your own garlic bread at home and avoid all the additives in the processed, frozen variety. It's the perfect accompaniment to a meal of mushroom pizza or Linguine with Clam Sauce (p. 190).

1 pound loaf Italian bread, whole
¼ cup extra-virgin flavorful olive oil
2 cloves garlic, finely minced
¼ teaspoon salt (optional)

1. Preheat oven to 350° F.
2. Split loaf in half lengthwise and spread both sides with olive oil, garlic, and salt (if desired).
3. Put halves back together and wrap in aluminum foil.
4. Place on baking sheet and heat for 10 to 15 minutes until heated through.

VARIATION

Make 1½-inch diagonal slices the length of the bread but do not cut all the way through. Spread or brush garlic oil on each slice. Place, uncovered, on baking sheet and heat for 10 minutes in a 350° F. oven.

YIELD
8 servings

PREPARATION TIME
10 minutes

COOKING TIME
10 minutes

NUTRIENT ANALYSIS
Calories per serving: 217
Protein: 0.05 gm
Carbohydrates: 32.3 gm
Dietary fiber: 0.9 gm
Cholesterol: 0 mg
Total fat: 7.3 gm (65 cal)
Sat fat: 0.9 gm (9 cal)
Poly fat: 0.8 gm (7 cal)
Mono fat: 5 gm (45 cal)

Herb
Bread

....

YIELD
1 loaf (15 slices, 1 slice per serving)

PREPARATION TIME
50 minutes + 2 hours rising time

COOKING TIME
1 hour and 10 minutes

The International Olive Oil Council created this wonderful herb bread. Serve with Minestrone with Pesto (p. 53) or use as a base for an albacore tuna sandwich with romaine lettuce and plum tomatoes.

½ cup scalded skim milk
⅓ cup extra-virgin olive oil
1 tablespoon sugar
½ teaspoon salt
1 cup warm water (110° F.)
1 package active dry yeast
*4½ cups unbleached all-purpose flour (or 2 cups whole
    wheat flour and 2½ cups all-purpose flour)*
1 cup chopped scallions
½ cup chopped fresh parsley
1 tablespoon dried dill leaves
1 clove garlic (or 1 shallot), minced
1 egg white, lightly beaten
¼ teaspoon black pepper
1 tablespoon cornmeal

1. In a small saucepan, combine milk, 2 tablespoons olive oil, sugar, and salt. Stir and cool until lukewarm.
2. Place water and yeast in a large bowl. Stir. Add milk-olive oil mixture.
3. Add 4 cups of the flour, stir well. Add enough of remaining flour to make a stiff dough. Stir and let dough rest for 10 minutes.
4. Knead dough on a floured surface until smooth, about 15 minutes. Wash and oil the bowl with 1 tablespoon olive oil. Return dough ball to bowl and turn to coat with oil. Cover and let rise in a warm place until double in bulk, about an hour.

5. Sauté scallions, parsley, dill, and garlic in remaining olive oil for 5 minutes over medium heat. Add beaten egg white to herb-garlic mixture. Season with pepper.

6. Punch dough down. Turn out onto smooth surface and let rest for 10 minutes.

7. Sprinkle a baking sheet with cornmeal.

8. Roll dough into rectangle, 9 x 15 inches. Spread herb-garlic filling over dough, leaving a 1-inch margin. Roll dough from narrow end, as if you were making a jelly roll. Pinch edges and ends of loaf to seal.

9. Transfer to baking sheet. Cover with waxed paper and let rise in a warm place until double in bulk, about 1 hour.

10. Preheat oven to 400° F. Brush loaf with water, place in oven, and bake for 1 hour until lightly browned. Cool on wire rack.

NUTRIENT ANALYSIS
Calories per serving: 165
Protein: 4.3 gm
Carbohydrates: 25.2 gm
Dietary fiber: 1.0 gm
Cholesterol: 0.3 mg
Total fat: 5.2 gm (47 cal)
Sat fat: 0.8 gm (7.2 cal)
Poly fat: 0.4 gm (4 cal)
Mono fat: 3.6 gm (32 cal)

Scones with Herbs and Parmesan

••

YIELD
16 pieces

PREPARATION TIME
15 minutes

COOKING TIME
15 to 20 minutes

These hearty scones take on the flavors of fresh herbs and aromatic cheese and taste wonderful when baking! Serve them with a light lunch of Tomato Herb Soup (p. 61) and fresh fruit.

2½ cups unbleached all-purpose flour
1 tablespoon baking powder
¼ teaspoon salt (optional)
¼ teaspoon black or white pepper
¼ cup grated Parmesan cheese
½ cup low-fat buttermilk (or nonfat yogurt)
⅓ cup extra-virgin flavorful olive oil
2 egg whites
2 teaspoons lemon juice
1 clove garlic, minced
2 tablespoons finely minced fresh chives (or scallions)
1 tablespoon minced fresh basil (or 1 teaspoon dried basil)
1 teaspoon minced fresh thyme or oregano leaves (or ½ teaspoon dried thyme or oregano leaves)

1. Preheat oven to 375° F.
2. In a large bowl sift flour, baking powder, salt (if desired), and pepper. Add cheese and mix well with a large wooden spoon.
3. In a medium bowl beat buttermilk, olive oil, egg whites, lemon juice, garlic, and herbs with a wire whisk. The lemon juice will curdle the milk slightly.
4. Add herb mixture to the flour mixture and beat with the wooden spoon until it forms a soft ball of dough. If too wet to handle, add more flour by the tablespoon. Flour

hands well, put dough on a floured board, and knead 10 or 12 times.

5. Divide dough into two pieces, roll each into a ball and place on an ungreased baking sheet. Press dough down to form 8-inch circles and cut each into eight wedges.

6. Bake for 15 to 20 minutes until lightly browned. Cool on wire rack for about 20 minutes before serving.

NUTRIENT ANALYSIS
Calories per serving: 119
Protein: 3.4 gm
Carbohydrates: 14.7 gm
Dietary fiber: 0.5 gm
Cholesterol: 1.4 gm
Total fat: 5.1 gm (46 cal)
Sat fat: 1 gm (9 cal)
Poly fat: 0.4 gm (3.6 cal)
Mono fat: 3.5 gm (32 cal)

Banana Oat Bran Muffins

Mar. 12, 1993

YIELD
12 muffins, 12 servings

PREPARATION TIME
10 minutes

COOKING TIME
25 minutes

NUTRIENT ANALYSIS
Calories per serving: 148
Protein: 4 gm
Carbohydrates: 17.8 gm
Dietary fiber: 1.4 gm
Cholesterol: 0.6 mg
Total fat: 7.2 gm (65 cal)
Sat fat: 1.1 gm (10 cal)
Poly fat: 1 gm (9 cal)
Mono fat: 4.8 gm (43 cal)

needs some sugar.

This recipe has the double cholesterol-lowering ingredients of olive oil and oat bran, plus added potassium from the banana.

1 large very ripe banana
1⅔ cups skim milk
⅓ cup mild, light flavored olive oil
1 teaspoon vanilla extract
¼ cup raisins (or chopped dates)
2½ cups oat bran
1 tablespoon baking powder
¾ teaspoon baking soda
1 teaspoon ground cinnamon

1. Preheat oven to 400° F. Lightly oil 12 muffin cups and dust lightly with oat bran.
2. Mash banana in a large bowl. Add milk, oil, vanilla, and raisins and mix well with a wooden spoon.
3. Add oat bran, baking powder, baking soda, and cinnamon and mix well.
4. Fill prepared muffin cups with batter. Bake for 25 minutes until lightly browned.
5. When cool enough to touch, turn muffins out of tins onto wire racks and let cool. Can be stored in the refrigerator for up to 2 days, or freeze muffins and thaw as needed.

VARIATION
Add ½ cup diced apples and/or ¼ cup chopped walnuts.

Blueberry Muffins

Favorites such as blueberry muffins become even more enjoyable when you know they're made with low-cholesterol ingredients.

3 egg whites
¼ cup sugar
⅔ cup skim milk
2 teaspoons vanilla extract
⅓ cup mild, light flavored olive oil
2 cups unbleached all-purpose flour (or 1 cup whole wheat flour + 1 cup all-purpose flour)
2 teaspoons baking powder
1 teaspoon ground cinnamon
¼ teaspoon salt (optional)
2½ cups (1 pint) fresh or frozen blueberries, stems removed and rinsed

1. Preheat oven to 375° F. Lightly oil 12 muffin cups and dust lightly with flour.
2. In a large bowl, beat egg white, sugar, milk, vanilla, and olive oil with a wooden spoon.
3. Sift flour, baking powder, cinnamon, and salt into the egg mixture and mix well.
4. Gently fold in blueberries. Pour batter into prepared muffin cups.
5. Bake for 25 to 30 minutes until lightly browned.
6. When cool enough to touch, turn muffins out of tins onto wire racks and let cool. Can be stored in refrigerator for up to 2 days, or freeze muffins and thaw as needed.

YIELD
12 muffins, 12 servings

PREPARATION TIME
15 minutes

COOKING TIME
25 to 30 minutes

NUTRIENT ANALYSIS
Calories per serving: 150
Protein: 3.5 gm
Carbohydrates: 20 gm
Dietary fiber: 1.4 gm
Cholesterol: 0.2 mg
Total fat: 6.3 gm (57 cal)
Sat fat: 0.9 gm (8 cal)
Poly fat: 0.5 gm (5 cal)
Mono fat: 4.1 gm (37 cal)

Orange French Toast

YIELD
4 servings

PREPARATION TIME
*10 minutes + 10 minutes
soaking time*

COOKING TIME
15 minutes

NUTRIENT ANALYSIS
Calories per serving: 465
Protein: 11.3 gm
Carbohydrates: 51 gm
Dietary fiber: 1.8 gm
Cholesterol: 137 mg
Total fat: 16.5 gm (148 cal)
Sat fat: 2.8 gm (25 cal)
Poly fat: 1.5 gm (14 cal)
Mono fat: 11.1 gm (100 cal)

Orange juice, skim milk, and egg whites help to make this a low-cholesterol treat for a special brunch. Serve with fresh fruit, yogurt, and all-fruit preserves.

1 cup orange juice
1 egg
2 egg whites
⅓ cup skim milk
1 teaspoon orange extract
2 tablespoons sugar
¼ teaspoon salt (optional)
¼ cup mild, light flavored olive oil
8 thick slices stale bread
1 fresh orange, sliced (for garnish)

1. In a large bowl and with a wire whisk or egg beater, beat orange juice, egg, egg whites, milk, orange extract, sugar, salt (if desired), and 3 tablespoons olive oil until well blended.

2. Soak bread in the mixture until liquid is absorbed.

3. Heat a skillet or griddle with 1 tablespoon olive oil. Cook bread until lightly browned on a side, turn, and continue cooking until second side is done. Repeat until all bread is cooked. Serve with a slice of orange for a garnish.

Pancakes
and
Waffles

Pancakes and waffles are light and golden when made with oats and olive oil. Serve with all-fruit jams, yogurt, and fresh fruit for a very satisfying, low-cholesterol treat.

1 whole egg
2 egg whites
1½ cups skim milk
¼ cup mild, light flavored olive oil
1½ cups unbleached all-purpose flour
1 cup quick rolled oats
1 tablespoon baking powder
½ teaspoon ground cinnamon
¼ teaspoon salt (optional)

1. In a large bowl, mix eggs, milk, and olive oil.
2. Add flour, oats, baking powder, cinnamon, and salt (if desired). Mix again.
3. Heat lightly oiled griddle, skillet, or waffle irons until hot. Pour ½ cup batter for each pancake or waffle. Cook pancakes until browned on one side and steam has stopped rising. Turn and cook until second side is browned. Cook waffles until lightly browned and steam has stopped rising.

YIELD
4 servings

PREPARATION TIME
5 minutes

COOKING TIME
10 minutes

NUTRIENT ANALYSIS
Calories per serving: 415
Protein: 14 gm
Carbohydrates: 51.6 gm
Dietary fiber: 2.4 gm
Cholesterol: 70 mg
Total fat: 16.7 gm (150 cal)
Sat fat: 2.8 gm (25 cal)
Poly fat: 1.8 gm (16 cal)
Mono fat: 11 gm (99 cal)

DESSERTS

Olive oil can be used in a wide range of dessert dishes. We have included cookies and several cakes that are low in cholesterol. Try substituting the new mild, lighter flavored olive oils for some or all of the fat in some of your favorite dessert recipes. These oils go very well in recipes that are blended with fruits such as apples, oranges, and bananas and with nuts such as almonds and walnuts. It allows the natural flavors of the fruit and nuts to come through without smothering their taste. Baking with light flavored olive oil will result in smooth batters that do not leave an oily taste. Traditional muffins and pancakes are especially easy to make using olive oil, since the oil, unlike butter or margarine, does not have to be melted first but can be mixed right in. As a bonus, this also saves the melting and washing up time needed when cooking with saturated fats. Once you try these recipes, you'll want to experiment with your favorites and turn your baking into yet another way to eat healthy monounsaturated fats each day.

Sesame-Almond Cookies

Make these sophisticated cookies with olive oil, sesame seeds, wine, cinnamon, almonds, and grated citrus peel. Here's a truly portable way to make sure you're getting your daily quota of monounsaturated olive oil.

1 cup mild, light flavored olive oil
1 2-inch strip lemon peel
4 teaspoons toasted sesame seeds
½ cup dry white wine
1 teaspoon grated lemon rind
1 teaspoon grated orange rind
⅓ cup sugar
3½ cups unbleached all-purpose flour
1 tablespoon ground cinnamon
½ cup sliced almonds

1. Heat oil, lemon peel, and sesame seeds in a large skillet over medium heat. Remove from heat and cool.
2. Remove lemon peel. Pour oil and seeds into a bowl. Add wine, grated lemon and orange rind, sugar, and almonds. Stir.
3. Sift flour and cinnamon together. Add to oil mixture slowly, stirring as you proceed. Gather the dough into a ball with your hands, knead once or twice until smooth. Set aside to rest for 30 minutes.
4. Preheat oven to 350° F. Divide dough into 18 equal pieces. Roll into a ball and flatten until cookies are about 3 inches across and ¼-inch thick. Bake for 20 minutes or until cookies are lightly browned and firm. Cool on wire rack. Store in a covered container.

YIELD
15 cookies, 15 servings

PREPARATION TIME
30 minutes + 30 minutes standing time

COOKING TIME
30 minutes

NUTRIENT ANALYSIS
Calories per serving: 277
Protein: 3.9 gm
Carbohydrates: 25.8 gm
Dietary fiber: 1.6 gm
Cholesterol: 0 mg
Total fat: 17.3 gm (156 cal)
Sat fat: 2.3 gm (20 cal)
Poly fat: 1.7 gm (15 cal)
Mono fat: 12.1 gm (109 cal)

Orange-Walnut Cookies

....

YIELD
36 cookies
(18 servings, 2 cookies each)

PREPARATION TIME
20 minutes

COOKING TIME
20 to 25 minutes

NUTRIENT ANALYSIS
Calories per serving: 160
Protein: 2.5 gm
Carbohydrates: 14.8 gm
Dietary fiber: 0.67 gm
Cholesterol: 0 mg
Total fat: 9.9 gm (90 cal)
Sat fat: 1.3 gm (11 cal)
Poly fat: 2.1 gm (18 cal)
Mono fat: 5.9 gm (54 cal)

These light, simple, fresh orange-flavored cookies are crunchy and not too sweet.

¼ cup soft tub margarine
½ cup mild, light flavored olive oil
¼ cup sugar
½ teaspoon ground cinnamon
2 egg whites
Grated rind from 1 orange
Juice of 1 orange
2¼ cups unbleached all-purpose flour (or 1 cup whole
*   wheat flour and 1¼ cups all-purpose flour)*
1½ teaspoons baking powder
¼ teaspoon salt (optional)
½ cup finely chopped walnuts

1. Preheat oven to 375° F. Beat margarine with wooden spoon until creamy. Add olive oil, sugar, and cinnamon and beat until blended well and fluffy.
2. Add egg, orange juice, and peel and mix well.
3. Sift flour, baking powder, and salt into oil mixture, adding a little at a time.
4. Add nuts and beat well.
5. Drop rounded teaspoonfuls onto unoiled baking sheet. Bake 20 to 25 minutes until lightly browned. Cool on rack and store in covered container.

Rum Raisin
Orange
Cake

This cake is easy to make and tastes much richer than the low-cholesterol ingredients would lead you to believe. Serve it for dessert with tea or espresso.

1 cup mild, light flavored olive oil
¾ cup sugar
Grated rind and juice from 1 lemon
Grated rind and juice from 1 orange
2 tablespoons rum (or 1 tablespoon rum extract)
1 tablespoon baking powder
2¼ cups unbleached all-purpose flour (preferably pastry flour)
¼ teaspoon ground cinnamon
¾ cup raisins

1. Preheat oven to 350° F. Lightly oil bottom and sides of an 8 x 8-inch baking pan, and lightly dust with flour.
2. With a wooden spoon, beat together oil and sugar in a large bowl. Grate lemon and orange peel and add. Squeeze lemon and orange juice and add. Add rum and mix well.
3. Sift baking powder, flour, and cinnamon into the oil-sugar mixture. Mix well.
4. Stir in raisins and pour batter into prepared pan.
5. Bake for 1 hour or until lightly browned, cake has pulled away from the sides of the pan, and a wooden toothpick inserted into the cake comes out clean.

YIELD
12 servings

PREPARATION TIME
15 minutes

COOKING TIME
1 hour

NUTRIENT ANALYSIS
Calories per serving: 310 cal
Protein: 2.5 gm
Carbohydrates: 35.6 gm
Dietary fiber: 1.3 gm
Cholesterol: 0 mg
Total fat: 18.3 gm (164 cal)
Sat fat: 2.6 gm (23 cal)
Poly fat: 1.5 gm (13.5 cal)
Mono fat: 13.3 gm (119 cal)

Chunky Apple Cake

YIELD
9 servings

PREPARATION TIME
30 minutes

COOKING TIME
1 hour

NUTRIENT ANALYSIS
Calories per serving: 322
Protein: 7.4 gm
Carbohydrates: 122 gm
Dietary fiber: 2.7 gm
Cholesterol: 28.4 mg
Total fat: 16 gm (145 cal)
Sat fat: 2.6 gm (23 cal)
Poly fat: 2.2 gm (20 cal)
Mono fat: 10 gm (90 cal)

This spicy golden brown cake is full of apple chunks. It is perfect to take along on a picnic or for a potluck dinner to share with your friends.

1 whole egg
4 egg whites
½ cup sugar
⅓ cup brown sugar, packed
2 cups unbleached all-purpose flour (preferably pastry flour)
1 tablespoon baking powder
1 teaspoon cinnamon
½ teaspoon grated nutmeg
½ cup mild, light flavored olive oil
4 cups peeled apple chunks (use a firm apple such as a Granny Smith)
¼ cup raisins, packed
¼ cup chopped walnuts

1. Preheat oven to 350° F. Lightly oil a 9-inch square cake pan and dust with flour.
2. In a large bowl, beat egg, egg whites, and sugars with a wooden spoon.
3. In a medium bowl, sift flour, baking powder, cinnamon, and nutmeg. Add half of flour mixture to egg mixture. Stir in oil, then remaining flour mixture. Batter will be fairly thick.
4. Fold apples, raisins, and nuts into batter. Pour into prepared pan. Bake for 1 hour or until lightly browned and a wooden toothpick inserted into the cake comes out clean.

Orange
Flat
Cake

This moist, flat cake is based on an Italian recipe and is excellent with tea or coffee or for a light dessert.

¼ cup mild, light flavored olive oil
½ cup sugar
2 egg whites
1 cup unbleached all-purpose flour (preferably pastry flour)
1 teaspoon baking powder
¼ teaspoon salt (optional)
½ cup skim milk
Grated rind and juice of 1 orange

1. Preheat oven to 400° F. Lightly oil an 8-inch square cake pan and dust lightly with flour.
2. In a large bowl, beat oil and sugar with a whisk. Add the egg whites and continue beating until well mixed.
3. Sift flour, baking powder, and salt if desired, into the oil mixture. Add half of the milk and beat well. Add remaining milk and beat again.
4. Add orange juice and rind (get all of the "zest," or rind, from the orange) and mix.
5. Pour batter into pan. Bake for 30 to 35 minutes or until lightly browned and cake has pulled away from the sides of the pan and a wooden toothpick inserted into the cake comes out clean. Let cake sit in pan for 15 minutes. Turn out and invert to cool on wire rack.

YIELD
9 servings

PREPARATION TIME
15 minutes

COOKING TIME
30 to 45 minutes

NUTRIENT ANALYSIS
Calories per serving: 154
Protein: 2.6 gm
Carbohydrates: 22.6 gm
Dietary fiber: 0.5 gm
Cholesterol: 0.2 mg
Total fat: 6.2 gm (56 cal)
Sat fat: 0.9 gm (8 cal)
Poly fat: 0.5 gm (4.5 cal)
Mono fat: 4.4 gm (40 cal)

Carrot Cake

YIELD
1 cake (12 servings)

PREPARATION TIME
30 minutes

COOKING TIME
1 hour 15 minutes

This is a light version of a classic carrot cake that uses olive oil and egg whites instead of butter and whole eggs. Serve it for dessert and pack any leftovers for a perfect lunchtime snack.

4 large carrots (1¼ pounds)
3 cups unbleached all-purpose flour (or 1 cup whole
    wheat flour + 2 cups all-purpose flour)
1 tablespoon baking soda
1 tablespoon pumpkin pie spice
1 tablespoon ground cinnamon
½ teaspoon salt (optional)
2 whole eggs
4 egg whites
1¼ cups mild, light flavored olive oil
2 cups sugar
1 cup unsweetened applesauce
1 tablespoon vanilla extract
1 cup raisins (preferably golden)
½ cup chopped walnuts

1. Preheat oven to 350° F. Lightly oil a 9 x 13-inch cake pan, or a 9-inch Bundt or angel food cake pan and lightly dust with flour.
2. Cut off ends, peel, and cut carrots into 1-inch slices. Steam until soft, about 10 minutes, in steamer with 1 inch of water in tightly covered pan or cook in microwave. Puree with potato masher or in blender or food processor, pushing down carrots with a rubber spatula until well pureed.
3. In a medium bowl, sift flour, baking soda, spice, cinnamon, and salt, and mix well with a wooden spoon.

4. In a large bowl, with an electric mixer or with a wire whisk, beat eggs, egg whites, olive oil, sugar, carrot puree, applesauce, and vanilla until well mixed.

5. Add flour mixture and beat for 2 to 3 minutes.

6. Fold in raisins and nuts. Pour batter into prepared pan. Bake for 1 hour and 15 to 25 minutes until lightly browned and cake has pulled away from the sides of the pan and a wooden toothpick inserted into the cake comes out clean. Put pan on wire rack and cool for 15 minutes. If sheet cake, leave in pan. If Bundt or angel food cake pan, invert cake onto serving plate to continue cooling.

NUTRIENT ANALYSIS
Calories per serving: 360
Protein: 7.8 gm
Carbohydrates: 74 gm
Dietary fiber: 4.0 gm
Cholesterol: 93 mg
Total fat: 5.3 gm (48 cal)
Sat fat: 0.8 gm (7 cal)
Poly fat: 2.3 gm (20 cal)
Mono fat: 1.4 gm (13 cal)

Biscuits for Shortcake

························ © ························

YIELD
8 3-inch shortcakes, 8 servings

PREPARATION TIME
15 minutes

COOKING TIME
20 to 25 minutes

NUTRIENT ANALYSIS
Calories per serving: 245
Protein: 3.7 gm
Carbohydrates: 26 gm
Dietary fiber: 0.8 gm
Cholesterol: 0.8 mg
Total fat: 14 gm (126 cal)
Sat fat: 2.1 gm (19 cal)
Poly fat: 1.5 gm (14 cal)
Mono fat: 10 gm (90 cal)

This recipe makes a wonderfully springy, easy-to-use dough for a classic shortcake. Top it with fresh or frozen strawberries, blueberries or peaches and a spoonful of non-fat yogurt.

2 cups unbleached all-purpose flour
1 tablespoon baking powder
¼ teaspoon salt
2 tablespoons sugar
½ cup mild, light flavored olive oil
⅔ cup 1 percent milk (or low-fat buttermilk)

1. Preheat oven to 400° F.
2. Sift flour, baking powder, salt, and sugar into a large bowl.
3. Add olive oil and milk and stir with a wooden spoon to form a ball of soft dough.
4. Knead dough about ten times on a lightly floured surface. Roll out dough until ½-inch thick. Cut six or seven biscuits with a 3-inch cutter or glass, rerolling dough scraps again and cutting rounds until you have eight biscuits.
5. Bake on ungreased baking sheet for 25 to 30 minutes until lightly browned. Cool on wire racks.

BIBLIOGRAPHY

Alabaster, Oliver. *The Power of Prevention*. New York, Simon & Schuster, 1986.

American Heart Association Nutrition Committee: Dietary Guidelines for Healthy American Adults: A Statement for Physicians and Health Professionals by the Nutrition Committee, American Heart Association. Circulation vol. 74 (1986), p. 1465A–1468A.

Aravanis, Christos, and Paul J. Ionnidis. "Nutritional Factors and Cardiovascular Diseases in the Greek Island Heart Study," in *Nutritional Prevention of Cardiovascular Disease*. New York, Academic Press, 1984.

Canola Oil: Properties and Performance. Winnipeg, Canola Council, 1987.

Composition of Foods. Agricultural Handbook No. 5. United States Department of Agriculture, Washington, D.C. Government Printing Office, 1976–1986.

Cooper, Kenneth H., M.D. *Controlling Cholesterol*. New York, Bantam, 1988.

David, Elizabeth. *Classics: Mediterranean Food, French Country Cooking, Summer Cooking*. New York, Knopf, 1980.

Davidson, Alan. *Mediterranean Seafood*. New York, Penguin, 1980.

DeBakey, Michael, et al. "Diet, Nutrition, and Heart Disease." *Journal of the American Medical Association*, vol. 86 (1987), 729–31.

Dumas, Alexandre. *Dictionary of Cuisine*. New York, Simon & Schuster, 1958.

Goldbeck, Nikki and David. *The Goldbeck's Guide to Good Food*. New York, New American Library, 1987.

Grundy, Scott M., M.D., PhD. "Cholesterol and Coronary Heart Disease: A New Era." *Journal of the American Medical Association*, vol. 256 (1986), 2849–58.

Grundy, Scott M., M.D., PhD. "Comparison of Dietary Saturated and Polyunsaturated Fatty Acids on Plasma Lipids and Lipoproteins in Man." *Journal of Lipid Research*, vol. 26 (1985), 194–202.

Grundy, Scott M., M.D., PhD. "Comparison of Monosaturated Fatty Acids and Carbohydrates for Plasma Cholesterol Lowering." *New England Journal of Medicine,* vol. 314 (1986), 745–48.

Grundy, Scott M., M.D., PhD. "Effects of Polyunsaturated Fats on Lipid Metabolism in Patients with Hypertriglyceridemia." *Journal of Clinical Investigation,* vol. 55 (1975), 269–82.

Grundy, Scott M., M.D., PhD. "Monosaturated Fatty Acids, Plasma Cholesterol, and Coronary Heart Disease." *American Journal of Clinical Nutrition,* vol. 45 (1987), 1168–75.

Hodgson, Moira. *The New York Times Gourmet Shopper.* New York, Times Books, 1983.

Kennedy, Diana. *The Cuisines of Mexico.* New York, Harper & Row, 1972.

Keys, Ancel, et. al. *Seven Countries: A Multivariate Analysis of Death and Coronary Heart Disease.* Cambridge, Harvard University Press, 1980.

Klein, Maggie Blyth. *The Feast of the Olive.* Los Angeles. Aris, 1983.

Levenstein, Harvey. *Revolution at the Table: The Transformation of the American Diet.* New York, Oxford University Press, 1988.

McConnell, Carol and Malcolm. *The Mediterranean Diet.* New York, W. W. Norton and Company, 1987.

National Institutes of Health Consensus Conference. "Lowering Blood Cholesterol to Prevent Heart Disease." *Journal of the American Medical Association,* vol. 253 (1985), 2080–90.

Nutritive Value of American Foods, Agricultural Handbook No. 456. United States Department of Agriculture, Washington, D.C., Government Printing Office, 1975.

Olney, Richard. *Simple French Food.* New York, Atheneum, 1974.

Rinzler, Carol Ann. *The Complete Food Book.* New York, World Almanac, 1987.

Roden, Claudia. *A Book of Middle Eastern Food.* New York, Vintage, 1974.

Root, Waverly. *The Food of France.* New York, Random House, 1958.

Root, Waverly. *The Food of Italy.* New York, Random House, 1971.

Simone, Charles B. *Cancer and Nutrition*. New York, McGraw-Hill, 1983.

Viola, Publio, and Audisio, Mirella. *Olive Oil and Health: A Research Compendium*. Crete, International Congress on the Biological Value of Olive Oil, 1986.

Visser, Margaret. *Much Depends on Dinner*. New York, Grove Press, 1987.

Vitale, J. J., and Broitman, S. A. "Lipids and the Immune Function." *Cancer Research,* vol. 41 (1981), 3706.

Von Welanetz, Diana and Paul. *The Von Welanetz Guide to Ethnic Ingredients*. Los Angeles, J. P. Tarcher Inc., 1982.

Wolfert, Paula. *Mediterranean Cooking*. New York, Times Books, 1977.

INDEX

ABOUT THE AUTHORS

SARAH SCHLESINGER is the coauthor of *The Low-Cholesterol Oat Plan* and *The Pointe Shoe Book*. She is a senior lecturer in communications at Towson State University, an adjunct professor of communications at Pace University, and a core faculty member in New York University's Musical Theatre Writing Program. Ms. Schlesinger began developing low-cholesterol recipes as the result of her husand's multiple coronary bypass surgery and has been involved in the study of the dietary causes of arterial disease since 1980.

BARBARA REED EARNEST is the coauthor of *The Low-Cholesterol Oat Plan*. She is the executive director of the Green Guerillas, a horticultural organization in New York City that helps community gardeners grow vegetables and plants in city neighborhoods. She is a Phi Beta Kappa graduate of Hunter College. Ms. Earnest became interested in low-cholesterol cooking because of illness in her family and began developing recipes with Sara Schlesinger using ingredients such as oat bran and olive oil.